BELIFE OR BELIEF

A Collection of Empowering Stories for Life Transformation.

DONNA KENNEDY

AND

CO- AUTHORS

First Published in 2020

Success in Doing Publications

www.donnakennedy.com

ISBN: 978-1-9160176-6-5

CONTENTS

ACKNOWLEDGEMENTS

I would like to acknowledge the fabulous co-authors in this book for their courage to empower and inspire others. It has been, and still is, an honour to have you on my team: Pete Lonton, Ken Falconer, Karen Fleming, Ed Martin, Hugh Hegarty, Joan McDaid, Jackie Mallon, Heather Lundy, Vivian McKinnon, Patrick Dillon, Christine McGonagle, Anne Canavan, Nadia Buju, Chris Wojnar, Tanya Cannon, Sharon McNulty, Therese O'Connor, Veronica Bodano and Pat Slattery.

I would also like to thank John Boyle for writing the foreword for this book. John and his wonderful partner, Gloriane Giovannelli, are simply amazing friends!

Thank you to Steven Kontra of www.webstop.ie for web design and importantly for his unwavering support and professionalism.

FOREWORD

by John Boyle (Boyle Sports)

The first time I met Donna Kennedy was in Dublin sometime in 2007. While it was much earlier in her career in the coaching, speaking and personal development field, one thing was clear. She was full of determination and a sincere desire to learn. Basically, she was, and still is, teachable.

My name is John Boyle, and I have some personal experience in what happens when you go from being unreachable to teachable. For me becoming teachable meant I was able to recover from the disease that was destroying my life and my health – alcoholism. While Donna was never an alcoholic, we found we had many things in common, like addictive behaviour and false beliefs that threatened to, and nearly did, destroy our lives. In order to heal, just like in the title of this book, we each had to first discover and then let go of the "lies" in our belief systems.

As a businessperson, founder and Chairman of Boylesports, Ltd., countless numbers of people have asked for my advice or guidance over the past decades. And why not? Learning what other people are doing successfully is one of the ways I grew my own business. But sadly, very few actually ever implement my suggestions. And even fewer ever take time to consistently make real use of their most powerful tool, the human mind.

In this way, Donna always stood out from the many. Not only was she determined to learn what to do, she was also always developing *how* to use her mind and to draw on its limitless resources. So much of this process is learning to consistently let go of what's not real and what no longer serves us.

While most books and teachers focus on knowledge and acquiring more information, Donna approached her growth on a much deeper level. But what exactly did she do differently?

Well, I observed in addition to learning what to do, she also chose to let go of what wasn't working. To face what no longer served her. To see the lies or the repetitive thoughts that would otherwise sabotage a successful career and life, and to stop giving them her attention. And yes, while she wanted success, to me it seemed she also wanted more. As far as I could tell, wanted it all! Just not in the way we commonly think of having it all. I saw that Donna was creating a destiny and a life that included not just success in business matters, but also in health, wellbeing, and peace of mind. What also stood out, was that she was (and still is) passionately committed to bringing others along with her. This inclusiveness, because it models the way life itself operates, is a large part of Donna's success. And also qualifies her to write yet another bestselling book, also supporting the other authors here.

So, when Donna first told me the title of this book, I was excited! Within the title itself, lies the very secret to releasing so much of our energy and intelligence— being willing to SEE and to let go of the lies we tell ourselves, the lies others have told us, and the lies that the mind and thoughts will tell us every day...if we allow them.

You see, these lies are the only things blocking us from uncovering and releasing our true potential. If we don't accept them, if we refuse to believe them and give any of our energy to them, we are automatically returned to our natural state. My understanding of a natural state is that this is when our minds are clear, our energy is freed out, and then we can apply that energy to any area (and hopefully all areas) of our lives. For me, I also understand the natural state to be when I am connected to the life force and intelligence that is already within me. And that is already within each and every one of us.

The great news is we can all choose to return to the natural state at any time. Yes, it may take time and the right type of work in order to learn how to let go and make proper use of the mind. But if my personal story, and of course Donna Kennedy's story (and the other stories shared in this book) are of any relevance or importance, it is that no matter what lies about yourself or about life itself you have been be-lie-ving, you can stop! You can let go of them and begin to create a different life experience.

Both Donna and I had accepted false beliefs to the point where we literally nearly lost our lives. And we both began the journey of seeing what is unreal, letting go and then applying our energy in better ways. There really is no magical secret. At a certain point you just do what Donna did. You choose to become teachable and to live in a way that honours the life within you.

I am delighted for anyone reading this book. If you can allow yourself to see what's not working and apply yourself every day to letting go, this book can help you change your life. As I write this, I am reminded of something I applied on my journey to recovering from severe alcoholism:

Question: How does it work?

Answer: It works if you work it. It doesn't if you don't.

So, if I were to offer the reader any suggestion, it would be to let go of what you think you know and what information you have accumulated already. If it were working, you would be exactly where you want to be right now. So why not become even more teachable? And let go. And work the insights and understandings in this book for yourself. Donna Kennedy is living proof, as are the other people here, that it works...IF you work it.

- John Boyle

CHAPTER 1
BELIFE or BELIEF

by Donna Kennedy

Right now, you are holding a powerful book, a tool that could potentially transform your life. 20 people, 20 life experiences, 20 perspectives – you are about to embark on a journey of self-discovery; some might even call it serendipity. In this book you will find hope, you will find light, you will find solutions and clarity. When everything seemed impossible for us, we found the possible within it. When everything seemed too big, we used it as a foundation for growth. We will share our learnings with you so that no matter where you are in your life, you can be confident that you can become more empowered to be, do and have all you truly deserve. And maybe by the end of this book you will choose to BE-LIFE!

*

Trapped and frozen in a silence of time, the darkness of the inside of my eyelids created an inner panic that I will never forget. The heaviness in every cell of my body told me that it could be my time to let go. But I didn't want to die, I wanted to open my eyes! My body was fighting me. It wouldn't let me open my eyes. It wouldn't let me move at all. It had pinned me to my bed like a lump of led covered in super glue. I was stuck and despite being acutely aware of it, and no matter how much I pleaded, my body was giving up on me. *'How could this be? I am in control of my body. I decide what happens and how it happens. This isn't right!'* I was petrified, and in that moment, I realized that the notion of control I had built up over the previous three years was nothing more than deluded ideology. I was going to die, and there wasn't a thing I could do about it. The irony was that my very own conscious, sometimes celebrated, decisions had brought me there.

For three years I had intentionally starved myself, rejoicing as the numbers dropped lower on the weighing scales, feeling as though I was doing a good job when I hit my weight loss targets. Never in a million years did I think I wasn't in control of the situation. I believed I could sit on the knife edge of life and death, which bizarrely felt safe, and control my body and what happened to it. I had grown to hate my body. I wanted to hurt it and punish it, but I always believed I could stop if I wanted to, well at least that's what I told myself. Feeling my bones sticking out was a comfort to me. It told me I was on track and in control. Bed sores, mouth ulcers, downy hair on my body, irritability, fainting, hospitalization – they were all just sacrifices for achieving my goal. Looking back, I don't think I even know what my goal was. I just knew I was on a mission that involved a lot of pain and a lot of reminders that I was on track.

But as I lay there on my bed unable to move, I knew that I was not in control of anything. I had gone too far. I couldn't shout out to my mother to save me; I didn't feel able to move my mouth to make a sound. I wanted to roll myself off the bed, but I couldn't even do that. I was stuck in a bubble of silence with no exit strategy and no hope, exhausted and too tired to fight. Gradually, a part of my me started to give up and I settled, finding a space in my mind to ask myself, 'Should I just let go? It might be easier.' I knew then that I could have slipped away, if I let myself, but when I asked the question something changed. I can't really explain it, other than I connected with something, a warm feeling, that was more loving and stronger than I was in that moment. It felt like an all accepting, life giving something surrounding me. I say something because it wasn't a big dramatic moment of having a life epiphany with angels hovering over me, it was a simple sense that everything would be okay, if I trusted it to help me to move. I had to let trust and faith replace the fear. And I did. Sometimes trusting something when you think you have nothing opens a gate for change. And I certainly needed that!

I gathered every bit of fight in me and I have no idea how I did it, but I moved. I couldn't get out of bed but at least I was awake. I lay there stewing in my thoughts and I realized that I had to change, even if I didn't know how. Honestly, part of me didn't want to change; my patterns had become so familiar to me that they felt like they were part of me, but if I was to live the only option I had was to change. I lay there until my mother eventually came into my room. She sat on the bed and I burst into tears. I told her how I hadn't been able to move and how afraid I was. Then I just blurted it out, I had been sexually assaulted at age 7 by a visitor who came to our home. It had been eating away at me – literally.

My family had helplessly watched me starve for years and pleaded with me to stop, not just to save myself but to stop the pain I was causing everyone around me. They saw my recovery strategy as "just eat" and they were right, that's all I had to do to be physically well. But my reality was that I *needed* my behaviour to cope. I couldn't talk about what had happened when I was 7 as it made it too real. It was easier to throw it into the back of my mind and put a lock on it. Starving myself gave me a distraction, somewhere to direct the emotions. I didn't know how to cope without my crutch, there was no way I was giving it up for anyone.

I started the behaviour when I was 12. At that time, my confidence was in tatters as I was being bullied at school. I desperately wanted people to like me, and as I was walking home from school one day a thought came into my mind, *'If I was thinner, maybe people would like me more.'* I went along with that thought for a couple of weeks, even though I didn't need to lose weight at all, and I lost 6 pounds. I didn't tell anyone what I was doing, I just focussed on the weight loss. However, I started to feel in control of my body (something I soon realized I had missed) and life took a dangerous direction. It felt like I had jumped on a rollercoaster, pressed the on-switch and then I couldn't get off. Things just got faster and more intense and my head was in an adrenaline spin. I began to exercise hard and I found that all the planning and weighing myself gave me a way to fuel out the 7-year-old emotions that had begun stirring within me. I felt anger boil and I hated myself. Nothing was going to take away my new-found coping tool.

Looking back now, I should have told the people then how I was feeling, and they would have helped, but when you're in the space of being emotionally hijacked, logic doesn't come into the equation. My actions were solely based on emotion, not logic, and the behaviour was fulfilling a need that I didn't know how else to fulfil. Control over one's life is a normal human need that everyone needs to have met in balance, but when our lives are thrown into chaos and we don't have the means to bring things back into equilibrium in a healthy way, it's easy to go for the second best option, doing the best we can, albeit unhealthy. In my case I didn't know how to put control back in my life in a healthy way. When it was taken away from me, I couldn't cope so I just responded and reacted, I didn't ask for help. I plummeted to a skeletal weight and I very nearly died.

Thankfully, I opened up to my mother that day in my room and later to the rest of my family, and with their support and admittedly a two step forward one step back approach, I regained my physical, emotional and spiritual self. With each step forward, I became stronger and more developed as a person. I learned to trust, accept, and let go of what wasn't good for me. Thankfully, today I am no longer afraid or frozen, I am free, and I live my life in healthy balance and natural flow. I feel amazing.

Over the last 23 years I have learned to navigate life and be okay in the territory of life's uncertainty. I have learned how to stand tall in the face of adversity and shine brighter than it. Would I change the past events if I could? Honestly, yes but the reality is I can't, so I chose to accept them for what they were, and I let them go. I chose to allow them to help me be a better person, and I have used the strength within those times to build a foundation for living my life with grace, dignity, and love.

In life we get two choices and ultimately which choice we make is our decision and responsibility:

1) We let circumstance overcome us and become us.
2) We become brighter than circumstance and shine.

We all get LIFE-TIME. I wasted some of mine. But I have learned that time is valuable. We should not ever waste it or disrespect it. We were born to use it to fulfil our potential, not disregard it. I have come to understand that challenges, circumstances, experiences, others' opinions, negative thoughts, and unproductive behaviour patterns do not define us; they are not our identity, they come from beliefs that take up space in lifetime. From the moment we are born we inherit *beliefs* from those around us. We explore what each day brings, and we are given a structure or script to live out our lifetime, which is all good and well in a healthy ideal world. However, if you look at the word belief you will notice that there is a *lie* in it. And because we rarely question what we are told as children, we take on lies as truths and just let the script run, life passes by and we go with it. Instead of exploring and shining our natural potential we learn to live out our life moments and become Be-LIE-Fers, not BE-LIFE-FORs, and often make bad decisions as a result.

If I was to truly value my lifetime I had to come down off my knife-edge and change my attitude and approach to life and time. I had to shed the old beliefs and the lies I had about myself and my worth. I

10

had to move out of the space of what I believed to be safe suffering. I knew it would be scary as the familiar is always easier, but I also knew that if I didn't allow myself to connect to the light within me, I would always live as a shadow or not live at all. By opening the lock on everything I had believed to be true about myself and the world (it was my fault, I must have done something to make it happen, my body was disgusting, nobody would like me anymore etc.) I could take full ownership for my life, for my behaviour, and all that went with it. I could learn how to love myself again, to feel that it was okay for me to be happy and unapologetically live a life I could be proud of.

When I decided to value my lifetime I began to understand that the true power of our lives is in the next breath, not in the past or in "coping" states. The past cannot hurt us unless we bring it with us into our future. Sure, we can use it to build a wall around ourselves and use it as a reason to tame our light, but if you really want to live a life with purpose, meaning and vision, you must consciously choose to let go of the lies you have been holding in your mind and BE-LIFE-FOR your purpose. Beliefs can cheat the soul. Your future is not in the past, so do not get tangled in lies that create a future as a replica of your past. Let go of what doesn't serve you now and make a *decision* that no matter how hard it may seem to move out of your monotonous "safe space" and into purposeful positive action, you will. You know what I mean by "safe space", don't you? That space you crawl into when life seems too big for you, or when how the worlds sees you seems to matter more than you do. That space really isn't safe, you know. It's simply repetitive and familiar. Ask yourself, has it ever made you genuinely happy or has it just made you comfortable? Comfortable is *not* the same as happy.

If you want to BE-LIFE, to feel truly empowered, you will need to move into unfamiliar territory, possibly with unknown outcomes or consequences. That might stir e**motion**, but the reality is you cannot ever move from one place to another without some level of feeling. And that's okay; you don't need to have it all figured out or mapped out, just become open to be seen in the world for who you are in all your authenticity, not for how you want to be seen. Embrace your wonders and imperfections, and if that feels uncomfortable too, just accept that it's okay to be uncomfortable and you will get there. Being uncomfortable, although it might not feel nice, means you are growing and expanding into your true potential. Keep your eyes focused on the prize – living your life as your best self! There were times (many times) on my journey when I was petrified, even to walk across the road or talk to people, but I had to stick with it to get to where I am today. The 'W*hat will people think if they saw the real me?'* got in the way. Does that question get in your way sometimes too? Well, here's the reality – you don't really care what people think of you, what you actually care about is how what they think of you might reflect back to you how you think about yourself. Read that again.

I didn't like what I saw when I thought about myself and I hated anyone who reminded me of it. I wasn't at ease within myself, I was operating from lies, so I manifested dis-ease in my life. Imagine being fully at ease with yourself, *to love yourself and feel* happy to BE yourself without judgement, to know you are good enough exactly as you are, to BE clear about your identity and allow others to see you stand without a crutch or excuse to fall back on.

I realize now that there is no such thing as a perfect human being; we are all just pieces of the same jigsaw, each different, but all as important and valuable as the other. However, without you present in your authentic form the bigger picture cannot be complete. So, if you don't shine and allow yourself to be clear about who you are, you will never connect to life in the way you were meant to, and you will never be seen for how wonderfully unique and important you are. And you are. You have a valuable purpose and you are here for a reason. Isn't it about time that you became the architect of your life, and BE-LIFE-FOR your purpose?

Slow it Down

Start simple by slowing everything down. Slowing things down allows you to regulate your life, and when you regulate you can elevate with strength and joy. You can clear a space to build what you really want. No more reacting or responding impulsively, just calmly initiating, building, and enriching your soul. Start to question your beliefs and become self-aware. Self-awareness is a powerful thing.

Stop for a few minutes now and let's get real from the get-go. I want you to write what behaviours you want to change and then write down the consequences of doing those behaviours so far. There will be negative consequences and positive consequences. Yes, positives! Did you know that we only continue behaviours that we believe (consciously or unconsciously) we get something from, *even* if those behaviours make no logical sense and even if we don't like how they make us feel. Become aware of your behaviours. Grab a pen now.

Behaviour/ Pattern I want to change:

_____

_____

_____

What has it got me up to now?

Negatives:_____

_____

_____

Positives:_____

_____

_____

If I do the behaviour:

I don't have to

_____

_____

It allows me to feel

_____

_____

I can

_____

_____

If I stop the behaviour

I will have to give up

_____

_____

I will have to stop

_____

_____

I will feel

_____

_____

It will mean

_____

_____

People will

_____

_____

People will not

_____

_____

For every behaviour we do or don't do we get something from because we believe it serves us, it serves a purpose. Do you think I enjoyed my behaviour? Of course not! It was painful, and I hated it, I wished I could stop, and I prayed for help to stop, but the behaviour got me something that took priority over wanting to get better or change. And as long as I believed in the gain, I wouldn't give it up. So, what could I possibly have gained from starving myself? Was it vanity? Well, any person with an ounce of common sense knows being skeletal is not attractive or fun. It gave me something much bigger than that. It gave me a sense of control over my life, a need that wasn't being fulfilled. Although it was painful and I didn't like it, it was meeting a need that I didn't know how else to meet. If someone was to tell me then that I wanted to keep the behaviour I would have said they were crazy, cruel even. After all I was miserable. However, although on one hand I didn't want the behaviour, a part of me did want it. It served the need I believed to be missing and it aligned with the beliefs I had about myself. It was only when I learned how to get my needs met in healthy way (you

16

will learn more about this later in the book) and let go of the belief that I needed anorexia to have control in my life, that I could BE-LIFE. If we don't be**lie**ve we need a behaviour, we don't hold on to it.

You could liken it to a plant trying to bloom. A plant needs certain things to have LIFE. It needs water, sunlight, soil, air etc. If it gets all it needs in balance, it will bloom beautifully, but if you take away one of the plant's needs, what does it do? You might say it dies. Well, maybe, but *first* it will do all it can to survive and get its needs met in balance. If it doesn't get sunlight, for example, it will twist itself towards the nearest source of light, looking miserable in the process. If it doesn't get water, it will soak up water from wherever it can find it, even from itself. It will do everything it can to bring itself back into equilibrium so it can bloom as it was meant to all along.

We are the same. We have needs and we look for ways to get them met, the ways we believe to be the best in any given moment in any given circumstance. The question is, in challenging times when things are unsettled do we just accept the situation and bear the consequences or do we do something about it to make it better? Do we allow ourselves to live in an unhealthy **lie** environment or do we get some e**motion** behind it so we can move out of a negative unhealthy way of living and **BE-LIFE**? That is the choice we are given every day. And how committed we are to taking action determines the results we get, good or bad. You must move out of your comfort zone to create change.

17

The Pendulum Effect

Isaac Newton, a renowned physicist, spoke a lot about motion. He identified three laws that I think are worth noting and thinking about here.

The first law defines the velocity of objects in response to forces, or in simple terms how fast something moves in a given direction when force is applied to it. The law states that if an object moves at a specific speed and in a straight line, it will continue to move at that speed and in a straight line, infinitely, as long as no other force acts on it, a bit like when you roll a ball forward; if you don't get in its way or throw it off track, it continues to move in the same direction. It could also be likened to when I sat on the anorexia rollercoaster and pressed go; I continued on the same path in the same direction until something stronger intervened. That intervention changed everything.

Newton's second law refers to the relationship between an object's mass, its acceleration, and the applied force. In other words, the bigger the object, the more force is needed to move it. So, the bigger a challenge, the more effort it will take to combat it BUT it can always be combatted!

Finally, his third law states that for every action there is an equal and opposite reaction. Your efforts will equate your results!

Now let's look at those principals in relation to how we can move a belief about ourselves and our lives into a mind-set that serves us better, especially during challenging times.

1) We are born into the world and on a clear track to reaching our potential. As trusting children, we do not question, we just continue on life's path as happy little BE-LIFE-FORs. It is only when a negative circumstance and the belief we have about it (i.e. something bigger than us) is forced upon us from our environment that we are sent in a different direction.

2) The bigger the belief forced upon us, the easier it is to throw us off course and the bigger the impact.

3) If we do nothing to challenge beliefs, or there is no outside intervention, we continue the behaviour or we get stuck in a state of inertia. This easily happens in childhood as we are more vulnerable. However, if we exert an equal positive force to what is given to us, by committing to focussing on good beliefs only, we can cancel out the impact of the negative beliefs. And if we exert a greater force, we can overcome the beliefs more easily and clear space for infinite possibilities.

This is where the importance of having good focus and energy comes in. It is especially important that we as adults recognize that just because beliefs may have been forced upon us in the past does not mean that we cannot become stronger than them in the present and future. We can, even when we feel we haven't the motivation or energy to. When I was stuck in negative beliefs, I had no motivation or energy to change them, at least that's what I believed and told myself. I just let it run without intervention. I believed I had tried and tried but the result was always the same — I stayed stuck. Then, with some revised thought, it dawned on me that saying I was trying was just an excuse. It takes little or no energy to try something. *Try* putting your hand in the air; don't actually do it, just try to do it. The fact is, trying is not focused or committed to following through to get a result. Commitment is essential to get a result. Deep down I knew I had energy, even if it was adrenaline-energy; I had just been using my energy to fuel my negative behaviours. I was just using so much of it in the wrong way that it was exhausting. I knew I had to let go of "trying" and move into the energy of "being and doing."

I was aware of the fact that feelings are not concrete things, they are states of mind that change moment to moment, depending on what is happening (internally and externally) at the time and how we steer them. I wondered if I could manipulate the horrible emotions I was feeling into something more productive of the same frequency, i.e. use them at the same level of power but in a positive way. What if I turned the anger I was feeling about life into determination to recover? Instead of being angry, I could become determined to be stronger than the person who hurt me. I could fight back by refusing to continue the pain and become determined to be amazing despite all that happened. I wondered if I could I use my stubbornness to persevere when I felt vulnerable, and if I could turn the feeling of lack into gratitude and abundance? I listed what I was grateful for and instead of focussing on the things I didn't have, I focused on what I did have. And if I started to roll a conversation about lack, I purposely switched to listing ten things I was grateful for in that moment. I couldn't think about lack and abundance at the same time. Essentially, I took back control but in a healthy way this time! With that in mind, I thought about all the feelings I was using to create negative behaviours and what I could turn them into. I had nothing to lose.

I purposely chose to tap into the same level of energetic force that I had been using to create dis-ease in my life and used it to create ease in my life. And guess what happened? It started to work! Little by little, day by day, I became a force to be reckoned with and eventually I became so strong that I threw the lie off track altogether and cleared space for a better version of myself to be-life.

As you read this book, think about what you need to do to move out of the beliefs that don't serve you into ones that make you feel amazing. In this book you will learn from many people but in order to really benefit from the information you read, you must become humble enough to be teachable and brave, and committed enough to take action on what will help you to become a better version of yourself. You have it within you to do it! The past is gone and there will never be a "right time" to change. You have been given the gift of the present, so take it as an opportunity to create something new. No matter what you've been through, or what story you've been telling yourself to keep you where you have been up to now, you have an opportunity now to create a better version of yourself. Look beyond the lie. Focus on making each moment count and the moments to follow will take care of themselves. You'll find answers here. BE-LIFE-FOR you!

CHAPTER 2

Finding the Flame

by Pete Lonton

In 2017 I'd had 37 ½ years of being average and living a lie. This lie was causing confusion, frustration, drifting and missed potential, all whilst living someone else's goal. Like so many people in life I did not know what I wanted to do with my life, I had not found my passion and I didn't know what my purpose was. I started to feel like a passenger on my own journey, watching it like you would do film on a cinema screen, even though I was the main actor. My schooling was what my parents and the system thought I should do. My job was what I thought was right and would give me the best opportunities and financial returns. Unfortunately, I simply never took the time to find or define that flame inside me, to understand what my real passions were and what I wanted. And I believe that I am not alone in that. Many people can go through life without ever actually finding their true passion or ultimate potential.

To quote Hamlet, 'to be or not to be, that is the question.' In this soliloquy Hamlet is asking the question whether it would be better to live or to die, looking at how miserable his life was amidst "outrageous fortune." I do not believe that death is ever preferable, however to not truly live and find the flame inside you seems like an immense wasted opportunity. I decided to put my focus on finding the flame.

At this tipping point in my life I found myself experiencing symptoms of depression, stress, anxiety and on the verge of burnout. Social media is amazing for spreading a positive message, and perhaps feeding the ego, but a virtual and commercialized world does little to assist when there is symptom overload and when you are living without passion. At the time, instead of slowing down and dealing with life as I knew it, I believed that self-care was something only the weak needed. I thought taking time out was frustrating and indeed it felt like a waste of time. The attitude of my conscious mind was to simply continue and work harder to overcome my fears, problems, and desire to achieve more. Now I realize I was searching to find my flame. I also understand that certain actions do not necessarily equal results.

Having a family, the trials of business, working harder and longer hours to progress and achieve more to support my family was all starting to take an increasing mental and physical toll on me. Fortunately, this was not the first time I had experienced these feelings; I knew from the previous time that I needed to make some changes in my circumstances and environment to create a new result. I was no longer willing to be a spectator in my life and knew it was time to take control. For the first time in many years I was unemployed and focused on finding my own passion and strength within.

I found myself asking deep and searching questions such as, 'Is this all there is?', 'Am I reaching my potential?', 'How do some people achieve so much more?', 'How can I get more time in my day?', 'How

23

can I get calmness and feel happier within myself?' and, 'What is the point of all this?'

> *'Change the Way You Look at Things*
> *and The Things You Look at Change'*
> *– Wayne Dyer*

It was time to empower my subconscious mind and become the person I was supposed to be and unleash my potential. In 2017 I found myself at a point in my life where I questioned the level of input versus the output. The results being achieved did not represent the goals, desires, wishes, ambitions or potential that I had. I was frustrated. We all know and accept that we can achieve more, however as humans we cannot help but look and compare ourselves to others. So why do some humans become world class athletes, geniuses, pioneers, and leaders in their field? I would hear entrepreneurs and speakers say, 'If I can do it, you can do it', but it felt like a throw away comment to me, that was until I decided to start accepting this comment and explore the actions and journey that these people had to get them to where they are today.

When a plant seed is created, it knows exactly what it wants to be; whether it is to be a plant or tree, that decision is already inside it. The blueprint, the goals and the structure of that seed has already formed, and its destiny is waiting for it. Could that be the same for us? Could it be that our future is already within us and our destiny is simply waiting for us to turn up and take control, to become empowered? When we talk about empowerment, it can be for ourselves, to ourselves, for someone else, by someone else or to reach a global goal.

In the world of meditation and on religious tracks they talk about the mind, body and soul. The body is made up of trillions of measurable cells but we cannot measure the mind or soul. Yet it is to the mind and soul that we often look when seeking answers.

In a world of so much noise, we are literally pumped news, opinion, and marketing 24 hours a day, if we let it happen! This is all presented to impact our values in the greatest possible way, to seek our attention regardless whether it aligns to our values or not. It can become impossible to listen and know what you really feel about anything when the noise becomes too great. The very phrase "mind your own business" is a great reminder to mind what you are doing and what you are allowing to influence your feelings and your own actions.

'Keep your attention focused entirely on what is truly your own concern and be clear that what belongs to others is their business and none of yours.'
– Epictetus

In my own journey, at 37 ½ years old I had reached a stage in my life where only I could answer the questions I was posing. As for all of us, only I could find the fire within me and only I could choose to do so.

In the book, *The Talent Code* by Daniel Coyle, the following is explained, 'The unconscious processing abilities of the human brain are estimated at roughly 11 million pieces of information per second. Compare that to the estimate for conscious processing: about 40 pieces per second.' This mere statement gives a great example to the nearly unbelievable volume of information we receive, but also the comparative power of the conscious (male) mind, versus the unconscious (female) mind to receive, process, recognize and filter according to priority, significance and risk.

When searching for the fire within, the fire in the belly, a good question to ask is that if we know how to change and be a better person, why do we simply not just go and do it? Perhaps it is not that we do not want to change, it's just that we don't value that enough or are not motivated enough to take the necessary action. But what if you did want to become a better person, do you think you would maybe then know what to do and be motivated to do it? I have learned that we need to find out what we really want, which will empower us to want to take all the necessary actions and more.

'To know that you do not know is the best.
To think you know when you do not is a disease.
Recognizing this disease as a disease is to be free of it.'
— Lao Tzu

Knowing

In dictionary.com, *knowing* is defined as; "having knowledge or information; intelligent, shrewd, sharp, or astute. Conscious, intentional, deliberate."

When it comes to finding our fire and passion, we do not always know with any certainty or clarity exactly what it is we desire. Knowing in itself requires experience, evidence under decision, thought and mind-set, based on our previous experiences. Within every human being is a subconscious mechanism that allows our bodies to function, to learn from experiences, and form a view of the world. When we complete a task successfully, we can say that we "know", that it was successful because we have seen it. When we have previous experiences open in our minds we can follow logic to say that we "know" what will happen as we have the same or a similar comparable experience.

Knowing is an invisible force, it's a combination of years of experience, opinions, ideas, failures and successes. But what we know has a limit in itself as can be demonstrated in the four quadrants of knowing:

1. Knowing that you know. When you have experience, facts, confirmation that you know something is true.

2. Knowing that you don't know. When you are aware that you lack the necessary knowledge, skills or experience to know if something is true or factual.

3. Don't know that you know. When something is known but you have not questioned it or become aware of something within your experience or knowledge.

4. Don't know what you don't know. When something is outside of your experience or you have not become aware of a fact, issue or area of life before. Alternatively, it may be that you think you know something but you are not factually correct in your thinking on a subject.

The power, opportunity and potential lies in the fourth quadrant but the risk of the ego, limiting beliefs and self-talk originate in quadrants 1 and 2.

You cannot empower somebody else, the same as you cannot lead a horse to water and force it to drink. Only you can decide what you want, what you are capable of, what you are willing to sacrifice, what your deepest desires, visions and expectations are. Empowerment is a state of mind. We step into an empowered state when we focus our mind and physical actions on achieving specific goals and or tasks that align with our mission and vision for our lives. When you know it is possible to achieve a goal, it's no longer a case of whether it can be achieved, but simply a question of what is required to achieve it and if you willing to spend the required time, energy and perseverance to make it happen.

There is an expression "to know and not do is really not to know," outlined by Stephen R Covey in *The 7 Habits of Highly Effective*

People. This is a great example of modern-day life; we have excess knowledge and opportunity but still we don't empower ourselves or take the appropriate action.

The invisible force of knowing is ultimately there to keep us safe but the ability to stand aside and test our knowledge, awareness and beliefs, is where the concept of change and empowerment takes place. As humans we often know what we want but in a greater way we more often know what we don't want. We know the difference between right and wrong, positive and negative, up and down, failure and success, but this is indeed subject to our belief mechanism and values. There is a concept that says everything you need to know is already within you, but the key part is to remember and apply that knowledge, which also links back to the power of knowing. Our subconscious and superconscious mind - that level of awareness that sees beyond material reality - has more capability and ability to judge, measure, evaluate, project and decide than humans will ever be able to realise or measure in a scientific way. Therefore, acceptance of subconscious and superconscious knowing is one of the hardest things to accept because it relies on an element of blind faith. The ability to trust and believe and have faith in the unknown is not a new principle because is not every religion and spiritual belief in the universe based on an element of faith and alignment?

Inside every one of us is a voice and often several voices. There is the voice of our inner critic, there is the voice of our better selves, but fundamentally there is also our true voice which comes from our

29

subconscious mind and is there to speak to us and guide us – but only if you let it. Voices and noises within our heads are all influenced by those around us; social media, world events, our families, and feedback on our health, wealth and expectation of success. One of the most powerful concepts can be the belief or the acceptance to say that I know that I do not know but I am willing and open to find out. Therefore, it is critical for us to have the space, peace of mind, capacity and willingness to listen to what we really want and know without fear of retribution, judgement, or failure.

> 'Knowing is not enough; we must apply.
> Willing is not enough; we must do.'
> – Johann Wolfgang von Goethe

Become clear and focused

Humans are goal-striving mechanisms that thrive in structure, efficiency, and achievement. In order to achieve this, clarity and focus are essential. For example, were you to drive a large vehicle through a congested town with no route, intention or idea of your destination, it would only be a matter of time before you would find yourself in a congested situation. Not only that but you would be able to be influenced by others, be open to opinion and become frustrated with your own situation.

A great example of being clear and focused is a space mission by Space-X "MARS & BEYOND: THE ROAD TO MAKING HUMANITY MULTIPLANETARY", the goal being to reach Mars safely and successfully, complete the mission and return home. All other details, specifications, questions, and queries are secondary to the mission. The beauty and simplicity of the mission alone creates a very clear picture, which binds teams and gives a sense of unifying purpose. There can be no deviation. There is a need for certainty. There is a point of no return on the project and indeed it can glean from the successes (and failures) of previous projects and also be a legacy for knowledge on future projects.

In the world of optometry, they talk about 20:20 vision and the ability to see clearly and to focus on certain objects. In nature the ability to see and focus on certain prey is an attribute that is afforded to hunting animals. To be clear and focused is key for us to be able to create and see a vision of ourselves and the mission and vision that we are each on. Through having this clarity, we can empower our mind and body to align with the true purpose and values of our soul. Knowing that you are on the right path, being clear and focused, generates a momentum, belief and energy that will shake off all doubt, uncertainty, and negative energy.

Build a Desire

At the moment of inception, a dream and vision are set into motion. As the cells multiply and cluster to form the various organs of the body and indeed the vehicle in which the brain and mind are to be held, the origin of the soul is a matter of opinion but it is true to say that every person and cell is unique. At that point your future is already within you. The cells of your body have set about to create the future physical you and indeed will carry on until the day of your ultimate bodily failure.

A passion or burning desire is a vision or concept of something that is so great that it can focus the mind and drive the body to its ultimate extremes. Subconsciously we can see desires in many forms through hunger, thirst, lust, greed and growth. In the personal development world there is a common saying, 'If you can see it in your mind, you can hold it in your hand.' The question is can you see it, can you see it well enough to desire it, can you desire it enough to be willing to do whatever it takes to hold it in your hand? It is true to say that our desires change in accordance with our values, phases in life, outside influences, and ultimately it may take until your later life to have the wisdom, insight and peace of mind to understand your desires. But like any child, understanding your true wants and desires is something that has to come from your "true self" — your subconscious mind.

It is important to say that a desire can be one of the most powerful things in the world. Also that good and genuine desires should be shared with others and indeed it would be selfish to not empower yourself and others around you to connect and create a life, network and vision so strong that the ripples in the pond may be felt for many generations to come.

Generate the Right Energy and Potential

Inside a bag of grass seed are thousands of seeds of potential. Within the bag and in store it is nothing more than seed. However, if that potential is seen, the groundwork is done, the seed is sown and the environment is correct then the hibernation of the potential is over, and thereafter empowerment has taken place and the seed has become a plant. This can never be undone. However, it also has the potential to generate future seeds. It is important to note that any seed or idea requires support from its environment to allow it to grow. Lack of sunlight, water, energy or belief is sufficient to stop the potential in its tracks. Potential is by its very nature an encased energy that can only be activated in the right conditions through want and desire.

As humans we are already about 1 in 20 million by the very nature of being a combination of that successful sperm and that opportune egg. The nucleus of an idea and potential are created at that moment of inception. The womb empowers it to be the best that it can be. Passion, momentum and ability are instilled from day one, whether it be consciously or unconsciously. As with every second of time, every cell in our body and every belief and thought, it cannot be undone. It can, however, form part of a greater thing or be wasted, to generate the fundamentals of change or be misused through lack of certainty or desire. Therefore, the potential can simply be said to have been used or wasted. There has never been a truer saying to understand potential than the following popular quote that is often attributed to Lao Tzu:

'Living in the past creates depression, and living in the future creates anxiety but living in the now creates purpose.'

How many school reports have said; "Could do better if they applied themselves" or "needs to concentrate more" or "needs to focus on what they're doing to achieve their potential," and yet still the individual does not respond or feel inspired. This could be akin to telling a dog to have more table manners or to eat differently but without reward or incentive.

The humble matchstick comes to mind. Matches were invented in the early 1800s and were seen as an amazing invention to have portable fire on demand. Despite its seemingly insignificant size and stature, one single match has the power and capability to create and destroy, depending on how it is applied. A match can be used to light the romantic candle for an intimate dinner or it could you be used to light a fire which could burn down a forest. How many matches or sparks of potential do you have within you?

Get passionate about your purpose

It is fair to say any Olympic athlete requires focus and attention to be at the top of their field. They require passion and belief to be able to fulfil their purpose, which is indeed aligned to their values and ultimate goals. By definition purpose is the reason for which something is done or created and a sense of resolve or determination. Some may call it a calling, some may call it natural ability, but it is often seen that a person who is aligned to their skill and ability to impact others, empower change, and fulfil their potential is indeed fulfilling their purpose.

By understanding your purpose and with the passion to succeed you will generate the momentum and flow necessary to achieve clarity and create certainty. Through taking such conscious inspired action, by the laws of the universe you must succeed.

Commit to Yourself

Commitment is the act of engaging our senses and has the potential to create certainty. Commitment can be seen as making a decision or indeed not making a decision, but it is a conscious thought and a decision to take a state of mind that if adhered to and completed will create ultimate success and the completion of that goal. Commitment in itself can be positive, negative or neutral. Through marriage we commit to our partner in the form of a promise and an intention that future actions, beliefs and wants will be undertaken. Commitment in itself is a process or a state of mind and requires the understanding that the potential is within us, the passion to undertake the task, the clarity of knowing where we are going, and the knowing that not everything in the future will be without fault or adjustment but should we continue to hold the burning desire then we have done everything possible to empower success.

In biology it is known that women are born with their lifetime supply of eggs at the point of birth. There is in the region of 1 to 2 million eggs already in a woman's ovaries at this time. There is no capacity to make new eggs, so the number declines each month. Perhaps eggs are like ideas; we are born with the seed or the egg, the idea or possibility is already within us and it's up to us to release them. Our job is to allow it to grow and unfold as it is intended, not to suppress or depress it. We must become passionate, persistent, and committed.

You only need to ask a young child about what they really want and you will see their natural passion and excitement. They will often be able to tell you straight away and as we see at Christmas in many homes across the country they expect to receive what they have asked for. Receiving a present, desire for a new toy or reaching a goal; a genuine passion is all consuming and the mind will go into overdrive to seek the goal. When we talk about "fire in the belly" we are talking about the passion or the burning desire that comes from within to reach our potential. The key is to never give up.

Think about a dog with a passion for a ball. When a dog is waiting for a ball to be thrown it salivates and shows absolute belief, focus, determination, and desire all in one very simple mission, "to get the ball." It will hold that pose, belief and tension without distraction until the objective is achieved. Can you think of a task or goal that you have worked on that showed such tenacity? We each have the ability to adapt and persevere even in the dullest of circumstances. The sight of an isolated tree growing strong on a cliff edge can cause us to stop and wonder in amazement. Despite the odds of a plant growing in that position, it has not only survived but it has thrived where others have failed. Could it grow better and bigger elsewhere? Maybe, but then it would be vulnerable to animals and other conditions. It has stood strong with limited resources and vulnerability but also limited competition and threat from other factors. As humans we can often find ourselves in places and positions that aren't ideal, however the power comes when you can accept your current position and to find that opportunity and thrive in the possibilities by empowering ourselves with conviction and passion.

In the globally acclaimed David Attenborough nature programmes the brutality and determination of nature is captured to show the trials and tribulations of animals in the wild in their daily journeys, struggles and ultimate fulfilment of their needs. Whilst some animals show the scars of previous battles, there is not the same emotional response or critical thinking that a human would attach to an event.

'We always overestimate the change that will occur in the next two years and underestimate the change that will occur in the next ten. Don't let yourself be lulled into inaction.'
– Bill Gates

The wonders of modern technology have allowed us to share knowledge and opinion, connect and inspire. We now have access to an extraordinary amount of information online. However, we need to consider that the subconscious mind may not be able to cope with this volume of information. It causes us to consider variation, different opinions, differences in values and the need for constant fact checking. In the field of counselling it is accepted that the counsellor needs to decompress after listening and taking on the views of others. How do you decompress each day to shake off the ideas and opinions of others to allow you to follow your own judgement?

In the book, *Chicken Soup for the Soul* by Jack Canfield, Mark Victor Hansen & Amy Newmark[1], Jack tells a story that nicely summarises the benefits of being persistent; *'Mark and I visited our very wise friend Ron Scolastico and asked for his advice. He told us, 'If you were to go to a tree with an axe and take five solid cuts with the axe every day, eventually even the largest tree in the forest would have to come down.'*

Keep it lit!

We are here for a short time not a long time. Like the years our life has many seasons on journeys we go through. It is often said that we over-estimate what we can achieve in a day and underestimate what we can be achieved in a year. The effect of compounding and consistent repetitive action can be an incredibly powerful in building up over time. On that premise then the saying 'Do something today that your future self will thank you for' becomes very poignant.

In Angela Lee Duckworth's book, *Grit: The Power of Passion and Perseverance*, she defines Grit as *'grit is passion and sustained persistence applied toward long-term achievement, with no particular concern for rewards or recognition along the way. It*

---

[1] 'Chicken Soup for the Soul by Jack Canfield (Author), Mark Victor Hansen (Author), Amy Newmark (Author)

combines resilience, ambition, and self-control in the pursuit of goals that take months, years, or even decades'[2].

Angela talks about how it is vital to show grit and when all else fails - to keep on, keeping on! Showing power and grit regardless of what's going on around you is a skill that can be developed through such persistence.

On the cross section of a log you can view the rings, measuring the years of age, of a tree. Each year or growing season leaves a mark on the tree and the size and strength of the ring depends on the impact of that growing season. The center of that log marks when the tree was first created and was weak and vulnerable. Each ring thereafter is built upon the last and compounds to make a bigger trunk with greater strength, capacity and breadth. Similar to our own lives, each year leaves a mark and impacts us in the form of wisdom, experience and memories.

By empowering others, you will by nature empower yourself. As humans we are naturally designed to help others and by helping others we in turn get satisfaction and feedback to know that we have done the right thing. The expression "the eye cannot see itself" refers to the fact that we can often more easily see another's skills, the positives and negatives. For this reason, we are often much better at empowering others than we are at empowering ourselves. It is also part of the reason we often benefit from mentoring or coaching by another. As a coach myself, I will often put myself in a

---

[2]. "Grit: The Power of Passion and Perseverance Hardcover" book, by Author Angela Duckworth.

position of needing to perform, putting myself under extreme focus and concentration, which in turn enacts my subconscious mind. Empowerment of yourself and others requires belief, motivation, burning desire and action.

'The mind, once stretched by a new idea,
never returns to its original dimensions.'
— Ralph Waldo Emerson

Feed the root not the leaf

Should you water the plants roots or the plants leaves? The common consensus is that it is always ideal to feed the roots where all the nutrients and water can be taken in by the plant. In this example, we can ask ourselves are we feeding our own roots, our values or are we feeding our leaves — our conscious mind and ego? The tree's roots are always the most important part to be able to set a wide foundation to support the trees structure and to absorb water and nutrients that will enable its growth. When a seed is planted the first thing that it will do is lay down roots and form a base in which the plant can stand. The bigger the plant or tree the wider and stronger the roots need to be to be able to support the structure. The roots are unseen and can take no credit for the activity of photosynthesis, receiving sunlight or being exposed to the outside world. Even so the roots can live without the leaves, but the leaves cannot live without the roots.

It is by going within and feeding our roots; focusing on our values, goals and vision that we can achieve growth and success. It is through a firm foundation and absorbing the right information and filtering out all the unnecessary noise that we can become clear and focused on achieving our goals and vision and remember that as Jim Rohn said, 'a tree doesn't grow half as high as it could.'

In summing up this chapter I would like to leave you with the following three simple concepts that have helped me to best understand and implement my passion and find my fire in the belly: Physics shows us that the amount of energy required to accelerate from 0-30 miles per hour is the same as the energy required to accelerate from 30-90 miles per hour. This shows us that when action is started, and momentum builds it requires less energy to go further and achieve more over time.

In Matthew Thompson's TEDx QUB talk in June 2019, he talked about the virtue of going deep not wide. After building one of the largest social media profiles in the country, Matthew decided to shut down the accounts to focus on having a deep impact on a small group of people instead of a shallow impact on many — a philosophy he describes as "Deep Not Wide." This was a great summary into how many of us may often find ourselves spread too thin and on the verge of burnout, a place that I found myself and having to face what he calls "the rocky shore." We find our desire in the depths, by moving away from the shallows and going within. By focussing our attention on our deeper relationships, goals and passions.

Within a tree there are approximately 300,000 matches. Each one has the potential to light a fire. In the midst of my burnout at 37 ½ years of age, I set out to find the flame within. At the end of the day all that I really had to understand and accept was that the passion, desire and knowing was already within me - as it is for all of us.

> *'You are who you are meant to be.*
> *Dance as if no one's watching.*
> *Love as if it's all you know.*
> *Dream as if you'll live forever.*
> *Live as if you'll die today.'*
> *— James Dean*

Find your flame, as only you can, and live with a burning passion and desire every day.

CHAPTER 3
Freedom of Mind

by Ken Falconer

The mind is a fantastic and wonderful thing. It can be your best friend or your worst enemy. Beauty, love, laughter, happiness and creativity all exist in the mind, but your mind can also be the dwelling place of anger, darkness and destruction. Our mind generates thoughts and these thoughts are the controller of our feelings and our emotions. Our behaviours, actions and reactions are interconnected to those feelings and emotions. It has been said - what we are what we become.

We all have a brain, which is a tangible thing, it's a part of the body; you can see it, hold it, it's an organ which houses the center of the nervous system. The mind on the other hand is a concept; it is different from the brain but dwells within the brain. I suppose the brain could be likened to a computer. Many years ago, when we bought computers, we had to load the operating system and all the programmes. Now a computer comes preloaded with operating systems and some basic programmes, the user then determines what other programmes are required, and installs these programmes, depending on their needs and requirements.

The mind can be likened to the data and information being loaded onto the hard drive of that computer. Some information comes pre-loaded. Like a computer, we have an operating system, and this controls many automatic operations, like our heartbeat, our breathing and many of our defenses and protectors. For example, our body sweats when it gets too warm, as the sweat evaporates the body cools down again. When too cold hairs rise on our forearms, we may start to shiver as a warning to danger as the body tries to induce heat. Shivering is the body's automatic response to coldness as your muscles tighten and relax in rapid succession in an effort to warm you up.

The feeling of hunger and thirst are automatic responses, again for our own protection. Consider the automatic process of eating – we may consciously eat and swallow our food, but what a fantastic set of processes are involved to release the nutrients, vitamins, minerals and energy from that food and produce waste product from those processes.

There is also a mind-body connection, as well as the previously mentioned automatic functioning. Other automatic responses and behaviours are triggered by thought processes. The mind can cause many reactions throughout the body as it communicates with it, down to a cellular level. This constant mind-body communication produces many physical outcomes, or symptoms. It could be the nervous excitement of a child on Christmas morning, the butterflies in their stomach as they enter the room where Santa has been. A similar feeling may be felt by a person as they face an audience from a stage. These are similar symptoms, but one is excitement based and the other is fear based. Maybe the speaker may have additional symptoms of dry mouth and trembling hands. Maybe you have experienced your heart fluttering, or you maybe get a little flushed, feel a warm glow in your chest, you may even blush when you see that person you fancy or love. Have you ever got "lost" in a book or in a daydream, where thoughts can, and do produce physical changes to the body?

After birth we are disconnected from Nature; it's almost as if when the umbilical cord is cut, the hard drive of the mind is switched on. We start loading information, we absorb masses of data from all our senses, we bring in information by what we see and hear, from what we smell and taste and from what we touch. We see light and darkness, this turns into colours, shapes, faces, objects. We hear sound, from the comfort of a heartbeat to crashes, bangs, voices, barking, tones and music. We learn smells from people and foods, and we closely link smells with taste. All these senses blend together and form a platform for learning and awareness together with the sense of touch, the feel of skin, hot and cold, your favourite teddy bear or blanket, that little hand grabbing, holding, and reaching out for information. There is so much information and data being collected, absorbed and loaded unto the hard drive of the mind.

We are programmed for survival in the culture and the environment that we have been born into, and this programming continues to the day of our death. Years of information is stored into the hard drive of the mind. This initial programming is both vital but also critical to the mind-set, belief system, morals, values, habits, feelings and emotions of that individual.

King Solomon, King of Israel from Biblical times over 900 years BC, was known for his knowledge and has been quoted in the Bible as saying 'Train up a child in the way he should go: and when he is old, he will not depart from it.' Almost 500 years later Aristotle, the Greek philosopher, used similar language when he said, 'Give me a child until he is 7 and I will show you the man.' The same quotation and observations have also been attributed to St. Ignatius Loyola, a Jesuit Priest in the early 15th Century. Modern day psychologists and scientists agree with these observations and declarations, and now through technology can measure the frequency and development of the brain to support these century old claims. So, what about Freedom of mind?

Programme of the Hard Drive

Just for a moment consider a man in his 40s. He is a little insecure, he is fantastic at his job, but he doesn't believe it; he often feels inferior to his peers and workmates; he judges himself based on his perception of the knowledge and qualifications of others. This man is always comparing himself to others, and often comes up short in his own estimation. At times he feels like an imposter. Yet he has never been unemployed throughout his whole life, and has progressed through life, with promotion after promotion. He is recognised for his work through official recognition and awards as well as surprise pay rises by his employers. This man strives for perfection; he gives his best, but only on his terms.

He hates criticism. He takes it personally. Other people's opinions feel like a personal challenge towards him. These opinions seem to threaten him in some way. He is good at what he does. Rather he is good at what he chooses to do. He gets results, measurable results, but when suggestions are offered to him, to help him improve his results further, he takes this advice as unwanted opinion and direct criticism towards him and his current performance. When you take this person out of his world of experiential knowledge and expertise, he becomes lazy. He procrastinates and finds a way to avoid things; he avoids new things, especially things that are perceived as academic. He will only do and choose to do things he knows he will succeed at, yet everything he has learned has been through trial and error – he is a "hands-on" learner, he has a "show me and give me a go at that" type of attitude. He is an amazingly fast learner in what he chooses to learn, he is persistent and resourceful. Throughout his many years of hands-on learning he could handle most of the trades within his career in the construction industry. He is by no means an expert in them all, but he can recognise and is aware of what good quality and quality workmanship is, and what it is not. He learns and feeds from those he respects, he is always aware of what is not acceptable to the point of looking for perfection, he knows the consequences of mistakes and poor standards and finds a solution for improvement.

This man has a life, a job and a lifestyle envied by many others, yet this same man is insecure to the point he has low confidence, he blushes when people talk to him and about him. He always takes responsibility for mistakes and mess-ups, strangely not only his own mistakes, but also the mistakes of others, he loads himself with guilt - after all he was responsible, wasn't he? He feels embarrassed, uncomfortable for other people who are being picked on. He hates unfair treatment and the awkwardness of conflict would provoke him to step in to help the weaker, or the person being treated wrongly. He hates injustice. He is riddled with guilt and insecurity, but is not a visibly angry person, however, when he is accused of doing something he didn't do, he defends his innocence viciously, and is aware he has this fuming anger trapped and fueled from deep within. Very seldom does this anger come to the surface, but when it does it erupts like a volcano. It only happens once every decade but beware of the spewing wrath.

He hates how people abuse his good nature and exploit other people for their own gains. He hates deceit and seeing people getting shafted unknowingly. This man has good morals, good values, he is honest, and when he deviates from this code, he fills himself with guilt. He has integrity and is empathetic towards others, especially those who are being treated unfairly and accused wrongly.

This man WAS me.

The man above was the product of his programming. It was that simple. I was brought up with good values, morals and beliefs. Remember we are all born into an environment and a culture and brought up by parents who do their best for us with the beliefs and information they have at the time. At the time of writing this I am 57 years of age; my childhood was a different era. Many of us who came from that generation were brought up very kinesthetically, we were disciplined by canes, straps, in fact any tool that made

48

discipline easier to enforce and therefore the subsequent learnings easier to administer, and before the younger more politically correct readers condemn this totally, it was the norm back then.

Our teachers did the same; many of them today would be in jail because of their disciplinary methods and their tools of calibration, together with their strategies of humiliation, like standing in the corner and other ways to segregate the culprit to set them as an example to the rest. The methods used back then were more severe than today, they were often kinesthetic, but this type of discipline was expected by the recipients in many households. There were consequences for bad behaviours, we knew it, but strangely we still took risks.

Just look at the language in the last paragraph, disciplinary methods, tools of calibration, strategies of humiliation, segregation, making an example of and of course expectation of consequences. I also used the word kinesthetic, it is a word I use rather than state the obvious, when force is applied or when infringement, abuse or violation has occurred. It softens the blow when clients realise, they do not have to relive details of their trauma. I learned it from a soldier who was describing his engagement while under attack when serving in the Middle East.

This was programming the mind through fear, guilt and judgement and it was the normal process. This programming was written into the mind and into the nervous system of thousands of children from an early age. It would be fair to say this was "normal" in many households, and it would be also fair to say the parents and teachers truly believed what they were doing was correct and the methods they used to teach and discipline their children was the approved and accepted method of that era.

I believe discipline is required and necessary for children. Children need to have boundaries and they need to recognize those boundaries. They need to know right from wrong, what is acceptable and what is not. Children need consistency; they need discipline, but through love, not fear, and never, ever discipline your children when you are angry. When a parent does that, it's not about the child and correcting their behaviour anymore – it's about the parent and their emotions.

I can say that in my 40s I was emotionally blunt; I was unaware of my emotions and my feelings. I simply could not understand them, I felt unworthy, I never felt good enough, I felt insecure, yet paradoxically I had pride in, and was recognised for my work, albeit as I have said before - the work that I chose to do. It was important to me that I chose my own path. I did not like being told what to do; there was too much risk, too many consequences by getting things wrong. If I had an interest and a desire to do something, then I would put the required effort into it to become good at it and get my results. Only then I would get recognition, praise and even the rewards that I craved.

I constantly needed external approval from others, I didn't have any inward confidence or self-belief, I believed I was stupid, I was told this many times by the person I loved the most, and this was reinforced by others, of course I believed them. Even the playground bully told me this. He was right, wasn't he? It matched my belief system. I hated education, I loved school, but the consequences of getting things wrong were so severe I didn't even try. I would never "study". The more you were made to study the tougher the consequences were. The words written in a report saying "could do better" brought terror to me, fears, shaking, sweats, and a lot of consequential pain.

I did not get involved in fights, I hated conflict, I was taught to 'turn the other cheek'. If I did get involved in any incidents, it just was not worth it when I got home. I suppressed my anger so deeply, but somehow, I found great significance by becoming the class clown. Doesn't everyone love a clown, someone who makes them laugh, someone who amuses others with their actions and behaviours? I reckon the clown is the opposite of a bully. I maintain that a bully is someone who does not feel significant but finds his significance in a negative way; by forcing his presence upon someone else. However, anytime I vented anger it was like someone had knocked off the valve of a pressure cooker, there was no stopping the spewing of steam. It was under pressure, it was volatile, and it was dangerous.

Running the Programme

Who we are is a direct consequence of our early environment and the choices we make through life. The series of choices we make are governed by our programming, our habits, beliefs and fears, together with our feelings and emotions and the thought processes behind them. It is fair to say traumas, setbacks and obstacles affect us and many things do happen outside our control, but it is also fair to say many blessings and opportunities also present themselves just as often, and just as regularly. However, what we see at any moment is totally dependent on our mindset and emotional wellbeing at that time. Thoughts produce feelings which in turn will affect our decision making, our actions and behaviours.

I came to a place in my life where things on the surface were looking good. I had a fantastic job, I had position, status, and recognition for what I had achieved. I was getting well paid, yet I had other issues away from work. I had been building a portfolio of properties, I had quite a few. Things were going nicely, I felt content, important, proud of what I had achieved. I had a great wife, four fantastic boys, all independent and working in good jobs, life was good.

I worked hard, probably too hard to the point of sacrificing time with my family. I worked all year to give "quality time" to my wife and kids, through two weeks of annual holidays. Young children do not know what quality time is, but they do recognize time. They recognize time spent with their parents, they recognize fun, playing, going to the park, the beach, picnics, happy times together, building huts in the garden and forts out of cardboard boxes. Keep your "quality'"time for work colleagues and adult relationships and just give your time to kids. They do not have to be taken on holiday, travelling for hours to foreign countries. They want to be with the people they love, spend time with them and to feel appreciated by them.

Things come up in life, important things, life changing events and one of these in my life was the recession of 2007 – 2008. I have stated before I was emotionally blunt. I had no emotional intelligence. I had my traits, my insecurities; I had my belief systems, good and bad. I had good morals and values and all the characteristics I have mentioned before. They directed my path and dictated my choices and my decisions through life. I was running on a programme that I was not aware of, but this programme led and controlled my life. It was as if my life was running like clockwork. My habits were consistent, predictable, regular and everything seemed to fall into place. When the spring slackened, I wound myself up again and continued my path of consistency, with maybe a little more energy. Some people refer it to the hamster wheel of life.

During that period, the world economy collapsed. I had worked in construction all my life, so it would have been common for people to personally invest in the booming housing market. During the years of growth, I bought properties and used the rising prices as leverage to buy more properties. As soon as I got the keys of one property, I was able to re-mortgage it for the deposit on another property. This was clever and was looking lucrative. Then the unexpected happened, the market collapsed, I was not expecting this nor was I prepared for such a change. Every property I owned went into negative equity. I transcended from a position of being asset rich to asset poor. It was if someone had just jammed my clockwork mechanism, I stopped functioning. I was stuck, I did not know how to respond, and then the real me, my feelings and emotions came forward.

All my insecurities came forward, all the deeper beliefs I held about myself were true. Although this was a universal problem, I was taking this personally. I buried my head in the sand as I did not want to hear the voices that kept reminding me how stupid I was. *How did YOU expect to be successful; you didn't deserve it.* All the beliefs I had that life is a struggle, things are hard, you're not good enough and the consequences of failure started to stack up upon me. I allowed myself to be filled with guilt, shame, and embarrassment. I blamed the world and everyone else; I filled myself with self-pity and resentment.

My head felt it was ready to explode, there were too many thoughts in there, and most of them were negative. I needed a distraction. My behaviours changed, I started to work long hours, ten to twelve hours were regularly put in. I was on a salary, so it was not a conscious effort to make more money, but this behaviour kept my head busy. When I was thinking and utilizing my mind through work, it stopped me from thinking about other things. There were consequences to this, I was getting rewarded at work with salary increases and promotions. I worked long hours. I was loyal to my boss, but I did not know how to wind down. When I was not at work, I felt lost and I did not know what to do. We had thirty days of holidays each year and at one point I was carrying half of them over to the following year. I felt lost and lonely on my days off. I loved my

Saturdays; I loved my bowls and after bowls I stayed in the bar. I worked hard, so I partied hard – well that is what I was telling myself. In reality I was hiding from my feelings and my perceived failures; I used the excuse that I had been there for the kids as they grew up and now, I was finding my own freedom. I was staying away from the people I loved the most, my wife and my kids. I was so riddled with guilt and shame because of what I had done to them so I was staying away from home. If I was not working I was bowling. How could I possibly sit in the same room as someone you pulled down with you, and what a bad example I had become to my boys? I believed I was a failure, I believed I was a bad husband and a terrible father. I was not fully aware of why I was doing these things, but I had enough justification to back up my actions and behaviours. I became the clown once again.

The 2007 economic collapse crippled many people immediately, not me. I spent the next 4 years with my head in the sand. I was struggling and surviving by meeting the deficit of my mortgage payments with my own money and my salary increase, until it eventually ran out. Re-mortgaging the properties and leveraging the rise in property prices combined with the ever-willing bank system made things easy and a great opportunity. I did not see a problem arising and did not face the problem when it did arrive or even seek to find a proactive solution. I was caught out. This confirmed how stupid I was. I believed mistakes had to have consequences, I deserved to be punished in some way and I was willing to accept those consequences – whatever they were.

I worked in an industry where problem solving, quality control and being proactive were simple tasks. Processes and procedures were put into place to save time, avoid wastage, increase quality and productivity. I was good at planning other projects and setting strategies and controls in place. Systems and processes can be built into any job. Once these are in place anyone can continue to follow the process and achieve the same results. Yet emotionally I did not understand my own feelings, I did not fully recognise the emotional side of my problems to be able to deal with them. I was being driven by emotions, yet I could not understand them or see them.

Changing the Programme

I now know the source of my thoughts and behaviours, and why I tried to self-medicate myself by overworking and enjoying a great social life, but I did not realize this back then. I now realize the choices I made were simply a survival strategy. After about four years of burying my head I ran out of money, I raised my head to consider and deliberate what had to be done.

What happened next was possibly the best and paradoxically the worst thing that ever happened to me.

I went to the bank to declare I had ran out of money; I had come to the point where one of my many mortgages could not have been paid. This was the bank who had watched my accounts diminish slowly over the past few years. When I approached them, they almost sneered at me, they said wait until we send you out a letter for non-payment. I had not defaulted on anything - yet. By the end of the month, as expected, I was £840 short for my payments. This was wrong; this was against all my principles.

My wife and I often joked about the first things that I always asked when I came home from work were, 'What's for dinner' and 'Is there any mail?' I had stopped asking about mail. I avoided it; often it would lie for weeks before I would look at it, it was a constant reminder of what I didn't want to see, what I didn't want to hear. I got the letter from the bank to tell me I had missed the payment; I did open this one as I was feeling guilty. I had defaulted and I knew it, and thought *Well, I am not saying that in print.* I took the letter to a solvency practitioner who said it was not strong enough, and that I needed a letter stating they were taking me to court. Court!

I had never been in trouble before; I had never been in a court. Court was for law breakers and criminals. I got my letter, a kind invitation on good quality paper with embossed corners and seals attached, but I did not attend, other hand-delivered letters invited me again. Again, I refused to go. I did not care about the consequences this time, they would do what they wanted, me going to court and pleading innocence wasn't going to help. I had made a mistake and I deserved to be punished. I suppose this was what I was waiting on, I had a deficit every month and it took approximately four years to catch up with me. Now reality was hitting hard. What would happen?

My head was pickled and my thoughts were dangerous; guilt flooded my head and my body, my self-confidence and self-esteem dropped to an all-time low. All the negative emotions I had ever felt seemed to compound and come forward, they enveloped me, I did not know what they were, I could not name them, but I did know I could take no more. I was confused; I was wallowing in a huge cocktail of many emotions and feelings that I could not even describe. My life was in danger, I could not see any other way out! I was in my garage weighing up the possibilities and ways to end the feelings...and then it happened − the Anger erupted. It was not a physical thrashing out anger it was more of a *What the f#@K are you doing?!! What are you thinking?!! Get back into the house and Wise the f#@K up!!* Someone was giving me a rollicking, and this time it was ME. My self-survival instincts had kicked in. I was so angry with myself, and this time rightly so.

This initiated a complete shift in my mind-set; there was a complete and a severe internal stir up from within. I realized the feelings I had were childish, even selfish. These feelings of feeling sorry for myself and all the 'poor me' crap I had been taking on board, together with all the "I am a victim" nonsense I was telling myself. I was stunned, I was emotional, but I felt and could see true gratitude for the first time. It was as if a cloud had lifted and I could see beyond. I felt a release of pressure; the anger erupted and emptied me from the pressure within. There was a lot more to deal with, but this was a great start.

The Cloud lifts

I could see a future, a positive future. I could see that I was part of that future and I could even take control of it. Why would I let circumstances dictate my future and wellbeing? I had a lot of things to sort out in my relationships, my work, my family, but I was the only one who could do that, not anyone else. I may not have been responsible for the collapse of the economy, but I was the only one who was responsible for my feelings. I was the one who was acting and reacting to what was happening around me, and none of it was personal, it wasn't about me, it was a global phenomenon. I was one of many others that found themselves in this same predicament. The wind blows on us all, the rain falls on us all, and the sun shines on us all. Universal things happen to everyone, what we make of, and how we allow them to affect us is down to us. If you allow your emotions and feelings to be governed by other people and external events, you will live a miserable existence.

The same mind that had tortured me was now helping me to realize what I had and what I always had. I had so much, but I was blinded, because I was wallowing in a pit of blame, shame, guilt, and self-pity. Tragic things do happen in life, but it is how we act and react to them that are important. I felt Freedom of Mind.

What does that even mean? Freedom of mind? I pondered and considered why this event affected me so much, yet others shrugged their shoulders and dealt with their issues. Why were they not reacting the way I was? How come others were able to deal with and offload their liabilities and I couldn't, or rather wouldn't. I realized I was emotionally attached to the situation and my emotions were the clouds and mist that blocked my vision and my judgement, but the sun had come out to burn them away. I could see a future and I could create a different future. I realized it doesn't matter what happens, it is how we react to it that is important, and now I was going to take ownership of the situation and my feelings.

Keeping the Programming Updated

I was living my life running on a programme that was badly out of date. My programming may have served me in the past, but it was not serving me now. This programme needed to be updated or changed completely. We have software updates regularly on our phones, laptops and computers, so it was time for my update – my current programme was dangerous. I had the warning that it was out of date, I could now see the benefits of a new programme and how it would serve me in the future, so it was time to invest in my upgrade, it was time to invest in me, to defragment – to organise and to optimise the hard drive of my mind. I spent money, I spent time, and I re-programmed my beliefs and thought patterns.

I know this language may seem strange, but this is exactly what needed to be done. I said previously we are a product of our programming, so it wasn't me that was the problem; it was the programmes I was running on. If we could change the way we think consciously, we could easily change our thinking processes to remove our anxieties, panic, fears, worries, feelings of low self-worth and low self-esteem. Yet this does not happen as easy as it sounds, it's because the problem is not a conscious problem. If it was a conscious problem, we would fix it immediately, wouldn't we? So, if the problem is not a conscious problem it must be a level below consciousness – a subconscious level. Why do some people find things harder than others? It's because they have a programme that matches that conclusion, things are tough, times are hard, I could never do that, life's a struggle. Are these people likely to succeed? We are what we think we are.

Making a Choice

I have been asked many times 'Why did you become a Hypnotherapist?' I didn't know fully at the time, but the main reason was that it was one of the ways I changed my programming, my thought processes and my beliefs. I had choices; I was able to deal with many old and inappropriate belief systems and pain points from the past. I used hypnosis to reprogramme my mind with positive new beliefs. I replaced the old with new information that I honestly believed and could accept. I became a hypnotherapist to deal with my issues, but also because it was so random, so unique, very few people understood it, so nobody could judge me. Believe me some tried, but they couldn't validate their opinion as they didn't have enough knowledge or information. I am now a trainer of hypnosis, as I believe it is a fantastic tool to allow change.

I mentioned I didn't have any emotional intelligence up until this point; many people recognise their emotions and even know why they act and react the way they do. For years I was not aware of who I was. I knew I had fears and insecurities, but they were just fear of judgement, fear of failure, fear of making mistakes. I had good morals and values but coming from a strict religious background any

61

genuine mistakes and deviation from the moral code and requirements caused confusion because they were embedded using the same processes. It is strange how I was able to reach the top of my profession in construction. I believe that was because I had another set of beliefs and confidences that backed up that part of my life, although I did need external approval for what I was doing. I required acknowledgement and could not accept or fathom my processes or procedures being questioned or being criticized. I was result-driven and my results spoke for themselves, so opinions from others, to me often remained invalid.

Dealing with your perceptions of the past will allow you to see and recognize the effect of your emotions and beliefs. When you gain this information, you become more emotionally intelligent, you understand your path better. You understand the consequences of choices and you realise for every action there is a reaction.

When you increase your emotional wellbeing you see things differently, you have a more balanced view on life, you make decisions based on fact, and you make decisions and make choices with more accuracy and clarity. Your choices are no longer based on emotions. You take action, sometimes massive action, apprehension, or fears do not hold you back when you have a desire for something so great. You recognize your vulnerabilities and when you make a decision, you commit to that decision. You face that challenge with discipline and absolute determination because failure to succeed is simply not an option, it becomes a choice. Success is the fulfilment of a goal after the required effort.

We must make choices, all our lives we have made choices and there are consequences to our choices, some good and some not so good. I decided to change my career. I had been helping others using the tools I had learned and the qualifications I had gained. When I realized why I felt and acted the way I did this opened a whole new chapter in my life, my passions changed. I loved my job; construction was in my blood from no age, some of my first memories were of me as a 3 or 4-year-old child walking in the foundations of our house. I am results orientated; in construction I saw measurable results - but I had to share my new knowledge.

What if someone existed just like me, but no-one was there to show them or guide them along a better path, a different and better life, one without clouds and mist. What if I could help others see more clearly and show them how to detach themselves from pains and traumas from the past? What if I could show others that anxiety is based on fears, that worry was only imagining something that they didn't want to happen? What if I could get these people to look at what they did want, rather than dwell on what they didn't want? I could show these people that they were created equal, the same as everyone who has ever been born into this world. What if I could show them, they are simply a product of their upbringing and past, and that your past does not define who you are? What if I could show them they have a choice to be, to do and to have anything they want?

I left construction, I had been a manager all my life, starting at the bottom, at the very lowest rung and climbed my way to Site Manager, then up to Contracts Manager and finally to Director of Construction in the Company I was working for. I made it even with all my insecurities, it wasn't easy, but it was worth it. I learned so much and have been blessed with so much throughout my life.

Everything I have ever done has been measured and now as a Business and Emotional Wellbeing Coach; I support my clients to secure measurable results. Just as IQ can be measured, so can Emotional Intelligence or Emotional Quotient EQ. From having little emotional intelligence, I have become an expert on the subject. I show people how to overcome their fears, doubts and apprehensions. I allow my clients to see the future with clarity and to be able to make decisions based on fact, not emotions. I was stuck; I felt lost, but now I understand why these things materialise and I can help others. I have a unique set of tools that give results and show people how to achieve the success mind-set and Freedom of Mind.

If you feel I can help you, please contact me and I will assist you in any way I can.

Kindest Regards

Ken

CHAPTER 4
Authentically you

by Karen Fleming

There is a calling and an awakening in our world today, life as we know it is changing. Many are now turning their attention inward, searching for purpose, meaning and clarity as we open to this new way. It's up to each of us to recognize how to co-create together, to connect with each other to create the world we want for our future.

As children we are molded by parents, teachers, religion, culture, and society. We develop belief systems and thought patterns that teach us to fit in with the world around us. We learn to adapt to our environment and conform to expectations which may cause us to gradually lose touch with our **authenticity**. On many occasions this involves conforming to standards or ways of fitting in. This version of us can be thought of as the adaptive self – the self that prioritizes fitting in, getting along and generally doing what we are told. Although adapting is not without value and purpose, we learn how to become functioning members of society but if you feel unfulfilled, connecting with your authentic self could help you create a life of abundance and fulfilment.

I call my authentic self my inner hugger, She is my creativity, she flows with life, kind, she loves freedom, music and dance, she knows how to let her hair down and hasn't a care in the world, she loves having fun and she loves life. She's the warrior within, the part of me

65

that stands up for me. She happily lives with a sense of adventure and joy, living each moment with curiosity and enthusiasm. She brings happiness to me in true form, and she brought me on her path for years. But then life changed and I became too busy for her.

Fear, which later brought inspiration, came into my world as a young girl when my mother took ill. One morning at the beginning of December 1987 she was diagnosed with MS (Multiple Sclerosis). During that period, I was scared of losing Mum, every night I prayed for her to come home, and thankfully with medical and nutritional intervention, and prayers, illness became wellness and she made a full recovery. Mum Is today for me a great source of inspiration in my life and my work and because of her I developed a great interest in the body and mind and how we heal.

As a young girl growing up, I loved to daydream and like most children I believed in fairy tales. I dreamed of having my very own magic wish bag, which I would reach into and take out whatever I needed. As a child latest but also a deeper wish. I was quiet and shy. I went to an all-girls catholic school. Then went to secondary school in Ballymun road. My parents were self-employed, I am the eldest of 3 girls, and when we were young Mam took pride in dressing us up. Every Saturday in our house was exciting, we had treats, watched TV, Mam put rollers in our hair, preparing us for family day out on a Sunday.

Later, in my teenage years, I liked the idea of modelling. Mam was excited about my portfolio; she was about to arrange it for me when

I gave her the news that I was expecting my first child. My son was born in 1996. I was 17 at the time. I had left school and grew up quickly. I didn't know a lot about life or who I was then, but I had worked in a creche for some time and cared for my 2 younger sisters so I believed I could be a good mum. I loved my son and vowed to myself that someday we would have the life that he, my family, and I would be proud of.

Within 1 year after giving birth to my son I decided to return to education to study business, I didn't have a lot of money, so I worked part-time. I was lucky that I had some good friends who helped me through. My friends, family and my son's grandmother's sense of humour were a support, and love guided him to become the smart warm-hearted man he is today.

Relationships were an area I needed to develop as I didn't trust easily. I made poor choices at times, mostly because I was connected to anxiety rather than true me. Sometimes I was depressed, I felt unable to cope at times. So, I decided to face it and began the journey of self-discovery and personal empowerment.

In my early 20s Dad and I attended a seminar ran by Tony Robbins – *Unleash the Power Within*. Here we completed a fire-walk and set goals that we wished to achieve in the future. It was a powerful happy atmosphere, I felt alive and happy and thousands of people attended. It was fun. They played loud music. I hadn't a care in the world for I believed in my own ability to create a life I wanted while at that weekend of success, personal achievement, overcoming depression despite obstacles in my way Following this, I began to embark on a new way of life, I quit smoking and became a vegetarian, within a few weeks I met my daughter's father. I joined him in a car sales business and we fell in love. Soon after we were engaged to be married and had a baby girl together and were overjoyed. My daughter was born in 2003, a bundle of joy. I now had the family and the lifestyle I dreamed of. She is a loving, talented, and creative young lady. She's almost 17 now and has recently begun her modelling portfolio.

Some weeks following her birth, I started feeling anxious and unworthy. Being a mum, partner and business owner was a great lifestyle and although I loved my roles, I felt somehow disconnected from my authentic self. I got so busy living my roles that I didn't let the true me come out to play. This was my inner hugger and it made me slow down again, to look deeper within and to stand up for my own joy and fulfilment.

I had experiences in the past that were troubling me; I had emotions which resurfaced and required healing. Your body doesn't lie, it knows. I had left a part of me behind I wasn't honouring her, the true me, she was lost and it was my job to find her, *'be true to yourself, truth will lead the way.'*

I joined an anxiety management group where I learned steps to recover. We were given a recovery booklet which contained the following poem. It has been with me for 16 years, reflects a little on my personal journey. I hope this can help someone (or many) learning to walk their own path of self-discovery.

Portia Nelson There's a Hole in My Sidewalk: The Romance of Self-Discovery

'I walk down the street.

There is a deep hole in the sidewalk.

I fall in. I am lost... I am helpless.

It isn't my fault. It takes forever to find a way out.

I walk down the same street.

There is a deep hole in the sidewalk.

I pretend I don't see it. I fall in again.

I can't believe I am in the same place.

But it isn't my fault. It still takes me a long time to get out.

I walk down the same street. There is a deep hole in the sidewalk.

I see it is there. I still fall in. It's a habit. My eyes are open.

I know where I am. It is my fault. I get out immediately.

I walk down the same street. There is a deep hole in the sidewalk.

I walk around it. I walk down another street.'

I fell a few times in life, but I learned that if you fall don't give up on yourself, try again. Find people who can help you, education and self- awareness were useful tools for me.

Some years later, still seeking to learn more about becoming the best that I can be, I found a wonderful friend. She dedicated her life to helping others to connect to their true self. Her energy, wisdom, and awareness were most inspiring. I leaned into our conversations and felt my energy rise high to learn about our true awareness and how vast it is, I began to access a happier place within. I learned how experiences we go through in life can be an opportunity to learn. When we are being the best we can be and by being in present moment it can have a positive effect on ourselves and influence the people around us. She helped many people through her teachings.

So, my personal development Journey continued. My relationship status with my daughter's father went through some difficult times, we decided it was best to be friends, my dream of becoming happily married changed from coming soon to hopefully someday. After a few years, still recovering from our separation, I began my Vape business, first by introducing product to a party of 10 people, and then I began attending a local market on a Sunday. The people at the market were a community of lovely hard working people, we had great time, even though it was dark mornings and freezing at times, I loved it, consistency and commitment brought me fun and rewards that grew from strength to strength. Within couple of months I opened a store in my local town. I was both excited and fearful about opening a store. It was during a recession, but I needed it to create a future for myself and children plus the excitement and enthusiasm was stronger than the fear. I decided to trust and enjoy the process rather than regret never trying. I questioned my values and if the business would serve my need to improve as many lives as possible. By staying true to my values, and with the help of friends and family, I made the right choices. I was helping people and part of something bigger than myself. My products make a positive difference to people's lives. This made my work fulfilling and therefore successful. I worked hard and enjoyed every minute. It is true that if you love what you do, it does not feel like work. Find your passion and purpose and follow it. My hope is that someday I am making a positive difference helping others to take the steps towards being the best version of themselves.

I formed a partnership with a man who has become a great friend today. We were from different culture and background which was both challenging and inspiring. We had the most interesting conversations, and in time we found ourselves in business together. We travelled to many countries to business events, educating ourselves and sourcing new products, met some wonderful friends. Sometimes when tough decisions needed to be made our communication was difficult, we both had very different leadership style, misunderstandings were many which we laugh about today, we could write our own book on our adventures, we discovered the best way for us to connect is to each other's authenticity, meet each other there. Because of him I further developed my interest in language, culture and life.

It took time but we have a great understanding of each other today and support each other on our journey. I'm grateful to him today for he inspires me to be the best me.

I had worked hard for many years and had total focus and dedication, my goal was to work on the business rather than in the business but hadn't quite got there, I learned the hard way about the importance of having life balance, running a business and having a family is very rewarding, making time for yourself is a priority, something I didn't do enough of and it began to affect my wellbeing.

A couple of years ago my world as I knew it was challenged, leading me to surrender to the reality of what I was running away from. I had a frightening experience. One night my home was broken into. My child and I were alone in the house. I heard the window smash downstairs, and I quickly checked my phone - it was 3am. I thought to myself, *this can't be real,* as I heard the footsteps come up the stairs, I froze in fear, looking around the room for something to defend us with... *I must protect us both.* I walked towards the bedroom door and looked out into the landing there was a man standing there, I was terrified, yet something inside me wasn't afraid at all. It was the warrior within, this part of me shouted to get out and looked him directly in the eye feeling like an animal ready to pounce to protect her cub. Fortunately, after a locked stare for a couple of minutes he turned and left walked down the stairs slowly and left the house. Shortly after that incident and due to stress in work, I changed. I felt stuck. I had become very serious about life and business. I worried at night about safety and at some point I was aware I had left behind my childlike innocence, my capacity to be curious and to have that awe of wonder, my love for living life with a sense of adventure and joy. Everything caught up with me. I lost confidence my ability and I had become a fragment of myself. I wanted to be happy, but had forgotten my teachings, life was busy, and I felt there was no escape. '*I must keep going, I must find a resolve*', I thought my Adaptive Self could help me out. Nothing I did made a difference so eventually, and only after an experience that changed my life, I opted to support my own authentic self. It began with the environment within first, and then the outer environment followed.

I didn't like being alone at night and one evening when I was alone, I began to experience a hallucination, which my doctor said was a psychotic event. After attending hospital to have blood tests, and a brain scan was carried out, I was delighted when the results showed up clear. The event lasted for a couple of months. I was non-verbal at the time, due to overactivity in my mind and I felt furthest away from harmony and peace than I had ever experienced. Fear was with me until I learned to move into a place of trust

I began to explore different ways to heal, I began supplementing, exercising and focusing on recovery. I began to make better choices in relationship with myself. Why? Because If you can love and heal yourself first, you can love another. How true and ironic was this at that time? For at first, I didn't get it, until it eventually all made sense. I knew my environment needed to change, the main one being able to stop and observe, and to let go and recognize that you are okay just as you are.

At first, I didn't get it, until it eventually all made sense. I had to learn to embrace my own personal power and create situations that were nourishing for me. Allow myself to be loved. It was time to see myself as loveable. Take responsibility for my own wellbeing and connect with my truth. The situation in front of me at that time was an exact reflection of this. How could I ever be happy, if I was at a deeper level inside believing I don't deserve happy?

During this time, I felt I had no power or control over my mind or the situation. *Was I going to survive this*? Then I asked the question 'How can I see things differently?' I began to let go and surrender to and pray for recovery, *'Can you please put this whole thing right because I know I can't?'*

Embracing the now, feeling what's real for me now, channeling the energy was he way forward. I was shown that I was in fact looking from the lens of false learned beliefs and behaviours at the time, and when I made the decision to take back control of my life everything improved. Hope, Love, inspiration allowed me to take the steps, heal the past, and let it go, then align my mind, heart and gut to follow what's best for me. I began for real to value myself and my health and wellbeing. The experience woke me up. *This was it, there was no going back for if I am well, I can help others too.'* Part of this healing is in embracing all of you. Make room for yourself in your life, you are important. Be yourself wherever you go. This takes courage, we don't want people to see our imperfections, I thought at times people were laughing at me because I had my own way, or I was in my own world, I said silly things at times, I was different and I wanted to be normal so I tried to fit in, but that's no fun because you're not being you so embrace you.. Sometimes I am funny, not because I'm great at telling jokes but because I'm just being me. Once thought of as a weakness is just what makes me Unique.

Thankfully, I have now embarked on a new journey of transformation and love with my authentic self. When I prayed for a solution a shift began to happen. I had previously held on tight to the fear of the unknown. Looking back, I wasn't trusting me. I had become overwhelmed with fear-based thinking because I didn't know how to navigate the necessary changes that had to take place, so ultimately the diagnosis wasn't that important in the end as much as the realization and perspective I have today.

One by one new insights began to unfold before me. I saw how my life happened up to that point. The seeds in childhood were sown in the disempowering beliefs such as *'I'm not good enough,'* They had played out through my relationships. I built a wall around myself to keep safe, but it kept others out. The seeds had been planted during the challenging experiences, however who was watering the flowers? Who was keeping the beliefs alive? Who planted them? – my disempowered self. I didn't know any better at the time. The beliefs were formed from a place of fear within to protect and care for the younger me, which then had served the purpose of keeping me stuck. I took the time with my inner hugger and began again.

'What I'm looking for is not out there, it is in me.'

- Helen Keller

When you wake up from the slumber you can begin to reclaim your power. We all have a light shining bright within. We are all resilient wonderful beings. The sun always shines within us but sometimes it can get clouded over.

It took some time for me to connect with my authentic self again. I believed if others in my environment were happy then I could be too, until I saw the illusion for what it was. Fulfilment is an inside job. I became happier in myself, put myself first, living from a true space. Aligning with my Authenticity began to affect others in a positive way. To live from the inside out means to be in the here and now, to stop people pleasing, being a victim of circumstance, being afraid to be you for fearing you're not good enough so instead playing small, access the part of you that is you.

I asked myself when would be the time to finally let go of the past and connect and trust that you will be okay, I began to build a new foundation through daily practice of love and gratitude. I began to trust myself again. When connected to fear you are not trusting or allowing any unfolding to happiness. Connect to the true amazingness that you are. I have come to understand that traumas are disconnection and the healing is the reconnection with your true self.

Last year in 2019, I bought myself a beautiful crystal vase. One day as I was changing the flowers and the vase slipped from my hand and smashed into many pieces on the floor. As I picked up each piece, I began to reflect those pieces as my life up to now. Imagine with me for a moment that each piece represents who you believe you are, the events in your life up to now and your past beliefs. You and I know we will never repair the vase to its original form as it was, and

76

we will head to our nearest store to replace it. In retrospect if you can imagine the broken pieces are reflecting your life and if you tried to glue those pieces back together what would each piece represent? Look at it this way, the vase holds the flowers, the place they live for a while, but they are not connected to the source of life. The wholesome authentic self is connected to the source of love and life, when allowed to be free. Soil, water, oxygen, and sunlight support it to maintain its natural state. So, the fact that the vase smashed gives you the opportunity to release the pieces of old adaptive you, for now you have finally found truth and opportunity and can begin allowing who you are to blossom. As you release the past emotions and beliefs, connect to your source and transform yourself.

In good time, with commitment and patience, you release piece by piece of who you are not and come into who you truly are. Carefully and consciously replacing the pieces with your self-belief, love, happiness, values, strengths and wisdom, inner knowing, and when completed the stronger characteristics of who you are rebuild your life.

Some people these days are feeling disconnected, fearful, vulnerable, and unsure about who or what to trust. Is this true for you? Are you seeking outside yourself for answers, have you let fear and limitations run your life? If so, when would be a good time to release that so you can live from your best self? By living as the Adapted Self, we can disconnect from our own innate support system, our life source. It can cause us to create an image of ourselves that we appear strong and "okay." If you know how powerful the story you tell yourself is in relation to what you experience in your life, what wonderful story would you create and live by? The universe helps us to achieve what we believe; it co-creates with you. What do you want? Believe it, feel it, achieve it. Know that you have within you the power to create good in your life in any given moment. Sometimes it's one step at a time and that's okay. Start today and be consistent.

A dear friend had a beautiful, rare set of crystal glasses, she kept it in a safe place in the hope that someday she would have a very special day to use it. She had waited years for her moment. One day as we chatted, we discussed what needed to happen to allow herself to have that feeling now? What if Today is the most magnificent opportunity? She decided that evening to prepare a nice meal with her husband and enjoy the glass of champagne together, they celebrated their life, and she found the courage to live the moment. So, ask yourself, what if today is that day? What if that crystal is a symbol of what's inside of you, waiting to be realized? Are you are waiting for when the mortgage is paid, the car is fixed, the children are finished college, or when something outside happens that will allow you to be happy? Fulfilment is something you can create now. It reminds me of a palliative nurse who once asked patients who were on their deathbeds about their biggest regret in life. Here's what they said: They all wished they had the courage to live a life true to themselves, not the life others expected of them, or the expectations they had of themselves. How long are you willing to wait to fully allow yourself to come out to play? To enjoy each day, to be fully YOU.

The stories we tell ourselves

To discover your authenticity is to become the observer of what your current story is based around. How do you talk to yourself throughout the day? Pay attention to the words you think and speak! How do they make you feel? What thoughts and feelings do you have about yourself and about others? What impact do these thoughts and feelings have on your inner environment? What negative beliefs do you need to let go of? What flowers do you need to water that encourage you? What weeds need to go? Write your answers here now.

_____

_____

_____

_____

_____

_____

_____

You have within your strength, compassion, resilience, and an imagination to help you be the best you can be. If your story does not make you feel empowered, tell yourself a new story, write it today, then read it aloud every day because you deserve happiness and success. What does the highest and best version of YOU look like? What feeling will this give you when you live it every day? What words, conversations and actions must you use throughout your day to be this best version of you? Who is the authentic you? When did or do you feel your most happy, alive and well? Who do u love to spend time with? When do you feel your most natural self?

Every day the thoughts we think, choose, and believe in, help shape who we become. Observe how you talk to yourself. You deserve to enjoy this life and now it is time to believe that and live by it. The inner environment is the most important environment; by creating a positive change within you it will also reflects outside of you and into your relationships. It creates space for the authentic you in your life, in your day, in yourself. Then ensure your outer environment aligns with this truth you find. Listen to your truth. Here are some suggestions that I have found to be life changing:

1) List 5 things that you are great at? Commit to do more of that regularly
2) Every morning, affirm the following:
   'I trust and embrace my true self,
   I love being the best me,
   and my life is a reflection of this.

3) Read your new story, listen to it, or visualise it whatever works for you.

4) Every night, write, say, or notice what you are grateful for that day. Capture the moments of joy.

5) Remember every day that we have one life. One day at a time, make it the best. Commit to being true to yourself.

6) What 1 change can you make today that allows your authenticity to support you and enhance your life?

7) If you feel challenged make your vision stronger than your problem. Have the vision infused with the feeling and think only about what you want and what you love.

8) Throughout your day remind yourself of and stay aligned to your best you. What's most important to you?

9) Aim always to bring balance back into your life, inside and out. Nourish you.

10) Make a positive difference to someone else, a smile, an act of kindness. Be you.

We are the co-creators of our own health, simply by trusting more. When making an important decision it can be wise to ask yourself if it aligns with your values. When I was a child, I wasn't allowed to walk to our local takeaway at night. However, on one particular night, I cheekily ventured anyway. I knew it was wrong, but I went anyway. Although it was fun to be out late at night, I had a strange feeling inside. When I came home, I had a huge weight on my conscience, and I burst into tears and told on myself. My mam found it funny laughing as she hugged me, but I couldn't hold it in. I felt so much better that I told the truth. Looking back now, honesty was a value for me, and we had trust within our relationship. When my value was aligned, I felt more ME. When we screw up, which we sometimes do, it's important to know that we can forgive, put it right to what is most true for you. Energy flows where attention goes, we always have an opportunity to align our vision with our desired outcome. We are together in this journey, it's our community, contribute to yourself, to others. Create a life of balance within and around you, your loving kindness makes a difference.

> *'To be yourself in a world that is trying to make you*
> *Something else is the greatest accomplishment.'*
> – Ralph Waldo Emerson

Whatever situation you are in at this moment, when you begin to have faith, choose love rather than what you fear. Everything we do in our life is based on trust, but the true trust is in yourself and your ability. You were created with love by love.

Consider nature for a moment; if you plant a seed, it will grow into a beautiful flower. My grandmother would nourish the garden flowers daily, she also spoke about flowers as a source to bring love and happiness within. Her nature is funny, loving, kind and strong. When my grandad passed she told herself to simply keep going. At 80-years-old, she made beautiful pieces of mosaic, this kept her connected to her happiness. She has love, she has hope, her innocence and mischievousness remained all these years. She has

82

light in her eyes and faith in her heart. Her humour and outlook on life is inspiring. Her flowers in the garden always blossomed as she loved and appreciated them. Next time you observe a sunflower, notice how they reach out towards the sunlight for nourishment throughout the day.

One day in conversation myself and a friend chatted about this. She loves sunflowers and informed me that when there is no sun, they turn towards each other for light. We can learn from nature to reach out to each other too.

Remember, how can a tiny seed blossom into a beautiful flower? What's the process that takes it there? What does the seed need to do or think or believe in order to become the tree?

With the right environment we can become the happy and healthy. We just need to water the seeds we wish to grow strong and trust the process.

My grandmother taught me about life experiences, working hard and raising her family. She created an environment that was supportive and loving. She loves cooking and she has a caring nature and would bake cakes for the community and cook for hours and enjoy. She didn't have an easy life, but she created her own happiness. Trust the process.

Hug yourself, and your loved ones regularly because it's one of the highest expressions of gratitude and connection, an expression of all the good in life. The more authentic you become, the less the material world becomes a source of fulfilment. True fulfilment comes from living in the present moment exactly as you are, enjoying the finer moments in life.

The big question I want you to ask yourself today is, when would be a good time for you to be the real you? What are you waiting for? Listen to the deeper wisdom of what brings you peace and take ownership of your life. Your life is your responsibility. Don't be afraid, be strong and have faith. Life can offer passion, excitement and acceptance. Love is the essence of life.

When you think and act from the love that is present within you, you will feel connected. When you feel lack of joy the missing piece is YOU – your awareness about who you truly are and what you are really capable of being, doing and having. If you desire to be your true yourself, if you want to return to LOVE, you can. Love always was and always will be, lovingly waiting for you. It's in nature's pleasures, the beauty of a rose in the garden, watching the stars at night, good food in good company, making love, a smile, a hug, a kind word from another, feelings of joy embraced at any moment. I would like to share some points that can help remind you.

-   Create a daily routine that supports you. Get your day off to a good start and stick with it.

-   Embrace the now, take regular moments throughout your day to just be, focusing on present moment.

-   Ask, what can I do in this moment to feel amazing now?

-   Recall a time when you felt most happy and loved. Ask yourself what you love about your life. What would you like to change?

- Connect with your inner wisdom throughout your daily activities, work and relationships.

- Remind yourself daily of your true value, bring it to your own life and to others.

- Play your favourite music. *Everybody's free,* by Rozalla creates great energy!

- Dance, take up a hobby.

- Be honest to yourself and your needs, never give up.

- Have self-compassion, love yourself.

- Nourish your body and mind.

- Choose the thoughts, feelings and actions that help you to be the best you.

- Allow your authentic self to lead.

- Trust in a Prayer. I have come to believe that the power of a prayer is important and is required in our lives, whatever prayer means to you.

In my life growing up, I had many great friends, and I share an innocent authentic love with one in particular. We spent a lot of time together. It was cute looking back; how innocent it was that we had a special place in each other's hearts. We were both U2 fans by the age of 10 and we still are today. Life changed for both of us and circumstances separated us, we didn't see each other for a long time. However, years later our paths crossed again. It was then after all this time that he knew me as I was back then, the natural authentic me, and I him. Ironically, our favourite song was, 'I *still haven't found what I'm looking for.'* In life, as it turned out, we hadn't found what we were looking for, however we had retained this friendship and mutual affection. I felt happy again. This helped me to reconnect with the part of me that I know to be truly valuable and joyful. I began to nurture myself back to health and wellbeing and begin a fresh start.

It took work, focus, and dedication but I had to change things. It wasn't easy, but in doing so I became more detached from the adapted me and more liberated in the true self. I found my inner wish bag that I had dreamed of as a child, in fact we all have it, it was there all along. I sat and made a wish. From that day on, life began again. It's never too late. I hold gratitude in my heart for all the people in my life who have lovingly supported and believed in me on this journey at the times when I didn't. And life begins today.

What if you just be gentle with yourself these days, talk lovingly to yourself these days? If you need help. reach out and connect with someone who can help you, to help you take the next step towards your greatness. You have it inside you. You have the key.

Learn to take things less personally, have fun throughout your day, laugh a lot (it's contagious), seek to enjoy the fun side of life. Life can be an adventure and we can create our own experience of more joy. Become it, live your day. now exactly as you are. Simply by being the highest version of yourself you could open others to their own joy, healing and awakening. The truth is you can. Let your true self shine, become the best you. You are amazing. Now get out of your own way!

Love is bigger than anything in its way.'

– U2

I would sincerely like to thank Donna Kennedy, Pat Slattery, my friends (new and old) and family for supporting me to become the best me and put the pieces back together in both life and business.

CHAPTER 5
The Good, The Bad, and The Rugby

by Ed Martin

It was December 2016 and I just left our solicitor's office, where my wingman had handed over the envelope with his personal cheque to buy out the balance of my loans from a vulture fund, who had bought what remained of my property assets from Ulster Bank, bringing an end, I hoped, to five of the worst years of my life.

The problem all started in 2005 in the back of a taxi. I was on my way to Kehoe's pub to meet my accountant, Damian, for a pint. We are former rugby teammates, and he was also a great friend. Damian has an incredible brain and skill in that no matter which of his clients he speaks to he has a complete grasp of their business affairs, as if he had studied their file in great detail just before they met, which he hadn't. I've always tried to surround myself in business with far more intelligent people than myself but also people I can get on with, Damian more than qualified on both counts. On the way to Kehoe's I was discussing property with the taximan. You see, back in 2005 property was what everyone discussed and we were all "experts" and he was advising me where I should buy, and in particular that I couldn't go wrong with Eastern Europe and Turkey; not only would I make a killing but I'd get a great tan as the weather was good there too. I was sitting there thinking that there was something seriously wrong with the property market, considering I was sitting in a taxi, listening to property advice (and no disrespect) from a taxi driver about how easy it was to make money in property. It was a bit like that famous story about Joseph Kennedy Snr, father of JFK, a wise share investor who sold all his shares back in the 1920s just before the crash when a shoeshine boy was giving him free tips on shares.

You see, I'm third generation property. My father wisely advised me, and I take his advice with me to this day, that all a long-term property investment is meant to do is to increase in value by a couple of percent per year. I've learnt that there are also short to medium term opportunities for people to make big profits but in some cases huge losses as a result of distortions in the market. There are four main distortions in the property markets; the world economy, the local economy, technology for example zoom and finally where the government introduce incentives or restrictive legislation (often politically motivated rather than economically motivated) that create a mini bubble or slide in certain property sectors. These distortions will sometimes provide a window of opportunity but your timing into and more importantly out of the market is critical. You need real experience and expertise to exploit these opportunities fully.

The conversation with the taximan was a red flag alert for me and later, over a couple of pints with Damian, I vowed to stop buying property. You see while property is a fantastic sector to work in, and if you ask me would I do it all again, absolutely 100%, it is also a complete rollercoaster ride, not only for you but also for those around you. Often you have to make fast nearly impulsive but always informed decisions to buy a property, often it finally comes down to your gut feeling that tells you it's the right decision. On three occasions I've bought properties without talking to Mrs. M first, which she has turned into wonderful homes. Buying and selling property is addictive, there is something different every single day thrown at you, deals to assess, solutions to solve, and people to meet; you need to be knowledgeable, even an expert in about a thousand different disciplines and I thrive in this environment, meeting people and having the control to make decisions based today on over forty years in this business. But back in 2005 I had to stop because property is anything but easy. And I did stop, well for a while anyway.

You see when you're involved in property deals all your life (I did my first when I was 18), it's very hard to sit on your hands for long periods of time, and although I had great intentions to stop buying property in 2005, two years later in 2007 I invested in syndicated investments. Syndicated Investments are where a group of investors participate in a fund to make an investment and because they are a group their buying power is much greater. However, in most cases you have little or no say or control in how the fund is run. I diversified into four such funds, none of them in Ireland, two of them run by the Investment Wealth Section of Ulster Bank (my bank of 25 years with money borrowed from the same bank), all secured by my very solid property portfolio. It seemed like a good decision at the time, but in 2008 the world economy changed when Lehman Brothers collapsed, and my 30 years of work started to unravel very quickly.

I had made two big mistakes that were going to cost me dearly. Firstly, I had lost my discipline by getting involved with syndicated investments. It's not my area of expertise and you are only a small cog in a big wheel with them. You have no input into how they are managed, nor have you any flexibility to get out at a time of your choice. Secondly, I had given away my control on two fronts, to the fund and to the Bank – the syndicated loans were supported by my extensive property portfolio. I went against my expertise.

In June 2011, my accounts were transferred from the main section of Ulster Bank to a special restructuring section of the bank called Global Restructuring Group or GRG. GRG was portrayed as a special section of the bank to help businesses that had fallen into trouble, with a view to rescuing them and returning the business back into the main stream of the bank, however history will reflect that it has a dismal record at this and in fact it was later described in the UK courts as a "profit center".

The minute we were transferred into GRG, the word *conflict* became a very big part of my life. I found GRG to be a highly aggressive section of the bank. Their stated aim may have been to find solutions and return accounts back into the main section of the bank, but statistics showed that they succeeded in less than 3% of all cases that were transferred and they folded a lot of solid businesses along the way.

When I look back, reflect and walk a mile in the shoes of the guy who was sitting across the desk in the GRG offices, rejecting proposal after proposal that our team put to him, I realize it had nothing to do with him, the banks needs were greater than mine, they simply had to balance their books .I came to the conclusion that conflict is where two parties want different things, but now I understand that with conflict the party who has control and whose needs are greater than the other party will prevail. Conflict is not the want but the exclusive need. Despite numerous high-end proposals and bringing in the very best experts, I was continually turned down and went through the long, slow and very painful process of losing everything that I had spent my life building up.

It wasn't easy to go home, after every broken proposal, face my family, shake my head, get into bed, try to sleep, try to get up in the morning, in fact just try to simply function without letting the situation encompass every aspect of your day and night for five years. I wonder now on reflection, like a death of someone very close to you, would it have been better mentally for me to lose the entire portfolio in one go rather than a slow drip feed process over five years?. They say that all our experiences are what we need for our personal growth however all this left me with was scars deep scars.

By the time I was finished with GRG in 2016 when they sold what was left of my loans to Cerberus, I lost more than 150 properties that I had owned or invested in. I remember at the time of those initial meetings with GRG wondering, like in sport had I choked in our presentations to the bank. During my rugby playing and coaching days I'd witnessed it on many occasions, maybe your place kicker, who has prepared and practiced for years for the moment when he has to deliver on the big occasion, maybe a kick in the last minute to win the game, and sometimes at that moment they just choke. I've seen it many times, but as I always say to the rest of the team you have to love your kickers, nobody else stood up to take the kick. However, at my first meeting with GRG I was confident I could deliver at that moment. We submitted our initial detailed rescue plan to the bank over a 45 minute presentation, it was meticulously prepared, I had conferred with industry experts in every aspect of the submission, I was very happy with the way the team (in particular my accountant Damian) and I presented our case on the day. GRG knew that we brought thousands of hours of experience and a reputation of delivering previously to the table. We were primed to perform that day. That day there was no choking in our presentation; it was on point and delivered in finite detail.

But when the bank then delivered their 5-minute-rejection of the restructuring proposal and told us to sell everything, I just sat there numb and panic set in. Panic is a hard emotion to describe. I found in that instance it hit me straight away, I knew I needed to do something, but I had no idea what or how to do it, so I just panicked. I found in the following months and years that it would kind of creep in on me unannounced slowly, and out of nowhere I would just begin to panic. It's like lying in bed and thinking there's a dangerous stranger in the room – it's very hard to think straight, move or make rational analytical decisions or choices during panic attacks you're paralyzed. Having been through these emotions, I now understand how people have let panic attacks get in on them to the extent that they take their own life. The stress just builds up and eventually breaks you. One of the bad things about playing rugby and the rugby community in general would be that we are slow to seek out professional help or talk about emotions. It's nearly as if it would be seen as a weakness and in the rugby dressing room before a match the last thing you discuss is your weaknesses. In hindsight and particular to men all I can advise is that if you need to go see a therapist go see them.

Things went from bad to worse with GRG. We had a follow up meeting six weeks later and this had allowed us to analyze the final outcome of the "sell all" GRG solution. Providing detailed, realistic calculations, we pointed out that there would be a shortfall balance, not a small one but a large shortfall. I remember they suggested that maybe the market would recover and thinking the gates of the clown factory have opened, this is 2011 there was not one single economic indicator to suggest that the market was going to change so the only way the values were going was down, unless they maybe supported us in some sort of enhancement program. I recently listened to the economist David McWilliams reference another 18th Century Irish economist Richard Cantillon who differentiated between workers and entrepreneurs. Workers work for a fixed wage, they sell their time to somebody for a fixed amount, whereas an entrepreneur buys something for a known price and sells it at an unknown price and that's the risk; they have no idea where the price is going to be when they go to sell it, so the entrepreneur must add or enhance the value. The ghost of Mr. Cantillon was not around the offices of GRG that day, as they responded negatively to our new proposal to at least enhance the property before selling. GRG would not support any enhancement program.

Having presented our calculations showing a large shortfall between what the sale of all the property could achieve in the economic climate at the end of 2011, my hands were now firmly tied behind my back and my main concern was for my family and the financial impact of a sell all solution or more like instruction would have. I asked what would happen to the shortfall if the market did not recover in the 18-month sales campaign. Would it be written down or indeed off? I will never forget for the rest of my life his response, he said they would empty my pockets, turn me upside down, shake me and if nothing came out they might leave me alone. I think one of my team asked did he say that, I'm not sure to be honest, my brain just froze, I sat there hunched, staring at nothing, numb, no thoughts, then panic – I had to get out of there. My breathing was gone. Is this where my 30 years of work was ending – emptied pockets? I must have got up, probably said something like we would get back to them, I don't remember. I don't remember saying anything to our team on the way out of the GRG offices, I must have given one of them my files, in fact I did, Damian gave them back to me a few days later. I just needed to walk and walk. The phone rang a couple of times and I could see that it was members of the team, most of whom I had played rugby with. Their concern for a teammate. I wasn't answering. After a while I knew they would be worried, that maybe I'd do something silly, so I texted them to tell them I was okay, even though I wasn't okay. Sitting here now, nearly ten years later, I'm thinking about all the people who maybe took that same walk who maybe did do something silly. It's an emotional pause for thought it's an emotional moment because there were many of us.

Early the following year in 2012 while coaching rugby I fractured my spine, which resulted in having to wear a steel brace 24/7 for six months. Sleep was tough with the brace on, if not impossible because every time I turned in bed the brace stuck into me and woke me up, a form of sleep deprivation that left me continually tired all day, every day for six months. Coupled with the panic attacks, this was mentally probably one of the toughest periods of my life. Up to the fall I had used physical fitness as a critical tool for my mental wellbeing and in this one innocuous moment a critical part of my mental therapy had to stop for six months. Ironically following the removal of the dreaded brace, the rehab program and strict adherence to it, set me up for life afterwards. I now have a great understanding of the importance and the limits of physical fitness as part of my overall wellbeing. I now tell people to remember to look after yourself first, it sounds selfish but you are far better equipped to help others if you, yourself are in a good place. During that six month period I realized the importance and need to become anti fragile when things go wrong and no matter what was going to be thrown at me I was not hiding, I owed it to those close who supported me to stay strong. Over the following years I learned to be an expert on how to compartmentalize matters. I think this was made much easier from my rugby coaching days where during the heat of a match you had to put all of the variables, the emotions, the crowd, the score etc. to one side to focus on a tactical change to make the team play better.

Accepting the non-professional support of others was key to keeping me emotionally okay, just okay, again like a rugby team; you stick together, you go to war together, there are players and coaches (in this case my family) that I will run through a brick wall for and some days you are lucky enough to win and come out the far side. I often think about the family, friends, individuals and professionals who stood by me during that difficult period.

I am reminded of the great Lions rugby coach Sir Ian McGeehan and what he said in the team meeting room before the 2009 second test match in South Africa. If you know nothing about rugby, the Lions Team is an unusual concept in rugby. All the odds are stacked against them winning. Once every four years, they are a team put together over a period of a couple of weeks, made up of players selected from four countries England, Scotland, Wales and Ireland, the coaches have only a very short window of time to prepare and gel together a team made up of historical arch enemies, who never play home matches but fly thousands of miles to other parts of the world to play against a team that has effectively been preparing for four years to play the Lions.

McGeehan, a great coach, recognized the difficulty and the importance of gelling a team together from four completely different cultures. Before the second test match he gathered his squad of players in the team meeting room, you could hear a pin drop in the room as he began to outline the sheer difficulty of the task ahead of them, he said to his players that should they win, against all of these odds they would in rugby terms create their own piece of rugby history and, having won they might see each other in 30-years-time, across a street and they don't have to say anything, there will just be a look that says *you were there.* The Lions went out that day and won.

And that's how I feel about those who were there to support me at that time, I see them I say nothing, but I know you were there for me. Special mention to my accountant and friend Damian, a rock of sense and humour in the very dark early days. I will never forget the day in late 2013 when I got the call that you my friend had collapsed in your office, never to regain consciousness nor when me and all your teammates lined up in James hospital like after a match to say our final goodbyes before they turned the machine off. We miss you. And the others, who without whom I may not have got through all this, I won't mention them by name, but you know who you are and I know you were there for me. Sometimes it takes a crisis to find out who your real friends and supports are, a special mention to Mrs. M in particular. I remember she gave me a stone, small, smooth, it would fit in your hand, with the inscription "Never Give Up." I keep that stone beside me every day. I also remember when I was at a particularly low ebb, she told me I was not to worry if we lost it all, especially not to worry about the kids who were brought up to be independent and resilient, that I was still the same person to her, the kids and close friends. Most importantly for me at that time she said she also had an unwavering belief I could build it all again with integrity and with her by my side. That meant a lot but it also gave me a singular goal to focus on.

I never fail in my admiration for women, their strength and their take on life. Historically if you look back at women during the World Wars they were on the frontline, without weapons they were the ones, while not active in the theatre of war, they were experiencing it and keeping everything behind the battle lines going. That was Mrs. M. More recently take the unprecedented pandemic of 2020, again women in our health service on the front line without weapons fighting an enemy that they cannot see, absolute heroes and respect. And no less Mrs. M, between 2011 and 2016; here she was an innocent party, not knowing the foe but still determined to hold the family together and keep life as normal as you can in very difficult circumstances. One small example that springs to mind was her utter determination that we still have our annual family summer holidays now not affordable. She set out to do house swaps with houses in all parts of the world. If you are not familiar with this concept there are various websites where you swap your house with other peoples' homes around the world. It meant for our summer holidays there were no accommodation costs, all we had to do was get cheap flights to the destination. Mrs. M was a whizz at this too. We went to great locations like Martha's Vineyard, San Diego, Spain, Portugal, a couple of times to Tuscany in Italy and had some of the best family holidays ever that cemented us as a family unit. Thank you.

These are your emotional relationships and then you have your commercial relationships and in particular there was my commercial relationship of 25 years with the same bank. I admit now I completely misunderstood that relationship. Again, like rugby over those 25 years at various points I had been in the trenches working through some tough times with some great bank managers assigned to my accounts. Two things changed that type of customer bank manager relationship, firstly the crash of 2008 and unfortunately for me my manager at that time was what I call a "fairweather" manager who when I needed him to stand up and be brave on my behalf decided he was not going to get his jersey dirty and allowed the transfer into GRG.

My advice to people starting out now with the banks is always retain control of your assets, retain the position that you can still make the critical decisions and the direction the business is going. Nowadays when asked for my thoughts in respect of your relationship with the banks I tell the story of a little bird, the Egyptian Plover, also known as the Crocodile Bird who lives and feeds off the backs of Crocodiles in Africa. We are all plovers borrowing, aspiring to succeed and survive on the back of the bank. It's a mutually beneficial relationship as long as you remember that at the time of crisis where the crocodile has to hunt or take evasive action you must remember that the croc will look after itself. The banks will always have short term thinking and hardly ever think beyond the next quarterly

100

results, always the here and now as opposed to tomorrow or long-term thinking.

So, anyone in business should remember that it's important to retain control. Also, you must have discipline. Back in 2007 as well as control I lost discipline, again critical in business. When you invest in property it's hard to sit on your hands for long periods of time but you must have the discipline to do exactly that, sit on your hands, wait and stick to what you are an expert in.

People ask me how I coped for five years where effectively my hands were tied and my life's works was evaporating before my eyes. I'll outline that now as well as give you my daily routine. First I would say to the Bank now 10 years later, it would serve them well to look back at the deal they could have gotten if they'd gone with us, as opposed to what the vulture fund paid them and at a broader level maybe reflect with some empathy on the social scars that they left on some very good people.

I would like to thank you, the reader for taking the time to read this piece and I hope in some way it will help or guide you. And rugby as you can maybe tell I've a great passion for the game of rugby, which I've taken to extreme levels at times, like when they were demolishing the old West Lower Stand in Landsdowne Road I went along and persuaded the contractor on site to cut my seats 138-139 out with an angle grinder, mounted them at home which I sit in when I'm watching matches on the television. I would like to sincerely thank the game of rugby and I encourage future generations to go out and play team sports of any sort. I was crap at rugby, but most people find when they play, be it Under 7s or upwards, that they are far braver and courageous than they thought they were. These sports expose you to both victory and defeat, you learn to deal with disappointments but you gather resilience along the way to accept defeat, to get back on the pitch the following week and test that physical and emotional self for another 80 minutes. Because it's a team sport you also learn the importance of tolerance. You cannot win a game of rugby on your own, you're depending on fourteen other individuals, so you have to be tolerant. So young adults who have played any of these team sports starting out in life and when hard times come along, as they will, they have a huge reservoir to call on to get them through it.

In my dark years one thing that was very important to me was that my reputation remained intact, reputation is imperative in the property industry. To this day I want to look in the mirror and like the person looking back at me. When it was all over we eventually refinanced out the remaining 2 properties through a commercial finance house headed up by guys who had previously worked in Ulster Bank, they subsequently made the comment that they remembered my case and that I had always remained honourable and kept my reputation intact.

But how did I get through it? It sounds easy but in the end I simply changed my attention, I used what had happened (where I felt I had been wronged) as an energy. In my own case there was many *uncontrollables* and you must put them to one side for that very reason, you cannot control them; accept them or they will sap your energy if your let them. My advice to people who have made mistakes or failed is to make sure not to withdraw after failure, learn from your failures but don't let them control you. I changed my attention to where I wanted to go rather than where I had been.

Before outlining my routine one thing I stick to religiously is to use the "do not disturb" setting on my phone from 10pm to 7.30am everyday I'm up at 6.30 so I am up nearly an hour before I look at the phone. Also the biggest mental discipline I learned during the bad times is that I do not allow problems to enter the bed, they must stay outside the bed, to be worked on first thing in the morning no matter how unpalatable they may be, it's what I call my frogs legs session – you know you'll hate them but they have to be done.

My day starts with short meditation, breathing exercises in the morning for ten minutes, and I exercise straight after (we are lucky to have a gym at home). During lockdown I set myself a goal of a 1000 ab exercises a day. (There is an 84-year-old South African golfer Sir Gary Player who does this so why not me?) I commence my day workwise with whatever problem I wouldn't let into the bed the night before my "frogs' legs" task. During the day I'm good at compartmentalizing and prioritizing what I can control and strive to find what improves things in the business. I think the Formula 1 Boss Ron Dennis once asked, *'Does it make the car go faster?'* and this is what we strive to do, improve our product for our customers (tenants). People often remark at how we go above and beyond for our tenants, but they don't understand that I'm fanatical about what the asset requires and in property the tenants are your assets, we always work back from who the end user will be when considering buying a property. Noel McQuilkan a great New Zealand coach I had the honour of working with when I started coaching once said "the ball is gold so hold onto it".

I'd describe myself as a very private person, a giver, I get a great buzz out of helping in particular young people on their property road, I'm also a very good listener but as I've got older and grumpier, I've made a decision that socially I will not spend time with people I do not want to be around and I try to cut negative people out of my life, they pull you down. My goals now are to leave a legacy not just for the next generation, my children but for their children both with property but also very much life's values and empathy for our fellow human beings. At around 5pm most days I go for an-hours-fast-walk where I listen to business podcasts or my music during which I crunch ideas or solutions to issues which I write down the minute I get back to the car. I write everything down which is another great habit. After that I turn off from work and prioritize family life and friends before heading to get a good night's sleep around 10pm.

Now back to the start of my story December 2016 and that envelope which rested on the desk in my solicitor's office, inside is the cheque from a private backer that would buy out my loans from the vulture fund. We still had another 21 days on the deadline set by them to close. I was glad that we had not come down to the wire on this deal, Cerberus are fair if you perform but you don't want to get on the wrong side of them if you don't perform.

It was Christmas week; my daughter was about to arrive home from New York and we were going to have one hell of a Christmas bringing down the curtain on the worst five years of my life.

The phone rang. it was John my Solicitor, *'Ed, are you sitting down?'* There was a long pause. *'There's nothing in the envelope!'* and I pick myself up I think to myself, *'Ed Martin this was your opportunity, you've now 21 days to get the money from somewhere else because there's nothing going to stop you getting away from the five years of hell you've been through.'*

That story is for another day...

CHAPTER 6
Facing Life with Courage

by Hugh Hegarty

Courage means different things to different people, for some courage is doing something that others would never consider doing like jumping out of a plane or working with dangerous animals or even joining the military and going to war. For others courage means doing things that others take for granted and do without even thinking about it like getting out of bed each morning, like getting washed and dressed and talking to people, like not ending your life. Just take a few moments and really try to imagine that the hurt inside you was so bad that the only way you could see to stop the hurt was to end your life. Imagine having a family that loved you so much, but for you that wasn't enough. Imagine having a beautiful and loving wife and two beautiful young daughters whose hearts you would break, but for you that wasn't enough. Imagine knowing the devastation that you would leave behind, the unanswered questions, loved ones blaming themselves questioning why you didn't love them enough, wondering what they did wrong, wondering could they have done more... But none of that mattered. Imagine planning your own suicide in every detail, so very carefully that even if you were seen no one would have the time to save you. I know it may be hard to imagine all of this because it seems so cruel and heartless, in fact some people even think it's selfish. For me it was reality, that's how low I had fallen into mental ill health. I don't believe I was being heartless. I don't believe I was being cruel or selfish. I believe I was doing the best I could with the knowledge and the resources I had at that time. Yes, I know even that may sound ridiculous to some people and my reply to that is, if all of this sounds ridiculous to you then I am really pleased you have not experienced the depths of mental ill health that I and many others have experienced. Thankfully, I am one of the lucky ones to have fully recovered and now I use the experiences of my journey and all its learnings to help others overcome many obstacles in their lives. So how did I end up in such a low position?

Mental ill health wasn't something that I had experienced in my early life, it was something that happened suddenly and without warning, well that's my memory, although others say that with hindsight there were signs. I was born in Derry in 1970, my mother and father were both hard working people and instilled great values in all of their children. Growing up on the edge of the bogside regular riots in the front street was normalised life for us. I say normalised because later in life I have come to realize that it was not a normal situation, it was not normal to watch that level of violence regularly, although some people believed at that time it was the only way to have their situation highlighted. The normalisation of such violence has left many with PTSD, and I honestly believe that everyone who lived throughout that type of regular occurrence was affected in some way by it.

My father owned a business delivering coal and had to display a sign saying essential services to avoid having the lorries hijacked and burnt. A hard-working family supplying a service to both Nationalist/Republican as well as to Unionist/Loyalist areas during the times of the troubles in Northern Ireland. Although it put him in a difficult position many times, my father was well respected in all communities. He ensured that his seven children respected people no matter what their religious or political belief was. He instilled in us all many good values including honesty, integrity and the value of human life.

My father was not a big man in stature but he was a giant in my eyes, he was my hero. He was generous to a fault and constantly went over and above what was expected of him to help others. However, within this hero of mine lay a sleeping demon that would steal him from us and ultimately lead me to the depths of depression. My father was one of five brothers who succumbed to a hereditary heart disease. He took ill initially at the age of 46 and the heart disease was diagnosed. Then five years later his illness deteriorated and within two years he died. My hero was gone at the very young age of 52, just three weeks from his 53rd birthday – way too young in my opinion.

Immediately my life changed, there was a massive void that never was, and never could be filled. I was lost and felt like everything had stopped for quite a while and even after that it was as if everything was in slow motion and fuzzy. I was married, a beautiful wife and two beautiful daughters, but I became oblivious to that. Life was going on autopilot for a while, work, eat, sleep repeat. I must have been a nightmare to live with because I made no effort at all, but I wasn't aware of it and that is the crucial factor, awareness is the factor that can bring about the most amazing and astounding changes, but I lacked that awareness. I lacked the awareness that my life was spiraling downwards. I had stopped properly interacting with people. Yes, I talked to people daily and at work, I talked to my family. However, I wasn't present, I was talking and hearing what was being said to me, but I wasn't fully aware of what was being said, or of what I was saying. It was as if my life was being controlled, in some strange way, by someone else and I couldn't control anything. I had gone from someone who was the life and soul of the party, someone who enjoyed life, someone who loved people, to a very dark shadow of my former self. I had become cold, unemotional, uncaring. I had become someone that, looking back now, I didn't like very much at all.

I was hurting and that pain was something that I have never felt before. Up to that point I had broken bones, I had been knocked down by a van and dragged a few hundred yards, I had scars from other injuries. I had experienced extreme physical pain but all of that physical pain combined couldn't compare to what I was feeling now. The pain inside wouldn't ease and it felt as if it was becoming more intense. I was hurting and I didn't know what to do.

In my early years I didn't see men display emotions. The normalisation of the violence I saw first-hand in the streets where I grew up and the tough guy image was one that stayed with me for many years. The off-the-cuff remarks such as 'Man Up', and 'Big boys don't cry.' Statements such as 'Be quiet', 'Don't say that';

whenever I spoke of how I was feeling conditioned my mind into storing all the emotional pain and hurt that I had experienced so it just built up. I wasn't alone in this experience as the majority of men growing up in the seventies and eighties and before were equally conditioned in the same way. We didn't speak about things that were bothering us, we "dealt" with it alone, we processed it alone and we overcame it alone, which generally meant that nothing was ever fully or properly resolved, it was pushed down in our subconscious minds and left to fester until it surfaced again.

This time I couldn't push this hurt back down, this time I couldn't deal with it properly, this time I could only see one way of stopping the pain. As I said before some people consider suicide to be a coward's way out, a selfish act, a way of avoiding facing up to reality. I can tell you that's simply not true. For me it was the only way that I could get that intense pain to stop. I didn't really want to die; I didn't really want to cause my family any further pain. I simply wanted my suffering to stop and I couldn't see any other way for that to happen. So, to those who believe its cowardly and selfish I simply ask you to close your eyes, imagine the worst pain you have ever felt and then multiply that by one hundred, when you can imagine that then imagine that you honestly and truly believe that there's no way out of this pain, that this is your life forever. Waking up every day after having had very little sleep, and the pain is there. The pain so intense all day every day that you become oblivious to everything else around you. The pain so intense that you could never possibly get used to it or learn to live with it, but it doesn't go away.

Yes, I know it's difficult to imagine that any pain could be that severe, but it can be, for me it was, and it was horrible.

The pain was so horrible and all-consuming within my mind, and my absolute belief that there was only one way to end the pain was so definite and resolute that I planned to end my life in order to end the pain. I now know that would have been a permanent end to a temporary issue, however at the time I believed the pain was permanent and getting more and more intense by the day and I could no longer take the pain so it was time to end it all. Thinking back on that it gave me some clarity and a strange sense of relief to know my suffering would soon be over. So, the planning of the finer details began, what was the best time, what was the best day, would I leave a note or not.

The day had finally come, my pain was going to be over, the sense of relief was exhilarating. I left the house for what I believed to be the last time and was so caught up in my impending relief that I didn't even say goodbye to my family. Walking to where my suffering would end, I met a man who looked like he was in a bad way. I talked to him and when I realized that he had the same plan as me to end his suffering I listened intently to his plight – the first time I had truly listened to anyone in quite some time. I listened to him and talked with him and helped rationalize some of his thoughts. Ultimately, I encouraged him to reach out for help, which I know he did because this man is alive and thriving to this day. In helping this man regain control of his life I still hadn't changed my own mind. I was good at giving advice but not so good at heeding

111

my own advice. That day I had left it too late and the place my pain would end had closed by the time I got there. Undeterred I simply resolved to go another day and complete what I had planned.

The second time I had planned to end my suffering I resolved that nothing would stop me. I got to the exact place where my pain would end, everything was in place, eternal relief was mine. At the very second I was about to complete the plan I had a vision of my father standing in front of me and an overwhelming sense of how bitterly disappointed he would be in me for going through what I had planned and I broke down and cried. I cried so sore that the pain and suffering seemed to fade only to be replaced with guilt. Guilt over what I had planned to do, guilt over the pain I was going to leave my family in, guilt over leaving my daughters without a father, guilt over leaving my wife without a husband and the most intense guilt of all... guilt over disappointing my hero, the man who had instilled in me the value of human life.

That was the awareness for me, that was the catalyst for the most profound change that would happen in my life. That was the turning point taking me from the depths of mental ill health onto a journey of self-discovery, a journey of personal growth and education that I could not have even comprehended at that time. The awareness of how low I had fallen was actually the relief that I had been looking for. I couldn't fall any further and when I realized that I also realized that everything could only get better. I'm not saying that everything was immediate in that second, but it was the catalyst for the awareness, the realization and the change that ultimately saved my life.

At that moment I realized that my life had spiraled out of control, that I had already been causing my family so much pain and turmoil. I decided there and the that I'd do whatever it took to change my life around and learn to become more aware of my internal dialogue so as I could pick up on any negative issues before they became a major problem. With the support of my wife I began to transform my mindset and therefore my outlook on life. I began to read and educate myself on how the mind works, I read positive psychology books, personal development books, self-help books. They were all great in their own way, however what I realized was that when I stopped reading this positive material things began to slip again. This gave me a whole new awareness, an awareness that a quick fix of reading a book or going to a workshop wasn't going to give me the changes I needed, it was a complete lifestyle change I needed and, as I had committed to doing whatever it took to turn my life around, that's what I did.

Whilst looking for the answers to how I can turn my life around I read many self-help and personal development books, I attended workshops, and what struck a chord with me more than anything else I had read and experienced was NLP, Neuro linguistic Programming. Neuro (to do with the mind), Linguistic (to do with how we communicate both verbal and non-verbal), and Programming (what we do with all the information we have available to achieve our outcomes). It all made so much sense for me. I had been processing the incoming information in a way that was giving me a negative outcome, therefore if I wanted a different outcome, I had to change the way I processed the information. Sounds simple, logical and straightforward, but it wasn't. NLP for me was the lifestyle change that was to transform my life, so I went and trained formally in it to master practitioner level and master coach. This was only the start of the journey for me, a journey that would see me use the skills and tools I had learned to help others change their life for the better. My clients now include businesspeople who come to me for business mentorship, people who have anxiety and phobia issues, people who come to me for wealth coaching.

No matter what my clients come to me for they are all looking to change something within themselves, even if they don't realize that at first. My life experiences and the training I have completed has put me in an excellent position to realize what my clients need even before they realize, but I don't tell them because that would be counterproductive. All of my clients want to know what they can do right now to bring about the changes they want. One of the downsides to the current society is that everyone wants a quick fix, an immediate result, someone to fix them right now so as they can return to "Normal". We used to post letters, they would arrive at their destination within a few days, the recipient would carefully craft a reply, which we would receive a few days after they posted, the whole process could take a week or two. Then came email which made it instantaneous, you can even get a notification when the recipient has received your email, and another when they have opened it. We get instant gratification in many areas that previously took quite a bit longer. We have fast food and microwavable meals, we have instant messaging through social media platforms, we have easy access to information through the worldwide web. We can order products online and have them delivered to our door the next day, so we have been conditioned to expect things to happen, if not immediately then within a very short period of time and with minimal effort.

The experiences I have had and the learnings from those experiences have helped me shape and transform my life in all areas. I have learned how to change my mindset from having a fixed mindset to having a growth mindset, I have changed my mindset around money, business, mental health and most importantly I have changed my mindset about my abilities; my ability to achieve what I want in life, my ability to be, do and have anything I set out to achieve, my ability to live the life I want, and I use all these learning to show my clients how to do the same no matter what it is they want to achieve. I help them become empowered to know that whatever they want they can and will get it. And I help them to realize that any worthwhile change or any goal of substance will require a strong reason why, vision, commitment, definiteness of purpose, planning and action.

So, when you are faced with any issue in life the most important thing is awareness. When you become aware of the desire to change, aware of the need to make changes then the process begins. When I became aware that my father would have been disappointed in me if I had ended my life, I became aware that my life had to change drastically. The first thing I did was to make a decision, a decision to commit to whatever it would take to transform my life. Change is the only constant we have and because I fought against the change, I lost control of my thoughts, I lost control of my ability to make decisions. When you have the awareness that something has to change then you must take plan to take control of that change before the change takes control of you.

When you have made the decision to control the change the next step is to work out your reason why. Why do you want this change? What will this change bring you? What will you have to give up to achieve this change? Every worthwhile goal will require a sacrifice of some sort. What will this sacrifice be for you? Will it mean changing your circle of friends? Will it mean changing your work colleagues? You need to assess all the sacrifices you will make on your journey towards your goal as well as the benefits the results and improvements, and decide if you are prepared to make these sacrifices and accept the consequences they bring. What do the benefits mean to you? Are you doing them for yourself or someone else? If your goals and the changes you are working towards are not for you, if they don't mean enough to you, if your reason why is not strong enough then you will be building the foundations of the change, the foundations of your goals on very shaky ground and if this is the case and the foundations aren't right then you will not achieve the results you initially planned for. On the flip side when you have the foundations right and have the right reason why, when you are working towards something you are passionate about then nothing will stand in your way.

When I was aware of what was wrong in my life and what needed to change, I then wrote down what I expected my new life to look like. I wrote down where I would be living, what I would be doing to earn money and how much I would be earning, who my circle of friends would be, who my mentors would be. I wrote out in minute detail what each area of my life would look like. Why did I do this? It's because a dream written down with a date becomes a goal, a goal broken down into steps becomes a plan, a plan backed by action makes your dreams come true. Therefore, until you write down your goals, they are only dreams. To make your dreams come true you must have a vision of what those goals look like to you, of how they will make you feel when you achieve them, of everything you will see smell hear taste and touch when you have achieved them. You must include as much details for every area of your future life as possible because when you are clear of what you want in life everything will happen, but only to the extent to which you are clear. Once you have the clarity of how your life will be its time to make a definite plan. This plan should be adaptable but should never compromise or change your ultimate goal. Once I had made the decision to do what it took to change my life completely, and when I had written down in every detail what this would look like and feel to me, this gave me the ability to visualise my new life properly. It also gave me the ability to plan what I needed to do to achieve my new life.

In planning the life that I had visualised I started with the desired end goal. I continually looked at how life would be when I had achieved every detail in the visualisation. I put a definite date in for achieving the goals and the began visualising that it was that date, that I was living that life and that everything was as I had imagined it would be. In other words when I visualised I did it in the present tense, living as if it was already true and I was already living the life I wanted, in every detail I could imagine. Throughout my journey and learnings, I learned that when you are visualising something you are using your imagination, your imagination is within the subconscious part of your mind, and the subconscious part of your mind doesn't know the difference between what is imagined and what is real. Therefore, when you visualise in great detail then your subconscious mind actually believes it has happened and this creates changes within your mind that prepares you to look out for things that will align themselves with creating the desired outcome. As Bob Proctor said, *'if you can see it in your mind, you can hold it in your hand '*. Everything we have has started out as a thought in someone's mind, they visualised it, they saw the end result in their mind and then they set about creating a way to make it happen. Therefore, no matter what change you want in your life, when you can visualise it in detail, you can make it happen even if you don't know how to make it happen.

I didn't know how to achieve the results I had visualised, but I knew it was achievable. I began with the end result and the date for which I set this to be a reality. I then worked back from that. My goal was a five-year plan initially so I knew exactly what would happen five years from now. Now I needed to know what needed to happen for this to come true. I needed to break the goals down into manageable chunks, so the overall big goal didn't seem so scary or unrealistic. I needed a plan of what needed to happen four years from now, then three years from now two years from now one year from now and six months from now. After I had the plan broken down, I set monthly, weekly and daily tasks to make sure I hit these milestones on the way to living the life I wanted. Once these milestones were achieved it gave me a sense of achievement and also a knowledge that I was on the right track and by continuing with the plan, and by taking action daily I would realize my goals.

Some of these steps may seem very simple and also straightforward and yes, they are. These are some of the steps that have given me the fastest results and the deepest changes in all areas of my life. I was at a stage where my fathers' death had affected me so deeply that I almost took my own life. Some of these steps gave me the realization that Death isn't the greatest loss in life. The greatest loss is what dies inside us while we live. The ability to change not just my own life but also to show others how to overcome any obstacle in any area of their own life was lying dormant inside me, just waiting for the right opportunity and the right time to appear. This ability wasn't just dormant inside me it was dying inside me while I was alive. Now I have made the decision that no matter what I will not wait until the "right" time, the "right" day. Now I take the time and make it right.

I want you to think now. What if...? What if you did make the changes? What if you did take the next step? What if you took control of your thoughts, your actions, your life? How much better would your life be? What if you reached out and asked for help? What if you dared to dream, and make that dream come true? At my lowest point I could only see one way to end the pain. When I reached out, when I asked for guidance and direction what did I get? I got awareness of where I was and where I wanted to be, I got visualisation of how my life should be, I got the confidence to plan and take action towards the life I want, and I got to live, I got to thrive.

No matter what your current situation a better outcome is possible. Reach out, become aware, visualise, plan and take action now and every day. Change your thoughts and change your life. The only way to predict your future is to create it.

CHAPTER 7
Realization

by Joan McDaid

Picture this, I am turning 40 and inwardly congratulating myself on how well I am coping with turning the big four zero. I have the husband, the children, the house and the job, but yet there's a wee nagging voice in the back of my mind that just won't leave me alone. Really is this what life is all about? Yes, I have the house, I have the husband, I have the children and I have the job, but I work really long hours and feel guilty for not being home enough. The house never seems to be clean and anytime my husband and I speak it's really nothing more than 'What time are you picking up the kids?' 'What do we need to get from the shop?', 'What are we having for dinner?' In these seemingly perfect surroundings, I never felt quite as lonely. I wondered how I was going to do this for the next 25 to 30 years until retirement. In all honesty, I was filled with dread and guilt. Surely this could not be the pinnacle of what I have been working so hard for, for so long?

Let me be clear from the outset, I love my family, they are my why, but the very foundations of my life, the values that were programmed into me for good outcomes (things like working hard to get a good job, having a nice home etc.) were the fundamental building blocks which I had built my life upon. Not being satisfied with the outcome of my life felt those blocks were starting to crumble. It wasn't because of anyone or anything, I just felt there was something missing, I had a core belief that there had to be so much more for me to be and give. I found myself suddenly without a focus, I did not know what the next goal would be, my life was slowly crumbling because I KNEW THIS COULD NOT BE IT!

It really is quite frightening when the very basis of the values of life suddenly come into question. I was afraid and really frustrated at myself that I couldn't just be grateful for what I had. Why was I always looking for more from life? Everybody else was happy, why could I just not settle and be grand? But as I was doing all this thinking, I noticed I didn't seem to be the only searching for more.

I saw changes in people I had known from afar, people I followed on social media. I didn't necessarily like their posts or leave a comment, but I was seeing a change within them. They seemed to be once like me but there were signs that they were changing, developing, moving on to something bigger. I didn't know what they were doing or how they were doing it, but I could see the signs clearly. Whilst I seemed to be stuck in the thinking-about-changing-phase, they seemed to have moved out of that and were living lives they wanted. Then I wondered if I was going mad. Was it a case of the grass is always greener, and I should be satisfied with what I had?

But at the same time, new people started to come into my life in unexpected ways, and I realized, based on the nuggets of information they were giving me that I wasn't going mad. There was something else out there and they just seemed to know how to access it. I needed to find out how I could. So somehow unconsciously I was asking the universe to bring me the people that I needed ...

I started to be more open to the information I was seeing around me, people talking about changes that were happening in their life. I started to take action on those. Then I saw an opportunity for learning, which felt right. I had started to listen to some life coaches and I practiced a bit of meditation for my mindset, without really doing any deep work. The information I was hearing spoke to me in some way and I became more curious to seeking out more information. I decided to get myself a life mentor, and a whole new world of possibilities opened up to me. The strangest bit was that this wasn't new information, this information had been around for centuries; somehow as a society we had become totally disconnected from it and many disempowered as a result. For anyone willing to look beyond the surface, this information is readily available to tap into its power. This no joke, kinda It shocked me to know that I had reached 40 plus years of age and I had never been told about this information, but even more importantly I was raising another generation that wasn't going to be aware of it either. I made a decision that my children were not going to grow up without this information in their lives. It was information that wasn't about academic learning and it wasn't about working all your waking hours; it was about working with the laws of the universe. Now before you think I've gone cuckoo, let me explain, for I too would have thought of them as a load of rubbish at first, that is until I began to actually understand them. These laws are not new laws, they have been documented and in existence since the beginning of time. even long before organised religion. and if you want to enhance your life, I suggest you learn about them. Thankfully, I came upon an opportunity to learn about them.

In the last few centuries we have become so reliant on organised culture to take control of our lives that we have lost any connection we have to who we are, where we come from and why we are here. And we walk around in a daze, building up a stock of material items to fill the emptiness within, not fulfilling the potential of our spirit and our soul

For me, I just couldn't put "Pandora back in the Box." it doesn't mean that at times I didn't think, 'Oh my god, how do I unlearn this information? This is too hard', but I couldn't because this information created a fundamental shift in my being; even if I wanted to put the lid back on I don't think I could, but what I will say is that I know the difference that it makes not only in my life but in other people's life too. And by channelling a little bit of this information I am so excited to see what I can do in the next 40 years and the difference I can make to people.

For me I made a decision that I was going to pursue this information and did a 6-month life coaching program. I started to study and try to apply the principles that I was learning. I started to learn techniques that helped me change my attitude and improve my mindset. I started to shift my thinking. Along the way there were many lessons; I learned about the way I had been living in such a closed mindset, only seeing my point of view and not developing my perception from other people's point of view. I started to consider the language that I used and how a lot of my language had negative connotations to it. When I started to examine where those thoughts had come from, I could see I had learned them as a child growing up from those around me, from people in the community and from media. When you listen to the radio; you listen to people talking as a society, we talk in the negative. I became aware of how everything around me was impacting how I felt on a daily basis.

I realized I was giving the power within my emotions to other people because I had such poor self-worth, I allowed other people's opinions of me (or my belief of their opinions of me) to affect me so greatly that it impacted my daily life. At that stage I could have sat and said, 'Oh my God this is a disaster I am hopeless' but I knew I wasn't. I knew that from the little I had studied already that these were things I had learned, they were just thoughts that I had repeated in my mind enough times, that it had become a habit and very often I was living in a cycle of lots of different habits. Have you ever arrived home from work and you can't really remember the journey home and you think, 'Oops how did I get here?' , that is because you were in habit mode, it was an unconscious thought on autopilot.

It became really clear to me that I was living my life that way. A lot of my habits on reflection were not healthily habits, not healthy for my mind, body or soul, so once I had acknowledged that and I knew there was more, I was only left with one decision – *Joan, you have to start working on those habits!* I had limiting beliefs that I wasn't good enough, those beliefs that if you have enough to get by you will be grand, you should just be content with your life etc. But why should I just be content? I was born for greater things, we were all born for greater things, we have just been so conditioned to think that mediocrity is the place in which we should live. Well, I now know that I did not come here to be mediocre, I came here to be great, I came to this earth to do good, to help people change their lives; it's not okay for me to sit back and not work on myself anymore. It was a real kick in the bum moment, to know that 'there has to be more' was so right. I wasn't mad. There is way more and it's up to us to grab those inner superpowers and make the most of them. When all of a sudden you realize that the world is your oyster, that you have everything within your grasp, that you just have to make a decision that puts fire in your belly, it's exciting! , The anticipation that tingles through your body is just phenomenal. And when you start to change your attitude, to bring people that a year ago into your life that a year ago I thought impossible is mind blowing.

When I look at how far my personal journey has come in a relativity short period of time, it feels amazing. I am grateful for the many blessings in my life every day, which before this I had taken for granted. I found that a daily, intentional practice of gratitude, set me up for the day with a totally different mindset. Looking for the good in a situation instead of dwelling on the negative helps to prevent me from falling into a spiral of negativity that previously could have impacted all aspects of my life disproportionately. Within this study I was building my resilience to the grind of daily life.

One of my favourite quotes on this subject comes from Bob Proctor:

'Harvest the good and forgive the rest.'
– Bob Proctor

During the coaching programme, I was challenged to reconsider my beliefs on many aspects of life, I would really love to share two of the most profoundly impactfully lesson for me:

1. What is wealth? For me wealth had become money and belongings. Through studying this it helped me to reconnect with wealth in its widest sense and moving away from only monetary terms. I realised very quickly that I had wealth beyond measure in my life, e.g. a family, a home, a job, running water, heat etc. Through my daily practices of gratitude, I grounded myself in being grateful for the abundance in my life and stopped thinking about what I lacked or thought I lacked. When you start to see yourself as someone with many blessings it changes the outlook on life for the better.

2. I am right, you are wrong = Perception

    I never really gave perception much consideration. I was studying it daily and some of the information really resonated with me. I would have been described as opinionated and generally seeing myself as right, there is no doubt this description is true albeit gives me the shivers to realise what a dreadfully ignorant world I was living in with this mindset. Through studying I came to the realisation that being right can mean many different things, it all comes down to how you see the situation. Just because I am right does not mean you are wrong, we are just looking at different sides of the same coin, both right from our individual starting point. Again, this is such a freeing place to be, I no longer felt a weight of needing to know everything, I just needed to move around the coin and see it from all angles.

I want to acknowledge that I do not have it all sussed every hour of every day and that's okay. I know, should I be lucky enough to live until I was a 100 years old, I still would not have it all sussed out because there's always going to be the ability to develop, learn and grow. At some level that is so freeing, to accept that you can always better yourself, so never give up learning. How exciting is it to know that every day you can wake up and be a better version of the person you were before because you've made a decision to grow and expand your mind and then apply it to your life? One of the

128

important takeaways for me has been that we can all learn; we can all listen but the application of these lessons for life is where the real growth is, this is when you really tap into your inner superpowers.

The first time that you realize you have reached a goal that you did not even know you could, it suddenly validates all the learning that you have been undertaking. One of my goals that manifested, was a goal I had set without even the slightest idea how I was going to do it. That was becoming an author, I wrote this goal on a piece of paper and at the time I knew deep within me it was going to happen, I didn't know how but I didn't need to worry about the how because I made a decision it was happening. Let's jump four weeks forward from me writing on that piece of paper without knowing how, I had been chosen to write a chapter in this book by somebody at that time I didn't know and who didn't know me... So for those types of events people might say 'ah that is chance', and maybe it was chance, but I believe I made a decision, I believe I connected with it, I believe the universe brought the right people to my life because I manifested the other people in this book to me and this was the journey for me. So, don't stop believing in yourself, you have unlimited potential within you if you believe in yourself.

Going forward I would like to share with you the 5 daily practices I try to include in my routine each and every day. These routines have helped me to tap into my inner superpowers and they may help you too:

1. Gratitude

I take 10 minutes every morning to list down 10 things I am grateful. This can be things already in my life but also future hopes and dreams. I write this into my gratitude journal and by committing to writing these I am sending my intentions out to the universe and accepting they will be fulfilled.

2. Attitude

I am mindful of my language and thoughts, that they are seeking out abundance rather than lack. I try to treat myself and others as the most important person in the world, so I leave people with the feeling of more following an interaction with me. I am tending the garden of my mind and keeping the weeds at bay, by this I mean that I consciously stop listening to negativity and the naysayers who want to keep the status quo.

3. Meditation

I meditate daily to quieten my mind. This has helped me to stop the constant noise in my mind and allow the inner voice to be heard. This practice has brought calmness into my life, helping me to tap into my higher mental abilities.

4. Decisions

I mentioned decision making several times here. I have realized there is power within making a decision; making a clearly defined decision sends out the signal to the universe that you are ready, open and willing, it also clears the mind of all the noise and chatter that can distract you from your purpose.

5.   Routine

I get up at 5 am daily to use the time in the morning before the house is busy and bustling to complete gratitude, meditation and study. Those couple of hours of calmness in the morning are some of the most productive of my day and it really sets my day up for success. Some days my body needs rest, so I accept that and move on, leaving the past in the past and allowing myself to be in the gift of the present.

Within each of us there are superpowers, take the time to find yours. You have invested in yourself by reading this book and I would like to thank you for your valuable time. I also want to acknowledge that as we go through life there will be challenges (I affectionately call them 'brain farts) and that's okay. Nobody's life is perfect. Sometimes it isn't always easy to make a transition from one of thinking to another but as long as you don't dwell on the challenges you will get there, and it is freeing. I really have to say breaking out of the prison of my own making that I had been living has been liberating. I hope you have picked up some takeaways for your life journey from my story. Peace and riches blessings to you.

Love J x

CHAPTER 8
Walk out The Gate

by Jackie Mallon

To walk out through the gate, you must first enter through it. What lay ahead of me, for the next 8 years was going to be a massive rollercoaster of experiences, emotions and a bigger task of finding me. With the sun shining, and in my pretty size 12 floral dress, smiling from ear to ear, I was so excited about the opportunities that lay in front of me. On the first day of my new role, bearing in mind, the Sales Manager at the Assessment Centre said, "I only want two years of service, and you are free to go for other opportunities in the company". With that carrot dangling in front of me, the world was my oyster. I had worked for this company before and held fond memories in my heart for many a reason. How did it all go so wrong? I asked myself. How did those opportunities fade so quickly? How did my excitement disappear so quickly and the lure of opportunity become a distant memory or maybe better explained, it was similar to a long hike across the desert with no water. On 4th July 2011, I walked into reception with a dream so big, with the feeling I was destined for so much more. I had a passion for sales and I wanted back into that environment. This company had everything I wanted, however, I did take a job lower than when I left 14 years prior. Was that a good decision? Should I have aimed higher? Did I sell myself short? This place of work not only held memories for me as an employee but also had great personal memories, my wonderful and amazing Dad had held a contract here for over 20 years. This beautiful man was my best friend, my hero, my mentor, my rock, the list is endless, he was my everything. Anyone who had the pleasure of meeting him, knew what a character he was, he left an impression on everyone. He had the kindest heart and the biggest smile, and gave the valuable thing called 'Time' to everyone. Nothing was ever too much bother, coupled with his fantastic work ethic. In fact, I emulated him in my career, and no better person to imitate but in my own way. However, on the !5th August 2001, my world came crashing down with a bang. My dad went through that same company gate that night, never to return. He passed away from a massive heart attack hours later. Words cannot describe that pain of loss. That night I also lost me, something inside of me died too, and the date will forever be inscribed in my heart. So how did I cope? I thought I was dealing with it okay, or was I just getting through a day at a time on autopilot? It was the latter - I know that if it hadn't been for my beautiful 6-month-old baby boy, I probably would have been lying beside my dad today. I was angry that God had taken him, how could he? Questioning why I had my son and not my Dad - how selfish of me, even to think like that, but when that gorgeous baby smiled with those big sparkly eyes, I knew God had sent me an Angel, knowing that I would find this loss in my life so hard. Selfishly I wanted both. Roll on 10 years, and there I was back in the same place, looking to reignite my career, but I hadn't planned for the pain and anguish it would cause me. Being that popular man, and everyone knowing I was his daughter, he used to say to them 'Here's my girl', I was such a Daddy's girl and he always made me smile. I had dealt with it, hadn't I? On meeting different employees over the first few weeks, welcoming me back and wishing me well, I hadn't allowed for all the other conversations and questions: 'I remember talking to your Dad, that night, just before he left', 'Such a laugh we had that night, such a character, what a shock when I heard later on', 'Telling me his friend had got him tickets for a sold-out match', 'How long is he dead now?' followed by shock. Nearly 10 years on, 'Must be near his anniversary.' Did I walk into a brick wall with a mighty bang? Yes, I did! Had I been pretending that I just hadn't seen him? This, I had not prepared myself for. I cried for two weeks solid, wondering what the hell was I doing. Why was I putting myself through this? And there, we have it, I found my TRIGGER to my GRIEF, 10 years of hiding and ignoring reality. Unbeknown to me, and you may wonder how did I not notice, I was grieving. What is grief? Like a baby, there is no manual and everyone deals and reacts differently. I comfort ate, with the environment I was in and the memories, and I spoke to no-one about it, as I was always the strong one. Within a year that size 12 dress turned into a size 20 with 5.5 stone on. I ignored that too, not that you could miss it, that mask I had been wearing had started to hide a lot more. If I had lost me before, I had lost even more of me. As a mother, what I ate, my child ate, I didn't notice, that he was also putting on weight. What mother does that to their child? One that is walking around in a bubble hoping the world will sort itself out. I was that girl who hid behind the smile, but inside I was falling apart, and how dare I give anyone a hint of what was going on. As the smile kept widening, my confidence was dwindling. It was a ticking time bomb, and I was responsible for when it went off. I hid behind my uniforms, an identity where I could be someone else and not the "Fat Girl', in my work uniform, I was the employee, in my pjs/tracksuit, I was the at home girl and in my baking clothes , I was the weekend baker. It was all causing me huge anxiety, not wanting to go out for fear of trying on clothes, people judging me etc. I was torturing myself, so I became a bit of a recluse as it was easier to hide at home - my safe place. Then on the 14th May 2015, my worst nightmare happened, I was at a family wake and no-one knew me! My heart was crying so hard inside, yet there I was with that smile, 'Oh, do you not know me, oh, that's probably 'cos we haven't seen each other in a while.' And the final nail in the coffin (no pun intended), was when my dad's best friend didn't know me and he was adamant he didn't. It was a moment of "ground swallow me up", it was horrific. Embarrassed I left, and I cried all the way home, knowing something had to change. The following Tuesday evening, I was facing the scales (and my terror barrier) at Slimming World, a small part of the journey to finding me. Looking back at that one photo I have of that time, I can completely resonate with their confusion, my face looked like it was either swollen or I was seriously allergic to something. That allergy was self-love. I hated what I saw in the mirror. Not only were people talking about me, but comments were being said about my son. He joined a personal trainer, and what a transformation, he looked amazing. He inspired me to go there too, and anyone that knows me, will know that me and exercise don't really go together. This was a game changer, I got the bug, not only was I going to the PT, I was also attending classes and slowly started to love the physical me again. How does this relate to the workplace you ask? Without sounding arrogant, I was very good at my job, but I was going nowhere. The team was getting bigger and there was definitely an opportunity for Team Leaders. Three Team Leader positions were advertised. Knowing, I would make a good Team Leader, based on prior history of running a team, my love of training, seeing the strengths in others and fantastic at getting results, I applied, in hope of one of the positions. The interview took place. Honestly, I thought I had applied for an MD job with all the questions, nearly, giving up halfway through. I didn't get a second interview, and took that quite hard (I was told at a sales event that my colleague, who was with me that day, had got a second interview, which made the rest of the event uncomfortable for me). There were some shocked people when they heard, but some you win, some you lose. What's for you won't pass you, right? It knocked my self-confidence, which already was on a downward spiral. This wasn't the real issue at that stage, for the team had been departmentalized and it wasn't the same anymore, the atmosphere was different, some people changed with authority. Here I was looking to progress my career, with an uncomfortable atmosphere. I wasn't the only one feeling it, however, it just wasn't sitting well with me. I loved working for this company, but the job search began, I deserved more. I was reliable, with a CV full of experience and fantastic results. I was given overall full performance after only 6 months, which very few would receive. I craved more, more responsibility, more of what sat in line with my skills. I loved problem solving, turning problems into solutions with productive results. Then, the day came when a job was advertised in another department. Gut instincts - Do you listen to them? Believe in them? Act on them? My instincts were doing a jungle dance whilst singing loudly, 'Do Not Apply'. Trust me, they were strong! Did I listen? Absolutely not! I applied! The job was on temporary hold until they got a manager. An email came out a while later, 'We still have your application, please advise if you wish to proceed?' If the jungle dance was loud the last time, this time, I think, there were nations of jungle dances going on. And again, 'Do Not Apply'. Again, I ignored it. I gave the interview of my life and got the job. Yippee, I was escaping, a new role, more money. Things were looking up, or were they? Was the actual job role as outlined on the job specification? It was not, it was half the role, and not the half that had excited me initially. So, for me, it wasn't a challenge therefore boring for me. Anyway, disaster struck, the job wasn't working out with the manager in line with the fact that the job wasn't what it should have been, and there I was going back to my old role. Thinking over everything that had happened, I decided to take out a grievance. Due to confidentiality agreements, I can't go into details, but the impact of this on my life was horrific. I was off work sick for five and a half weeks, all the sick leave I was entitled to at the time. I was called to the Occupational Health Doctor and I broke down, it was all just too much. She advised that I attend counselling sessions on the healthcare policy before coming back to work. On the same day, I got chatting with our Acting Manager who advised me that, she was giving me a problem area, as I was the only person who could sort it out. And it was where I flourished. At last, someone who saw my potential! She was a breath of fresh air. The counsellor saw me twice that week, to help me to go back to work and gave me breathing techniques etc. That Monday, I heavy breathed the whole way down the motorway trying to be positive, I entered Reception, and on chatting to my friend, I burst into tears. I literally, couldn't stop. It was the fear of meeting the people I had a grievance out against. It was traumatic and my lovely colleagues thought I didn't want to come back to the team. Again, it was a bit like my grief, where it was all held in, no one on the team apart from the manager knew what was happening. Things started to change, I wasn't sleeping, I was dreading going in to work every day out of fear, I was exhausted, and there were days I didn't even know how I got home. This wasn't who I was. I always strived for perfection (a limiting belief) and was the girl behind the smile. This was something much more difficult, I was physically and mentally drained and I started to make mistakes. I even requested a seat move for fear of these people passing my desk, and I was told, to get used to it. Finding the smile was harder to conjure up and my emotions were very upfront, a side of me, not a lot of people had seen. Fast forward, I was to do something for a rep. On a normal day, it would not be a problem. I forgot what I was supposed to do, she asked again and I forgot! This was so not like me; I was so customer and service focused. I was so organised and thorough in my work. She reported me and I was pulled for the error, which was proper order, but knowing that this was not my standard, I got asked how this would not happen again, how humiliating! Honestly, it was one of my weakest moments at that time. I broke down in tears saying, that this was so not me and that things were getting to me, and so forth, but they knew this wasn't my standard but still questioned my ability and no empathy given. Something had to give, or things were going to get worse, so I took a week unpaid leave to just sleep. It was exactly what I needed. But that, wasn't the end of it, on return, I was facing the grievance panel, during which I encountered major panic attacks. It was like judge and jury, there should have been oaths taken, as I was being made out to be a liar and witnessed colleagues stabbing me in the back, their lies and deceitfulness hurt. I lost in the end, but it wasn't about winning, it was about my integrity. And for me, an unfair decision. With the impact it had on me, I dropped the outstanding grievance, I didn't have the energy to go through another one. From then on, I believe there was a big bold black mark put beside my name which held me back. I wouldn't change a thing, because I will always defend my reputation, and every life lesson, is a learning and growth. Sometimes you have to get comfortable, with the uncomfortable. Then a Team Lead role came up again and there was no second interview, even with the team routing for me, and given my knowledge and expertise. Hey ho, I just had to take it on the chin. At a later stage, I went for the role again and got another No! Hand on my heart, did I really want it? No! The team had changed even more, including a person who would accuse me of bullying her, not once but twice. Bullying someone? Now, that was a laugh, I was that busy in work I hadn't time to speak to people. She produced a list of dates for months and months but no witnesses, the same thing had happened to others prior to me. Was this a repeated pattern, just the individual changing? The sickening thing was that the mediator was taking her side and demanding an apology from me to keep the peace. Apologise for doing nothing? The blinkers were put on from that day forward, and I was afraid to look at people. Walking on eggshells began. The thing is, despite all that was going on, I chose to stay there and for that I had to take responsibility. I was and am at any given time there because of my choices. Sure, it was a handy job, 9 'til 5, 20 minutes to and from work, a 20-minute break, an hour for lunch, a pension, healthcare, etc. The money was crap and I wasn't happy but I sat in the knowing of a comfort zone. There was a lot more going on, a lot more rejections, a lot more opportunities denied, a lot more paths and projects blocked. Through all this, I guess I started to take things personally and beat myself up, I had feelings of not being good enough etc., and I became very frustrated with it all. I reacted instead of responding, and not always in a good way. I was pulled because I started to say I hated my job and wanted to leave. Why was I being questioned, when ninety percent of the team didn't like their job role and were a lot more vocal than me? Was it because I was a high performer? Was I sending out negative vibes or was I influenced by the negativity of the team or were people discussing this change in me? This drove to me to look at my CV and see which jobs brought me joy. One job stood out more than the others, the one, I always said if I was asked what was the best job I had, it would always be that one. That day, I decided I wanted to be a Foodservice Business Developer, bearing in mind this current company didn't have the role. But I am an opportunist, and I could see how this could work, with a vision for increased sales, knowing, I was the one that could do it. You can imagine, not everyone saw my vision, in fact, no-one saw it. Remember, no one needs to get your vision, only you! At this stage, I knew nothing about setting goals, visualising etc. I could only see the end goal. When IDP (Individual Development Plan) time came, my plan was to work alongside people to learn more about how my vision could work in line with the company ethos. I was driven and, it excited me but no one got it. Working in line with the Sales Manager who arranged some exciting activities. I attended head office meetings etc, and I was buzzing because I was learning. In January 2018 I had another meeting with the Sales Manager, a lot of ideas dispersed out including leading a project team. Excitement was an understatement but still the fact remained, we don't have that role. My answer was always, 'but I will be ready when we do'. If you have a vision, see it and believe it's coming, it can appear, maybe not as you expect it, but it can work out better. Obstacles are put in our way to encourage and stimulate our growth and learning. In July 2018, something changed. The Sales Manager requested that I change my IDP, even though this should never happen. They didn't have that role, which then became known as my "Imaginary Job". The only person who believed in me was me. I just needed one person to believe in me more than I believed in me. Leaving the office that day in disbelief (maybe disgust would be a better word)., I wondered why people were interrupting my career flow? A few days later, I recommended to my manager that for me to move forward with my dream, I was going to put Field Sales on my IDP. She was so excited saying she had waited 5 years for those words and she would action ASAP. All along, I had stated I was only interested in one division. I knew there were no roles at that time in that area but at least I had put my interest and intention out there. Within days HR were doing a telephone interview, then an online test, then a group interview and then they invited me to an interview. An interview for a job role I didn't apply for, which was funny! I didn't get that role, and I was told I would have to start at the bottom, despite having worked in the role before for the company and yet watching other people walk in, and not start at the bottom. It seemed there were different rules for different folks, I just had to keep my vision at the forefront. Why was this happening to me still? I could still only take this personally. Everyone I worked with, appreciated the work I did, which was always over and above, so why was I stuck in the same position? What was I not seeing or doing? Within a few months, a 9-month role had been advertised for the division I wanted. I thought the heavens had opened and the angels were singing Hallelujah! and thought, this is it! I went for the interview, despite there being good vibes, I didn't get the role. History repeating itself? The HR girl didn't want to ring me, she felt my pain. For me, that was it, this was another obstacle, only this time, I chose not to apply anymore. Enough was enough! I got home and boy did it hit me like a bolt of lightning. I felt so worthless, which led me into having a really bad panic attack. Thankfully, I knew how to control them, as I had suffered with them after my dad died. But this time was so different, in a scary way. I was walking to the door to get some air and my body was genuinely walking in front of me, like an out of body experience. I thought my number was up, and that I was going to have a heart attack like my dad. On cue, a friend rang, and talked me out of it. It was frightening, I just couldn't catch a breath. After a sleepless night and a pity party, I rang in sick. My manager advised that I take a few days off, so that I could get back to the good place I had been in. She empathised with me as well as being in shock with the news. What does she mean by in a good place? With everything going on, it had a big impact on my life, I had changed, I had become someone I didn't know anymore. My opinion was that the world and everyone was out to get me, and I was the most negative, opinionated person you would have met. I was hurting so much, and I couldn't express it any other way, I didn't know how or who I even was anymore, I was a mere shadow of myself. To people who listened to me without judgement at my pity parties for hours, weeks, months on end, I hereby openly personally apologise, if I drained the life out of you. But you listened and believed in me and I promised myself, that on the 1st of January 2018, my New Year Resolution was to be "Positive Annie". Coincidentally, I came across Reset the Happiness Project on

143

Facebook, run by a lovely lady and now a good friend, called Gemma Heaton. I purchased her journal and with great advice and tips, and every day I wrote 5 affirmations and 10 gratitudes. This simple exercise would be the start of the amazing journey of finding me, and to be a complete life changer. It came wrapped in hope, faith and love. I was open to anything at this stage. I hadn't done anything like this before, but things started to magically change and others started to notice before I did. People were saying that I had changed, that I was glowing. I was like, 'No, I haven't!' but the thing was, I was changing, and I was glowing from the inside out. People laughed at me, calling my journal my Bible, because it was always with me and I was constantly writing in it. Yes, I was the person who had laughed at a colleague doing this practice 20 years earlier. Looking back, I wish I had taken her advice on board. It is true, that at first they will laugh at you and then they will ask you how you did it - Fact! And they did ask! These practices are not airy fairy, as some may say, they are life changing. The quote on my first day of journaling was 'Day One or One Day, you decide?', it was day one of the rest of my life. I practiced powerful I AM declarations, affirming good things about myself every day. I AM, are the two most powerful words although the words that follow it, are even more POWERFUL! I now know that you are what you tell yourself, so watch how you speak to yourself. I had been telling myself things like, 'I AM not good enough or worthy enough... I AM fat' etc. Those were the words I used to tell myself and believed them Now I tell myself, 'I AM good enough... I AM worthy...I AM deserving .... I AM living in a healthy fit body.' Look at these statements. Which sounds better? What are you telling yourself every day? So, what is gratitude? It is being thankful for what you have, and it too, is powerful. A good exercise is to write 10 things you are grateful for every day, and it can be anything. I struggled with it at first. Imagine not thinking of anything to be grateful for. Now I can write pages. 'I AM happy and grateful for ... water... my home...friends/family...my job ...the birds singing ... music.' Gratitude can be taken a step further, and you can write 5 things in the present and 5 things in the future as if you have them in the present, it takes a bit of time to get your head around that one. During those few days, which I admit were tough, I was extremely grateful for my Reset Journal as it gave me hope, love and faith. I would have been lost without it, as it gave me the tools to continue to focus on my future rather than hold another pity party. I just love quotes, and during those few days, all the quotes just seemed to be relevant for me, at that time. But one quote appeared from the lovely Jay Shetty, and it lit something inside of me. It gave me a new perspective; it was like someone had flipped the switch on. This quote is how I look at any challenges now - I hope you enjoy it as much as me, maybe use it, it's a game changer.

'Swap "Why is this happening to me" and replace it with
"What is this trying to teach me?" It will change EVERYTHING'
- Jay Shetty

This quote made me realize that the company wasn't my future, and to stop torturing myself over it. I just had to have faith and belief in my dream and it would come. The dreaded Monday to return was looming, and I just knew I needed something to help me go back. Meditation called me, and I went to my first mediation session that Sunday evening - what an experience! I know this talk of affirmations, gratitude and meditation is very new to some, and airy fairy to others. I thought the same but it really works. Don't knock it until you try it. I came out buzzing and ready to take on my return to work. The following morning was a different story and my instincts said, 'put your makeup in your bag', but I didn't not know why. What could I do to increase my vibe during that dreaded drive to work? That answer was Justin Timberlake and 'Can't Stop the Feeling' on repeat. It's my go to song, my feel-good-and-raise-my-vibe song. I played it on repeat for a month, until I thought there must be something else. Then I found morning motivation talks and I think Denzel Washington and I became virtual good friends, but those words he spoke started to impact my day, in a marvelous way, saying 'You are a masterpiece', 'Win the Morning, Win the Day' to name but a few. On arriving at the office, no one spoke to me. I'm sure they didn't know what to say, I just wanted to cry. My friend gave me Rescue Remedy and Ping! But as the remedy wore off the anguish was returning. At 1pm I walked out the door for lunch, but I just couldn't hold it in anymore, and I cried to my car. In that moment, I decided I wasn't going back. I phoned my beautiful Godchild, as I wasn't coping too well. I couldn't speak through the tears. We had a good chat and got some great advice, it settled me. Now I knew why I had the make up with me! On it went and back to work. Going home, I decided to go to meditation again, only this time something happened that would change my thinking in a big way. After the session, the lady was chatting about auras, mentioning that suicide was coming up. That was my lightbulb AHA moment. It was in that sentence that I realized how strong I was, during everything that I had been through and all the rejections etc. If this had been someone else, they could have been burying them the week before because not everyone has the strength or belief in themselves to take so many knockbacks. I was like a new person; I knew I deserved more and better. The next day, the change in me was evident and when my manager said, 'Talk to me', I simply replied, 'I will be focusing on getting a job out of here, I can't give anymore to those who don't share my vision.' The thing about this company was that you didn't really have a voice. You could have a chat and put your opinion forward but the response was like an automated one. Most of my conversations were about a pay rise as there were people getting paid more than me. Funny, in December 2019, I got Laryngitis for a period of 12 weeks, 8 of which I was off work. I lost my voice, I'm sure to the joy of many as I am a wee chatterbox, but the spiritual reason is, not saying something you need to say - how true was that. Those 8 weeks would change me so much that I really did need a telescope to look back. During that time, I found Louise Hay, a book called How to Heal Your Life, this book was so invaluable and it had exercises to do. These were about dealing with your inner child and understanding limiting beliefs. It was the chapter on work that really resonated with me, especially when you aren't loving your work environment. Her advice was to be grateful for everything you have and what your job gives you. And now for the best bit, my new inspiration, Mr. Conor McGregor. I know, you either love him or loathe him. I have learnt so much from this man, and one day, I hope to thank him personally - I guess I watched every video on YouTube, and his documentary Notorious, which I could probably act in. Estimating, I probably watched it at least hundred times. What I love and learnt about him was his work ethic, his faith, his belief, his small circle, his passion, his goals, his dreams, following his heart, his information on the Law of Attraction on how he had read *The Secret* and put all the advice into action, his confidence, his determination, his drive, ignoring other's opinions and his visualising. I have taken on so much of these. He speaks with conviction and doesn't doubt for one minute. For me, self-image was an issue, because I had given my power to others and I was doubting my affirmation of being good enough. However, I now realize it was just other's opinions and a reflection of them. I had applied for jobs that I didn't want, externally, just to get interview experience because I doubted my ability. The funny thing was, I was getting down to the final two, proving there was nothing wrong with my interview answers. An opinion is only acceptable if it is moving you forward, and I was being halted. I returned to work in February a different girl than I was in December. On return I had to do my appraisal, yet again I give myself the highest scores to which they

148

tried to knock me back, but this time I just replied, 'Your opinion of me doesn't matter, this is what I am.' For the first time, in a long time, I knew my power was back. My gripe was still the salary, but this time was a bit more positive, they were looking at it. My confidence was growing every day, and my belief in myself was growing stronger. I just kept saying 'it's coming soon.' By this stage, I had walked on fire, broken arrows with my throat, bent bars, did board breaks and a glass walk, it was all so empowering. I have since been to several seminars and reading a lot more books like Think and Grow Rich, The Science of Getting Rich, Psycho Cybernetics to name a few, and online courses and mentoring programs. I was learning and growing every day. In early June 2019, a meeting was called to tell us we were getting a pay rise. Everyone got the same percentage, which meant the same people were still getting paid more. I asked for a word and asked about the extra. Again, the answer was 'No'. So, I went to walk out only to be told, 'there is a big world outside that gate, Jackie, a company who will pay your value and worth.' I was shocked, as this statement did not sit in line with company values. But a voice spoke to me saying 'You will never discuss your pay with her again' and on the way to my desk, it said 'You won't be here much longer'. Now that was interesting because I hadn't applied for anything. Have you ever heard those voices with messages? The following Thursday morning, I awoke to a message about a job opportunity, and within two weeks, I had a telephone and personal interview. I knew in my heart that this was my job, the one I've dreamt of, believed in, and written in my future gratitude intentions. Expect the unexpected. Yes, the job was mine! On the 31st July 2019, I walked back out that gate, with pure gratitude for the experiences, good and bad, because I wouldn't be as strong today without them. I had experienced things I never dreamt of doing, I had pushed myself, I had grown, I am more aware, I believe in me because, anything is possible. The girl behind the smile, now owns that smile with pride, and it's quite contagious. Smile and the world smiles back. I continue to learn every day, and more importantly I changed my attitude. The world is a much brighter place. Behind every dark cloud is a rainbow. Oh, and that job title was Foodservice Business Developer, so be careful what you wish for, thoughts become things and dreams do come true. My best advice is to Be You, Believe in You, Keep Smiling and Keep Shining and NEVER GIVE UP! Always have goals to strive for, be the best version of you, showing up every day for yourself. As Wayne Dyer says, 'When you change how you look at things, the things around you start to change.' What a quote! The only person who can change you, is YOU! A year on, I am a different person, even a different person from yesterday, as I choose every day to learn and grow. Am I still faced with challenges? Of course I am, but I deal with them differently with a different mindset and attitude. Even doing this chapter, I struggled with imposter syndrome but also questioned if I was good enough? Yes, I am good enough! And if my message helps just one person then I have achieved my goal. You can, be, do and have anything you want when you have the courage to take that leap, and keep believing in you and your goals. Like the line from the film, *The Pursuit of Happiness*, 'Don't let anyone tell you, you can't do something, not even me!' This line reminds me of my dad, the man who always had my back, to whom, I dedicate this chapter, because no matter what happened in my life, he always got me to see the good in it and me. I am truly blessed to have had great teachers in my life, my beautiful parents. They taught me to Never Give Up! Today is a Great Day to be YOU!

CHAPTER 9
Letting Go

by Heather Lundy

I drove home from dropping my daughter off at school knowing that I was going home to ask my husband to leave our family home. The end of our marriage took many years, and this would be just yet another step in a process that would see not just the breakdown of our relationship and marriage but also the breakdown of our family. I stopped at the garage to get petrol and cigarettes. I also bought a can of diet coke then drove home. The house felt brighter to me and I sat down at the dining room table and smoked a cigarette before picking up the phone. My husband answered on the second ring.

Just a few months before after returning home yet again and as we got ready for bed, my husband turned to me and in a moment of horrifying clarity he said to me; 'It's all gone very Greek.' It was so true and the truth cut like a knife. I started to look only at what was happening; the words being said, the actions and behaviours that were being taken or shown, the actions not being taken. So much was revealed to me and many of those Shakespearean tragedies started to make increasing sense to me on a gut rather than intellectual level. The truth cut away at my hopes and dreams with the sharp pain of living in conflict and pain.

Our marriage and family life had become a tragedy. The chaos had to end. The best thing seemed to be to ask my husband to leave and for me to remain in the family home with our children. I had known for a long time that this day may come but had always hoped that it wouldn't. The family system is so important to us all as human beings and in my roles as wife, lover, and mother I had done all that I could to try to keep things together. The truth was that change was needed and everything that we had tried - and we had tried many, many things - had not worked as behaviours continued to get repeated that led to many breaking points over the years.

The end of a marriage takes time, for me the decision to end my marriage was strongly resisted by me and then came all at once. I refused for so long to even consider our marriage ending, I had made a commitment and honestly believed at that time that love was not the problem. As I tried everything over many years to save and fix the marriage and family relationships I became more and more entrenched and invested in my marriage and our family being able to work through things. I was so focussed on not separating that I lost sight of just how difficult and how far off track that the marriage had become. I was so focussed on fixing the problems and changing behaviours – mine and others' - that I forgot the error of that position.

I had so much hope and have never lost hope for the best for all of us but in finally facing the truth of my situation and taking action I let go of trying to control the outcomes. I knew this may be the very end of the line and the heartbreak and pain was indescribable. I had palpitations, I felt my heart break in two and felt like it was ripping on a daily basis. I felt sore all over and ached and ached. I knew all of this was linked to my marriage breakdown.

In the final years of my marriage and our family breakdown I was so focussed on a solution and a vision that only included us all being together in a family unit. I kept holding on while all around me was falling apart. And then I heard those magic words for the first time – let go if you can. I would be told the same thing three times by three separate therapists assisting us as a family, couple and individually as I tried to save my family, but finally, I was willing to see that I had choice and that there was another way.

As the wife, lover, and mother in our family I fully embraced the role of family fixer. I had been so focussed on keeping us all together, trying to be all things for my children, trying to be all things for my husband, trying to make everything better. I drove myself to distraction along with everyone else. I soon manifested all manner of physical symptoms from the pain and heartbreak of knowing that our family was breaking down and that I would have to leave my husband. In the final few months I had constant headaches, lost weight – a lot of weight. It seemed the worse things got at home the more people commented on how well I looked. When I look at photos from the time, I cannot see that, only the strain and pain in my eyes, which seem large and very black. Over time even our children started to ask for us to break up, yet when it happened I was unprepared for the great physical and emotional pain that I would feel, I had thought I had already been through the worst of it.

Days after the first family therapist told me to let go if I can I made a choice. I chose to let go of any idea that our family would not resolve our issues. We are both intelligent people – we can do this. That was my thinking at the time, so I went ahead and booked a holiday that we had been planning for our family. And we renewed our wedding vows.

Now just six months later, here I was living on diet coke and cigarettes and after two more therapists had told me the same thing (Let go) and yet another fight within the home once again that morning. I was constantly feeling anxious and walking on eggshells. I knew that today was the day and knew I had to make a phone call to the man that I loved and had spent the best part of 20 years with. I picked up the phone and said it had come, the time that we both knew might come and that I needed him to move out. I still had hope that things could be resolved, and I held tightly, so tightly to that hope. I packed his bags and after a meeting with work colleagues at our home the next morning he moved out.

The pain was alleviated, and I entered an extremely surreal time. Over the immediate next few weeks, I focussed on home and the children. I was surprised as the family home settled, the atmosphere slowly and then very quickly transformed for the better. It just felt different – clearer, easier and the fear dispersed. At night however I hated going to bed alone, I would lay two pillows down my side and fill a hot water bottle. It was at night that I would often wake with my heart tearing in two. I developed a lump in my left breast and was advised to get a mammogram. Not this, not now was all that I

155

could think. I started to pray, continually, *'God, not this, not now, not this'*. Looking back, I am so, so grateful for all my friends who were fully there for me throughout this time and refused to let me keep my story or how I was feeling to myself anymore. They planned coffee dates, had us over for dinner, called in and most of all just made me laugh and laugh and learn to laugh at the situation and remember all that was good and focus there as things evolved and developed in whatever way that it would. I am also so grateful to many of their husbands and the men who stepped in and helped in so many ways and for the many encouraging reminders to keep my "head-up."

When a mammogram was needed it was my husband I called immediately, we made an appointment at a local clinic and just the next day he took me to the appointment. The sense of separation was apparent as we sat side by side in the waiting room and he didn't join me behind the curtain as I was examined. He drove me to the mammogram at a nearby cancer charity head office and back to the clinic for a scan. Just three hours later we received the extremely welcome news that it was not cancer and left instead with a treatment plan.

For the next few weeks we discussed how we wanted to be reconciled but soon the blame and excuses would start again. I finally came to realize that I had been so busy trying to keep everything and everyone together that I had refused to see that they all needed me to let go. I was until that moment still in denial and had been living in denial for so long that I had become unable to see and most importantly I hadn't taken the actions that had been needed and now here I was at the end of the line; scared, exhausted, heartbroken and it was time to act.

I ended our marriage in the only way that I could at that time. I went no contact and let go of all hope and expectations, knowing only that life could and would be good again. It is extremely hard to end a marriage but I have learned through our family breakdown many of the dangers in denial which showed up in a number of ways including;

- Feeling unable to think; I often felt like my brain was burning or literally rattling around in my head. I found making decisions and finding clarity difficult during this period of time. I understand now that this was due to the extreme ongoing stress that can be experienced during a marriage breakdown.

- Feeling uncomfortable in my own skin; looking back it was almost as if I was shedding a skin as my life changed. I often felt nervous and anxious.
Everything was changing and our family life began to feel fake and like a show.

- Feeling extremely fearful most of the time; I cannot stress this enough, in the weeks and months immediately before and after I ended our marriage I felt terrified most days. This is a real energy block

157

and was something that I had to work through over time.

- Physical symptoms including palpitations, panic attacks, aches and pains. On many days I would feel like my body was breaking in two and felt my heart ache and tear on a regular basis. I felt this was very much due to the marriage breaking down but I still talked to my GP and had any physical symptoms checked medically. Medically I was fine but the pain was very real.

It was only in facing the truth and taking this step and more importantly starting to speak up and stand up for myself and children that I was able to find a new vision for my future. Once I had faced the truth that my marriage had to end, life started to open up again and new paths started to reveal themselves. I became able to accept and hold the two opposing truths that I could love my husband and that our marriage did not work, accept that many of the relationships within our family had broken down.

I let go of any control over the outcome and chose to act only in mine and our children's best interests. To keep moving forward and make the best choices that I could without any thought to what choices or actions my husband may or may not make, but face them as they came and make the next best choice always. This enabled me to refuse to try to control anything and determine to speak of my experiences. In making these decisions I was able to keep going, to get up every day and make new plans. Daily life changed very little for me with the daily routine and needs of three children and a full time job taking up much of my time, I had always taken the bins out, made dinner, helped with homework and mum's taxi was always busy. In many ways my life became easier. There was a new clarity and a focus on mealtimes and planning good times for us as a family of four.

As time passed I was able to accept just how difficult our home and family life had been whilst we remained married. In the last few years of our marriage my husband had left many, many times returning after a night or two. And I had let him. I had to ensure that this would not happen again and break completely the cycle that we had been operating in repeating generational patterns that although we could identify we had both been unable to break whilst still in a relationship together.

I felt that my husband felt blamed. I just felt completely exhausted and in deciding to end the marriage I found that I had to go no contact. This was an extremely difficult decision for me and one that I struggled with until our family finally faced rock bottom. If things were going to change then I had to play my part and at that time that meant no contact.

'When I had nothing more to lose, I was given everything. When I ceased to be who I am, I found myself. When I experienced humiliation and yet kept on walking, I understood that I was free to choose my destiny.' – Paulo Coelho

In the decision to divorce I faced many hard next decisions. I had to be able to rely on myself only and be the leader for our family. No contact is a well-known tool for many couples who aim to end a difficult relationship that is not in the best interests of either party. Our family dynamics were not working and impacting our children greatly. No contact became the only option available to me after three years of concerted effort to save our family, marriage and relationship. There are three things that helped me through this time:

1. Accepting, fully accepting, that I could still love my husband whilst choosing to no longer be in a relationship with him.

2. Doing only what would most benefit our children and me at any given point in time. I tried always to choose with faith rather than fear.

3. Focusing on the present time only and allowing within my mind the knowledge that things would not always be like this – "this too shall pass" became a mantra as I allowed the process.

To any family facing divorce all too often, as in our case, it is a family breakdown. I was terrified to step out of my marriage for so many years and it was only when the risk of staying became greater than the risk of leaving that I finally had the courage to act. I acted swiftly and decisively at the very end. Almost three years later I am in awe that I was able to do this and know that it is thanks to the many good people that I surrounded myself with and in continuing to learn, understand and hold a better vision for our family.

I let go of any thoughts of what should happen, I let go of the man I had loved for 20 years, I let go of any expectations that I had of him as a father, husband and lover, I let go of my roles as wife and lover, I let go of the other half of our family and many people that I had loved and shared many good times with over the past 20 years, I let go of all expectations and took it one day at a time.

I cleaned the house, I packed up his clothes, I took down our family photos, I put them back up again, I put away our wedding album, I threw out my wedding dress, I slowly stopped looking at my wedding and engagement rings, I talked to my male friends, I talked to my female friends, I made new friends. The children and I would hike every weekend, we walked and laughed for many miles together, we had movie nights, games nights, pizza nights, we had people over for coffee and dinner, school exams had to be done, parties attended and so life carried on.

The two greatest gifts to me through that first year were a great therapist to hold my tears and a great solicitor to help me speak my truth and stand up for myself and our family. I spent a lot of time looking at myself and my choices in continuing our marriage, trying to save our marriage and now in ending the marriage. And in all this, in all this time and in focusing only on the needs of our children and myself I found that I could accept it all. I could and do forgive it all, myself included and I started to feel hope and love and joy again. I have listened to and accepted our children's experiences and I have seen our family change and develop.

Growing up I had watched so many people become stuck because of relationship or marriage breakdowns, people who were still bitter and devastated by the horrors of a divorce that took place maybe 5, 10 or 20 years before. I decided that would not be me for the sake of all involved. I am so grateful to the divorced women and men who helped me and shared their stories with me – one thing most shared was that they had wasted many years feeling bitter or resentful; how the mention or sight of their ex would still cause them pain and rage. I tried everything to shift the pain, and thankfully I found things that helped.

Meditate daily.

I had been meditating for many years at the end of most days but now it became a twice daily practice, a ritual and routine that helped me to be at peace for at least one hour every day. I joined a meditation group and learned more meditation practices. I made new friendships and most of all loved meditating within a group. I needed to let go of the pain that was giving me dis-ease. Intentionally calming my mind allowed me to focus better. It gave me head space to create ease within my life again.

Acupuncture, Reiki or massage to help shift your energy.

Anytime that I felt really low or exhausted I would book a massage and without fail it helped me to feel cared for. The physical touch was helpful and I would book either an energizing or relaxing one depending on what I needed. I slept much better for the next few days. I also benefitted greatly from Acupuncture and in particular Reiki treatments from friends. I was open to trying everything and I could feel my energy shifting through such treatments; in particular, feelings of guilt or shame being released, I would feel lighter and the churning in my stomach would stop.

Talking to friends and learning to laugh more.
I opened up and talked to my friends all the time about everything, including sometimes the divorce but mostly just having many great conversations. I talked to my female friends and male friends and it was critical at this time to have that type of support and talk about my feelings and experiences with both men and women who had my back. Most of all the best part was all the laughter, the jokes they sent on a regular basis and just laughing together.

Do things you enjoy with people you enjoy spending time with.
On a day to day basis I didn't feel that I had much energy during much of this time and naturally pulled back from most people and activities. I did only things that I enjoyed doing, tried things that I thought might feel good and spent time with people that I could easily spend time with. By that I mean I focussed on being places and with people where there would be little challenge and no conflict. There is time for challenge and I love to spend time with many different types of people but for around a year I benefitted most from being around people who felt like sunshine to me – whoever they were and wherever we found each other.

Always think what is best for me – it is necessary to put yourself first.

I found this really hard. I am surprised looking back just how much I struggled with this. It's a message often repeated due to its inherent truth – put your own mask on first. The more that I took good care of myself and the better I felt the better I was able to lead my family, be a good friend, a better neighbour and a better colleague.

Accept that the behaviour and choices of the other person are only about them.

You have no control over anyone else and if you have a divorce like I have you quickly learn through that process that you have no control over it either. This can be very freeing if you let it. I found a great solicitor and established some much-needed boundaries. Then I sat back and tried to respond rather than react to whatever would come. In accepting the other person's behaviour and choices I found that I had more courage to really consider how I wanted to behave and the next choice that I wanted to make. I also understood that my behaviour and choices would be all about me.

Watch lots of funny films! Laugh as much as you can.

Belly laughs are the best, I spent countless hours laughing out loud at Michael McIntyre, Sarah Millican, Peter Kay, Tommy Tiernan, Tadgh Fleming and watching funny films – in particular any including Kevin Hart and The Rock, for their comedic value - obviously. And I always felt great afterwards.

A great therapist and a great solicitor.

A great therapist to cry to and hold you accountable and a great solicitor to help you best navigate the divorce process. Invaluable. I wouldn't have been able to discuss things with friends the way I could with a therapist and it also protected many of my friendships to be exactly that, friendships. For one hour every week I could cry snotty tears and explore the depths feeling better afterwards and with strategies in place. My therapist at this time was someone new and for me only; holding me accountable when I needed to be, questioned me and listened in ways that helped me leave many of my experiences in the past.

I am so grateful that I received a recommendation for my solicitor and made the appointment immediately. I was gently guided through the separation and divorce process by a solicitor with great understanding, experience and compassion for the family unit. In particular my solicitor and their colleagues helped me to speak up and stand up for myself and my family.

Make a new plan, get a new vision. Write it down.

All my plans had included my husband. In order to change my thinking and in order to see a new future I had to think about the future that I wanted. On a weekend away with a friend I took part in a journaling class and started to imagine the life I wanted using paint, photos and words. I got a mentor and for the first time in my life wrote down my goals across every area of my life. I wrote a life script, completed vision boards and really started to picture a new world and see that life would go on in a new and better way. I also found it really fun.

Just keep on keeping on.

And when you can't, lie down for a little while. Then get up and keep on going again. It is only recently that I have found myself surrounded by people who understand the kindness in allowing yourself to stop briefly, to stop when you are tired and lie down when you need to rest, take a walk or take a day off. It also has given me the ability to quickly feel better and proceed in a positive way much more quickly. For many years, I would put off stopping until I became ill or depressed, when it would feel that I just couldn't go on and would take me weeks to feel better.

I have benefited from making new decisions and different choices. In the first two years I focussed only on myself and our children and moved away from the FOG of fear, obligation and guilt. I now put all my energy on my own life, career and money and ensuring that our children have what they need and are supported through their own goals and dreams. I have no-one to negotiate with on a daily basis and have found freedom and clarity to achieve what I want to. I have been supported by my work colleagues, family and friends. I have managed to pick up the pieces and move on and had to do it for myself. I now accept other people's choices and the person that they show me immediately – something it has taken me 40 years to learn.

I now focus on all the things and people around whom I feel really good. Together, my children and I have been on so many adventures and travelled to many places that we have always wanted to see, we did the Uni tours travelling much of England, went to Harry Potter World, had spa days, family adventure days and in everything have found great joy as a family of four. I have met so many people and life has opened up to me in ways that I couldn't have predicted. I know that I have remained fairly closed to a love relationship and that is my next step – maybe, hopefully. I would love to be able to meet someone that I can have a loving, successful partnership with and where I can allow myself to feel safe and protected.

In the meantime, life continues and life is good.

'Listen close to me
Anything can happen, child
Anything can be.'
- Shel Silverstein

CHAPTER 10
Embracing the Magic Within You

by Vivian McKinnon

Yes, I made it! I was behind the safety of the couch and nobody saw me. I looked down at the glass on the floor and picked it up, lifting it so quickly that I almost spilt it all over me, I swallowed the drink as fast as I could before anyone could catch me and take it from my hands. I cannot even remember tasting it, but I knew that this would be the answer. During the months of parties I had been allowed to attend, I watched, with great excitement, the effects it had on others around me, the magic liquid in the glasses and cans that my mum, dad and their friends drank . I left the glass behind the couch and returned to the party.

Within 5 minutes I felt a warm glow, I felt a sense of belonging that I hadn't felt before, I felt capable and confident, and I started to become the joker of the party, a role I adapted to quite well. It took the focus away from what was really going on, the adults around me were laughing and egging me on to sing a song and give them a dance, and I had absolutely no issue in fulfilling their wishes.

Back then I felt my life was about creating a distraction. My mum and dad sat laughing and joking with their friends and encouraged the behaviour and I could see they were proud of me and what I was doing. There and then I made the decision, I could be a performer! A significant part of the party, I could boost the fun and laughter that rang through the walls in the dimly lit living room of the upstairs council flat that we called home had been made available by simply drinking the magic liquid.

Home is a funny word, it's where we are supposed to be safe, where we are supposed to be nurtured and taught how to be human, where our needs are met, and our wants are created, where fitting in is replaced by belonging, and a loving embrace heals the wounds of the day. As an 8-year-old child that first experience of alcohol, or the magic liquid as I fondly named it, had created a real home, it melted away all the pain within my muscles, it stopped the sicky feeling in my tummy and settled my overactive mind. It felt safe.

Looking back the problem began in 1972 when I was just 8 months old. It was a beautiful spring morning, sun in the sky and the smell of fresh cut grass was in the air. My sister, Jacqueline, had just turned 5. As my mum lifted the table, she asked my sister to lift the chair and to remember to close the door to ensure I could not get out. I was in my baby walker and exploring the world at such a pace that if I ran over your toes, I was miles away before you felt it. Like any 8-mosnth-old in a baby walker, faster than the human eye!

As my mum and sister turned their backs, I made my bid for freedom and thundered towards the front door, whizzing over the threshold and out into the fresh air. As my mum turned to come back towards the house, she heard a neighbour yell and rush towards the bottom of the stairs. Thrown from the baby walker, I had tumbled from the top to the bottom and just lay there screaming. Luckily, my bones had not yet fused and formed, so I only suffered bruising and swelling, but that experience was to set the tone for a confusing and

169

traumatic childhood. I experienced several traumatic incidents in my early childhood, covering every form of abuse you can imagine, mostly because of being left in vulnerable and unprotected environments. My mental and physical health were massively compromised.

At one point, I developed big ugly sores on my forehead, that looked like ringworm. Then one day I had a blinding headache. I could not stand up, the light hurt my eyes and they were red and puffy, I was pure white, and my glands were swollen. My mum called the doctor to the house, as I could not even hold my own weight. I was no stranger to the doctor because my mum took me there regularly regarding sores, tummy aches and wetting myself during times of stress.

The doctor arrived and was very annoyed, he took one look at me and said, "I've told you before, she is doing this for attention. You have called me all the way out here", he went on. My dad had heard enough. Having seen my mum become almost paralyzed by the doctor's words and behaviour, he threw him from the house and warned him to never come back. By morning, my symptoms had worsened, and my dad called in another doctor. That doctor sat for a bit, checked a few things, and gave me a diagnosis of rubella (German Measles). I was confined to a room, in the dark, and no-one was allowed in. No one explained what was happening, so I thought I had done something really wrong, I remember crying and thinking this was that last straw, I could never be the boy my mum wanted and that I was going to be given away, I was just too much for them to look after. I felt that since my brother came along in 1973, I was a burden and there was no need for me anymore. Everything that had or was going wrong was my fault.

Not long after that my mum's drinking became a "thing". She had used alcohol to cope before, as she experienced several challenges in her own life. My gran had taught her that alcohol helped you cope with life's adversities. My gran taught her that when things became too much, alcohol could shield you from all the nasties in the world and create a place of safety.

My mum used to work behind the local bar, which made drinking easy for her, but it also made drinking easy for me. When I was around 13 she would give me and my friend 2 bottles of special brew and 2 bottles of K Cider. My friend and I would go to the woods and mix them together, a lethal combination but when I drank it, I was that confident, witty 8-year-old performer. This was also around the same time my dad went on strike from the coal mine.

The strike of 1984 added huge pressure on our family, financially and socially. Men who returned to work were shouted at in the street, children were beaten up at school and called "Scab". My mum really started to struggle, and having no money added pressure to the situation. Her drinking began to escalate quickly, at a frightening pace, and so did mine. She would often be found in the street, having to be rushed to the hospital.

At this point I was introduced to cannabis. I found it numbed the racing thoughts and dulled the pain I had experienced.

By 17 I'd moved out of the family home and was living with my boyfriend. Within no time I was pregnant and married. I married because I did not want to bring even more shame onto my family by having a baby and not being married. At that point in my life I knew everything, my boyfriend might have had issues in regulating his emotions and he could be a violent bully with others, but not me, he loved me and I thought I would heal him with my love and in turn he would look after me.

This relationship was an eye opener, every belief I had about myself was confirmed; I was projecting all my internal pain and disconnection onto everything and everyone around me and found myself in a really dangerous relationship, full of volatility and abuse. In 1992 at 20-years-old, I plucked up the courage and left him. I had left before and went back to my mum and dad's. My husband would then visit my mum at the pub, buy her alcohol, turn on the tears and get her to bring him to the house where he would do the same to me and get me to go back with him to our house. He was always full of promises that he would change and that my son and I would be safe. So, this time when I left, I was presenting myself as homeless at the local council offices. My son and I were placed in a homeless hostel. After a few weeks, a friend of his, who had also been placed in the hostel, informed him I was there. Thankfully, this way of rehousing women fleeing domestic violence has been changed.

My husband appeared at the hostel, gained entry through his friend, then made his way up the stairs and kicked open the door of my room. He appeared in the room holding a knife and began to beat me. Covered in blood and in a blind panic I fled, I ran down the street and hid in an alleyway, but then remembered I had left my son. When I returned 5 minutes later, he was gone and so was my son. I panicked and phoned the police and a warrant was issued for his arrest. He was caught within an hour, arrested and my son was returned to me. There and then I knew I couldn't live there anymore as he would just keep returning, he had no fear of the police and I couldn't take the chance of being forced through fear to go back to him. I decided the streets were the safest place to be, he probably would not find me there and I could be free from him until I gathered my thoughts. I was homeless and on the street with a 1 year old. I was also now awaiting the court case for attempted murder and kidnap which had been brought against him by the police and my legal team.

I remember feeling so alone, feeling like I had no one except my little baby boy and I was failing him so badly. I couldn't even keep him safe and warm. I wanted to provide the best of everything for him, yet I couldn't even put a roof over his head. I had such a sense of not being good enough, thinking that if I can't look after myself, how the hell can I be in charge of his little life? That said, I remained stubborn and refused to let anyone in or get help, they could just hurt me even further and I couldn't allow that to happen. At court my husband was found guilty of grievous bodily harm and given a community service order and a fine.

It was around then that I was introduced to ecstasy, amphetamine, cocaine, and crack cocaine. For the next decade, my life became a blur fueled by disconnection, secrets, and avoidance that I allowed to hold me hostage in the hope of it all going away. On Christmas day in 1997, after a sober drug-free pregnancy I gave birth to my beautiful daughter. I hoped her birth would stop the cycle, and it did for a while, but then after lies, secrets and heartache between myself and her dad I went back to my old friends, alcohol, and drugs. Addiction was my cycle, it was vicious and endless, yet dependable and always there to pick up the pieces.

In October 1999 I woke up in the intensive care unit of Edinburgh Western General Hospital, at the ripe old age of 28. I had been rushed to hospital with suspected meningitis.

As I woke up and before I opened my eyes I lay there, just listening to the beeps from the surrounding machines and the running commentary from the harsh internal critic who was first on the scene, as usual, with her less than complimentary run down of where I had gone wrong and ridiculing my decisions, my flaws and failings. Only this time she was accompanied by a new voice, a softer, quieter, kinder voice who was simply saying *'Please stop this, just rest, take your time and just rest.'*

I left the hospital with an inner knowing that my life had to change, I didn't know what or how, but I knew I needed to change, in order for my life to do the same.

The hospital ran all sorts of tests and found nothing, the doctor put it all down to a viral infection, what he never knew was the lifestyle I was leading and how I had used and abused my body with alcohol, drugs, food, men — anything to release the pain and to *feel* something, so in order for me to see my 30th birthday, I decided there and then to make that change.

Now the thing with change is that it's not just as easy as just saying it, it takes work, hard work, commitment, resilience, hope, personal control, kindness, connection, understanding and gratitude, which initially made this quite hard for me as I didn't believe I had any of these traits. However, what I did have was grit and determination to stay alive. I persevered and I became involved in life in new ways, I really worked hard at it and at age 30 I walked over 100 miles of the Great Wall of China raising thousands of pounds for a Scottish based charity who support families whose lives have been impacted by disability, mental health and addiction. I went there with 52 people who I had never met before. Each and every day I woke up half an hour earlier than my room-mate and sat in front of the mirror and spoke to the part of me who controlled the panic I had felt in my life up to then, I made it clear that they had half an hour to appear or to stay away for the rest of the day as I had things to do and people could not see this version of me. I mean, what would they think?

In my 2 weeks in China I never had any panic attacks, I had a few wobbles but again the softer kinder voice appeared and said *'Aw come on, you had your chance this morning just let her get on with her day.'* When I came back from China I had a huge realisation. *'What if I am in control of this stuff and not the other way around? What if I keep this up and it all goes away, what if ... ?'*

175

For the next few years, I was dedicated to figuring things out, still using cannabis every day and alcohol and cocaine at the weekends but getting there and learning more and more each day.

In 2004, aged 33, I began to volunteer for a charity called MOVE ON within a project that supported young people who had experienced the care system, young people who had been looked after and accommodated and who were at the start of the transition to independent living, I could relate to these young people so much, and in a way I suppose I was at the same point, trying to become independent from the internal voice who until then had ruled so much of who I'd become.

Within 6 months I was coordinating the project, I started to see myself, and my capability through someone else's eyes, I believed I could, and even when I challenged it to look for the lie that lay within, the lie was that this ability to make a difference and use my skills to help others was new. The truth was it was not a new thing, it had been inside me all along, I just hadn't accessed it properly yet. By now my body ached, my back, shoulders and neck were, at times, almost locked in spasms in my mind desperate bid to distract me from my mental pain by creating these manifestations in my body. This subtle but important shift was the repressed emotions way of necessitating symptoms.

A colleague at MOVE ON introduced me to floatation therapy, a therapy that involves lying in 25 centimeters of body temperature water and half a ton of Epsom salts. Once I got over myself, I stepped in and lay down. I was suspended in this warn comforting environment, allowing my central and peripheral nervous system to glide into rest and digest mode, for me, this was a very unique and quite profound experience. And after just one session my approach to my whole world changed. The reality is, we spend approximately 80% of our energy fighting the effects of gravity, but in this amazing environment I was free from that, allowing the 80% of energy to turn inwards. Floatation provided a space free from distraction, a space free from all external stimulation where I was able to just be. Being free from mental and physical pain I was able to creatively imagine what my life had the potential to become, free to realise that I wasn't my story, I wasn't the person the internal critic kept telling me I was, and that she was only saying that to move me to action, to start a fire in my belly and get me to push back, I suddenly realised I pushed against the norm all my life, I didn't conform and did things my way yet for the last 33 years of my life I had listened to this running commentary of fear, rejection and hopelessness, and suddenly, almost immediately, I was full of hope, full of excitement and insight.

When I emerged from the tank, I wanted to know exactly what had just happened. I was full of questions and was firing them like an AK47 rifle. The float center owner said *'Yeah it's such a beautiful spa treatment'* I said *"No, no, no ..what you have there is the most amazing mental health intervention'* When she couldn't answer my questions I left the floatation center that day knowing something fundamentally within me had changed and I realised I had to find out exactly what that experience was, what it meant and how I could bring it to others. I realised that day that the magic was within me and had been all along.

In 2007 at aged 36 I reengaged with education and challenged the real monster, the 2 most ingrained beliefs I had, the belief that I was stupid and not good enough!

I went to college, then university, and began to understand who I was and to explore my purpose. Around the same time, I reconnected with an old boyfriend who I had spent time with when I was not long back from China.

Back then the inner critic decided he was too good to be true, so he had been swiftly dumped. There had always been a part of me open to having him beg me to come back, but he never did. So, 8 years later when he came across my radar I was like, '*Right let's see what he is doing with himself now.*' He had moved to the North of Ireland and we decided to meet up. Within 2 months I made the decision to move from Scotland to Ireland to be with him. Part of this decision was to change my environment, because although I had changed so much for the better, my environment had remained the same.

I was still Aunty to the village and being dragged into other peoples' drama when I had learnt to manage mine. So, in August 2010 I ramped up the journey to the core of me, the journey from the head to the heart, and it brought me to County Down in Northern Ireland. In April 2011 we got engaged and in November 2011 we exchanged vows on the beach in the beautiful resort of Rendezvous in St Lucia, just the two of us. In January 2012 I found out I was pregnant, and we had Sonny on the September 11th, 2012. Whirlwinds have nothing on us!

For the first 40 years of my life I covered my battle scars, I carried them within, hidden in my attempt to deny that they existed. Not yet understanding these were my badges of honour.

I tried to remove the parts of me that I deemed were broken, bad, or dangerous. I believed the generational story of struggle and disconnection and lived up to the character genealogy had been written for me, until I decided that I had almost died for the last time. Only then did I begin to cement the foundations of change.

I realised most of the *beliefs* I had about myself, and the things I *believed* about others all had a similar core, an exact middle point that was glaringly obvious when I looked at with a new approach to life. Looking at it now, the word *lie* was embedded in the 2 words before me.

Then suddenly I stopped and focused on my breath. To expire we let go of our last breath, so, surely, we are inspired by our first breath. Every breath in between is an opportunity denied to so many. like a golden thread weaving you from one stage of life to the next.

I began to realise the most powerful nation in the world is the imagination and we carry it with us all day, every day. Its willingness to serve can bring us all we could ever want or need. All we need to do is just ask.

I realized that my experiences since stepping out from behind that sofa at 8 years old had been created to teach me about flexibility, to get me to commit to myself, to show me hope and promote kindness from within, to invite me to explore the meaning of resilience and how to grow and thrive. These experiences did not mean I was wrong; it was all my fault and I was a bad person. It simply meant that every decision I had made was the right decision, for me, at that time, with the resources I had available. If they were not, I would have chosen something else. You see, even when we think we do not have a choice, it is actually the one thing we always have. I started to I forgive myself for believing the internal critic, for fighting against her in my attempt to silence her, instead I started to embrace her, challenge her, give her the respect, acceptance and safety she had been desperately seeking for far too long.

I went into private study and explored cognitive behavioural therapy, neuro linguistic programming, time line therapy, clinical hypnotherapy, havening technique, SPECTRUM performance and emotional coaching, and I began to really understand who I was underneath all the layers of guilt, shame, fear, hurt, sadness, anger. I began to unearth my true purpose, my intention for life.

After lots of subtle encouraging nudges and comments from my husband I took the leap of faith into self-employment. He always went on about how he believed in me, how I would be able to do it hands down so when push came to shove and I made the decision to open my own wee therapy world I, said *'If you believe in me so much then give me your savings to start-up'* And without lifting his head from the computer he said, *'Yeah okay, great investment.'* I was like, *'Shit, this is real now!'* My idea of having a therapy room with an adjoining float room quickly grew arms and legs. My

180

£25/30,000 project suddenly became a £100,000 project. I was scared, I was full of emotion and unsure of my capabilities, while at the same time forcing myself to believe *'This will work, it will all be great.'*

To cut a long story short, In September 2015 I opened Northern Ireland's only floatation center, *Hydro-ease*. I gave up my full-time job, I spent my husband's £27,000 savings and placed myself £66,000 in debt and chased the dream. I kept my eyes firmly on my ability to serve and how this vision would bring healing to the people of Northern Ireland. I then shushed the naysayers out of the picture. I developed an approach called the R.A.F.T (Reconnection and Floatation Therapy) Program, where I blend and layer the skills and tools I've discovered on my journey to inspire others to reconnect to their self and deliver this in unison with floatation, supporting people to heal. I hold space for *adult children* of substance misuse parents to empower them by making sense of the impact their early life experiences and informative years have on their motivation and ability to move freely through life.

In setting up and developing all of this I've discovered a funny thing; when I took my leap of faith, those who were closest to me become risk averse on my behalf, they quickly identify the ways in which I might fail, yet almost strangers were cheering me on from the side lines.

I became a businesswoman, an entrepreneur, titles that still make me giggle to this day 5 years later. I sat one night and thought, *'What if I approached my internal world like a business, if I mediated between the "versions" who live within the skin of me?'*

I began to identify each one, I wrote down their strengths and their challenges. The frightened child, the class clown, the rebellious teenager, the abused wife, the resilient empath, the strong warrior, the emotionally secure guardian, the passionate and the fiery adult and realised they are prototypes of who I have become, without them there is no me!

I looked at how they all played a part in my life, and as such deserved the recognition for getting me to where I was. I wrote down how they cope and how they appear when they feel they are needed or being threatened.

I then visualised a board room, a *huge* boardroom with oak doors and a large oak table, beautiful art on the walls, luxurious carpet on the floor and crystal water decanters on the table. I visualised myself as I was that day sitting at the top of the table with my electric blue suit on, my hair and makeup done and my biggest. *'You're-getting-a-promotion'* smile. I visualised inviting each one of these versions into the room, one at a time. I warmly welcomed them with a hug and invited them to take a seat. I asked how I could support them, what I could do to make the most of their skills, what they felt their strengths were, their challenges and how I could empower them to rebuild their *self*. I apologised for shunning them and their efforts and began to gather the information about how they operate. They spoke about how they hijack the body and the mind, and what I could do to work with them on this They spoke in detail, with excitement and compassion. There were tears and tantrums and whole lot of healing.

You see, in life people will share their pain with us, their guilt and their fear and beautifully wrap these up as gifts of love, connection, and acceptance. Once we accept these as ours and unwrap then over time, we realised these beautifully wrapped gifts are full of broken glass and they cut to the core.

As a child our care givers, or prominent adult figures, show us the world through their eyes teaching us how to operate within it. We very rarely challenge these models that we are shown or make that connection to our core, seeing it as too fragile, too painful, too raw. We often overlook the fact there may be more to this life than we have already uncovered. We take reactions from others and give them meaning by comparing and contrasting them to previous experience, to make sense of now. Never affording our self the diversity of opportunity. My internal critic demanded so much attention to survive, until there was a new kid in town, and she turned up back in 1999 in the hospital bed and simply said, *'Please stop this.'*

I want you to know you have the freedom to challenge everything you think you know, I want you to know you are not your story, instead you are who you choose to become. Just because others may expect less from you does not mean you cannot be more, do more, have more and totally break free from your own shell to not only grow but thrive.

Now, closing your eyes, I'd like to invite you to picture yourself looking in a mirror. Look to your head with all its power, knowledge, and fascinating capabilities. Listen to your gut with all its power, knowledge and fascinating capabilities, I mean how many time has your gut spoken, or not spoken, and it's voice or silence been exactly what you knew to be true? Now imagine they both make a pathway to meet, to connect and show you the way, to bring you into the flow of your life. As they meet in the middle and connect at the heart, feel the connection as the power becomes compassion, feel it as the knowledge becomes understanding and the fascinating capabilities become the ability to love yourself. That path may be long and windy but it's the most empowering journey you will ever embark upon.

When you open your eyes have a good look, a good look at who you really are. You are not your experiences, you are not your programming, you are not your mum or dad, you are true and authentic and full of possibility.

No one else has been with you 100% of the time —*you* have. No one else knows all your experiences and outcomes — you do. No one else can connect to your innate excellence and love you just for you — you can.

When you open your heart and realize this, you will begin to become your own best friend, and, knowing what that's like, ensures you can wholeheartedly share it with others. Be the friend you would like to have, the friend you sought in your own times of need, your own personal friend who can share the silence within and be at peace with it.

Focus in on the courage and strength that has enabled you to survive; the very fact that you are reading this book means you have a 100% success rate, nothing has killed you so far and you've survived the lot. You are amazing and all you have done in life has led you to where you are right now. Just know this — YOU ARE ENOUGH!

CHAPTER 11
A Pot of Stew

by Patrick Dillon

Growing up in family of 4 children and being the only boy, life as you can imagine was hectic for my mother, having to look after 4 young children was a task in itself leaving very limited time for individual love and support. This allowed us children to grow up not dealing with emotions properly and therefore were uneducated if you will on how to build coping mechanisms. I believe now that not properly dealing with your emotions can lead to difficult roads ahead for adult life, in my case domestic violence.

I can only describe it as a pot of stew, let me explain. All the ingredients that you need to make a pot of stew represent your feelings and experiences (both good and bad) such as happiness, sadness, anger, frustration, jealousy, low self-esteem, love, hate, ego and passion, provoking, pushing buttons, drugs and alcohol abuse etc. With a continuous buildup and no release, the pot overflows, possibly exploding, and you end up with a hot mess in your kitchen (your life), however if you deal with all the negative feelings and remove them from the pot you can be guaranteed to have a beautiful tasty dish at your kitchen table.

Within a relationship one has many feelings, some are on the surface and some are under the surface. Some people within a relationship can bury their feelings, preferring not to deal with them or talk about them, this could be due to fear of judgement, fear of rejection, shame, regret, hurt, bitterness, uncovering lies and deceit and feelings buried so deep that they are erased from their memory. At first it would appear that a person is all full of love, kindness and compassion and they have big dreams, however as they relationship progresses all the nice ingredients slowly dwindle, and the harsher feelings raise their heads.

This happened to me. At 19 years old, I was lucky enough to meet and amazing girl and fall in love. We moved in together and life couldn't really be any better. I was a second-year apprentice electrician, had my own house and car, and although I had big dreams of becoming a millionaire, I was really happy and comfortable with my life.

I had been smoking/abusing cannabis since the age of 15 and never saw it as a problem, since I was smoking cannabis when we met, I never expected her to want me to change or stop.

As the honeymoon ended and the years passed, paranoia slowly started creeping into my thoughts, when she was out with a friend who was well known to get around or when she was out alone with her male friends. This started to cause arguments, due to lack of trust and jealousy on my behalf. I began to give her very hard decisions, such as, *'it's your male friends or me'*, and since her love for me was so strong, she picked me and stopped spending time with her male friends. Now looking back, I can only imagine her resentment building towards me. However, this was only the beginning, as she became part of my family, when my family had disagreements, she started to take sides, and since I gave her hard decisions to make, she began to return the favor, and I stopped talking to most of family for a few years.

So if I can paint a picture for you at this point and put all the feelings and emotions into a pot, just like you would put ingredients into a pot of stew, we have a pot with love, passion, happiness, paranoia, resentment, jealousy, lack of trust and cannabis abuse, and as you can see it is starting to become a recipe for disaster, and it didn't stop there. As all these feelings and emotions gathered momentum and tempers began to flare, we both knew each other so well from spending so much time together that we knew how to push each other's buttons. Arguments started to get fiercer with words, the screaming got louder, and it became a competition of who could say the harshest thing to hurt the other person the most.

Although this is starting to sound like we hated each other, I had seen this type of behavior growing up and assumed it was normal in a relationship What I hadn't been taught growing up was how to. deal with these emotions. I was taught to give each other the silent treatment, brush it under the carpet, never speak about it again, it will all blow over and everything will be back to normal after a day or two, until the next argument happens, and with each argument it would escalate more because the previous argument wasn't dealt with properly. It was like a ticking time bomb waiting to go off, the words got more personal, tempers flared and we started to really get into each other's faces, as we screamed daggering insecurities and faults at each other, that's when it started to get physical.

Having being the perpetrator of a domestic violent relationship, I can honestly say from experience that the guilt and the shame of my actions ate away at my core for six years after the relationship had ended, the love I had for that girl was the best feeling of my life and I wreaked it because I didn't know how to deal with my emotions or communicate properly. Although that was the darkest time of my life and I did things totally out of character and said things I didn't mean. I wanted her to feel the emotional pain that I was feeling. Until one day enough was enough for her and she packed her bags and my 18-month-old son's bags and she left. It was a wake-up call. I mean how could I put my hands on the one person that I loved so dearly? What was I doing? What was I thinking? Was it just me to blame, was it how I was brought up? Was it her? Was it my friends? Was it the cannabis? In hindsight, I was always looking for someone or something to blame when in actual fact I was the one who made that pot of stew, I WAS THE ONE TO BLAME AND ONLY ME. We all have our own minds and for the majority of us we know right from wrong, I can't sit here and tell you that because I witnessed domestic violence as a kid I thought that's how you treat women, I KNEW exactly what I was doing and even though I knew it was so wrong I continued to do it and continued to let myself live in a world where I was always right and everything always had to go my way. But it had to stop.

If I and everyone around me were to have a somewhat decent and more peaceful life, I had to stop, find out why I was doing and how it all happened, and I had to deal with how it affected not only me but my ex-partner and my family. Hitting your partner is the result of the problem but not the problem itself. I needed to get to the root of why I was doing it in the first place.

I plucked up the courage to go to counselling to try and sieve through what was going on. Through this avenue I found that I had many issues stemming back to my childhood that were buried so deep I had forgotten all about them. There were other issues where I felt I couldn't say anything or get involved in but it would have concerned me and I never got a say in it, this was hugely imbedded within our immediate family culture (to brush everything under the carpet and to sugarcoat everything). At the young age of 15 cannabis was introduced into my life and for a few years I thought it was a way that I could block out my feelings and get away from it all for short while, this obviously I learned was not the way to deal with my emotions but at the time I didn't know what dealing with.

It also set me on a different journey, to find out why I would feel the need to hurt somebody I loved so dearly, and I was determined to get the answers. I knew the only way I was going to get my answers was to swallow my pride, pull back the carpet and let the skeletons out of my closet of the shameful actions that I had done.

As soon as I started talking the weight of the world started to lift off my shoulders, it was never going to take back what I did and it never will, but it began the process of finding the answers I so desperately wanted, and it started to free me from the personal self-sabotage I was subjecting myself to in private.

It takes more courage to admit what you did wrong than to suppress it and allow it to grow like a cancer inside you. You must deal with each individual ingredient and only put into the pot what you want. It didn't take a genius to tell me that the paranoia was coming from years of cannabis abuse, however, I did learn that being jealous is caused by comparing yourself to somebody else, for example, *'He's funnier than me, he dresses better than me, he drives a better car then me, he has more money than me or he has a better job than me.'* All these thoughts are negative thoughts and if you catch them as they enter your mind you will eliminate the jealousy and that's one less ingredient in the pot. Trust or lack of is caused by your own insecurities, hurts from the past that's not directly linked to the person or the situation your bringing them into, and if that's not valid for these circumstances then leave it out of the pot.

Resentment is caused by manipulating somebody to do something that they do not want to do, and why would you do that to somebody that you love?

Growing up with little or no understanding of feelings and emotions or how to deal with them, I learned from the visual aspect of what I saw. When two boys at school had a disagreement, they sorted it out with a physical fight, when my sister and I had a disagreement we sorted it out with a physical fight, and when my parents or my friend's parents had a disagreement it also turned into a physical fight. Although I knew this was wrong, I had become accustom to it The screaming and shouting were deafening at times, the banging of doors, the noise of objects hitting the wall after been thrown, the sirens of police cars and ambulances, the barring orders and seeing grown mothers and fathers crying. I knew deep down it was all wrong, but I never really questioned it or tried to understand it. The last thing I ever thought would happen is that I would become the violence I didn't like, but I did for a time.

After it happened I dealt with it in the same way I had seen it been dealt with in the past, I brushed it under the carpet, never spoke about it again, and thought flowers and chocolate was the perfect way to say sorry, and it did work for a while.

My whole life had fallen apart and to be honest I deserved it, I had lost my job a few months earlier which affected my ego to be the bread winner in my family and the security was lost to be able to provide for my family.

I wasn't talking to most of my immediate family and now the echo of an empty house all day every day had brought me to my knees, I remember one specific day lying in bed at 3pm unable to stop crying begging god to give me back everything that I had lost or take me, but if that had of happened I would not have learned anything.

It was time to change, in order to change I had to question my actions and what caused me to act this way, I had to hang my head in shame and tell somebody what I had done, so I started with my immediate family. The disappointment on my mother's face was devastating and the anger from my sister was so strong I thought she was going to kill me herself.

Today I can honestly say that although I can't take back or change my past, I am more educated on how and why I acted that way and how to make sure that it never happens again in the future. As I grew older and became more understanding of my surroundings and my life, I realized that I was letting history repeat itself within my relationships and I knew I had to get help to fix this. This was made very clear to me when my ex-partner plucked up the courage to walk away and take my son with her. It was a pivotal part in my life as I didn't see it coming, in my selfish ways I always believed that she would never leave, and boy was I wrong! If I am being honest, she actually did me a favor because had she not done what she did when she did it, I probably wouldn't be here today to tell my story. I will mention here that after she left and I knew in my heart it was forever, I sank so low that I thought of no other way out only to end my life, thankfully my family were there to catch me as they could see me eventually falling so hard and they were not prepared to let me do what I wanted to do.

I sought out help from many different counsellors and drug addiction support groups, I also found many answers through talking to my family, especially talking to my mother and father. it was only when I felt confident enough through counselling that I was able to talk to my mother and father and it was only after I had forgiven myself and them for the negatives in my life that I could move forward in a happier environment.

For me counselling was a life saver, I had never received counselling in my life before, so it was a new and frightening experience. I quickly learned that I could be free and speak about who and what I wanted without hurting anybody's feelings; this allowed me to breath freely and thankfully I couldn't stop talking. With each session I grew more confident and became very self-aware of what I had done in the past, how it happened, where it came from, and more importantly I started to forgive myself, which opened up a road for me that I never thought I could travel. I started to believe in myself.

Self-belief and self-worth are huge and difficult emotions to swallow, most of us don't actually believe we deserve to have self-belief or indeed deserve to have self-worth. It often stems from negative situations that happened in the past, it could be from not being told enough how much you are loved and how well you are doing, be it in school or how much of a good friend you are or how much of a good child/son you are, either way it stems from not being nurtured with positivity early in life and it snowballs into your adult life with you still believing that you're not good enough.

Self-belief is probably the most important ingredient to put into the pot first, I find self-belief has a rebellious affect against jealousy, if you have self-belief, you will never compare yourself to anyone else and therefore jealousy and self-belief cannot mix in the same pot. Self-belief also increases self-confidence, self-esteem, self-worth, and the trust you have in yourself to always treat your partner the way you would like to be treated

I also find it has a lot to do with accepting yourself for who you are, what you look like, the family you came from and your ability to accept the past, everything else in life can be changed, if you don't like where you live, change it, if you don't like the car you drive, change it, if you don't like the job you're in, change it, and you don't like the relationship you're in, change it. What I am trying to say here is that if you accept the things in life that you can't change, well then self-belief already exists and reinforcing it with positive affirmations and achievements from your past, will help you achieve more, grow your self-belief and other peoples judgement won't affect you anymore.

If other people (or yourself) try to bring you back to the old you or punish you for what you have done in the past, they will only be able to do that if you allow them to. You and only you have the power to allow that happen.

Thankfully, I can now raise my hand and take responsibility and accountability for what I have done in the past and I have, and I can say those words, that for some people proves difficult. I AM SORRY. I keep myself focused on all the good in my life now, and quite frankly I didn't realize that I had so much good in it because the negative dark stuff was shadowing it for a long time, and as mentioned above the talking and counselling lifted a smoke screen if you will. It allowed me to see through a clearer glass.

I found these little tips can help to stay focused

- Deep Breaths
- Exercise
- Surround yourself with positive people
- Eat a healthy diet
- Make time for family and friends
- Make alone time for yourself

195

- Keep a diary of your feelings and reflect every so often
- Keep your faith, talk to your higher power (if you have one)
- Read positive affirmations everyday
- Be kind to yourself
- Forgive yourself and others (holding grudges is like an anchor around your waist) (LET IT GO)
- If you feel overwhelmed and can't seem talk to family or friends, seek outside help (TRUST ME IT WORKS)
- Identify negative emotions such as guilt anger and frustration and replace it with something positive like being kind to somebody you don't know, texting a message to that someone that you love or repeating and affirmation to yourself of how strong you were to admit that you made a mistake.

Having dealt with my past and what it has done to not only me, my ex-partner and my family, I can now stand tall with my head held high, there was always that niggle in the back of my mind, always afraid, afraid if someone brought up the toxic relationship I had with ex-partner. Now because I have nothing to hide, because I have taken responsibility, I have been held accountable, and more importantly I have apologized and forgiven myself. I can now move on and focus on making the tastiest pot of stew anyone has ever tasted.

My advice would be to stay conscious of what is happening in your life and ask yourself how things will serve you. You have probably punished yourself over and over again for mistakes (I know I have) and there is no need to punish yourself anymore. If you have dealt with the mistake you made, you have changed your ways, rise above it, and stay focused on being the best boyfriend, partner, or husband you can be.

CHAPTER 12
The White Feather

by Christine McGonagle

As I am approaching my half century on my 49th year, I reflect back on my life at all the situations that have brought me to where I am now. The joys, the tragedies, the heartbreak, the ill health, and the financial strain of life; not forgetting the family, genuine friends and the nay sayers.

From all these life lessons, the first was the joy at the birth of my first born, my one and only daughter Emma. From there on followed five sons, all of which I am equally proud of. They make me smile, tug at my heart strings, each and every day. They have been the reason that I wake up in the morning, put on my shoes, hold my head up and face the world. I have had many trials to face in my life and my children have been my saviours.

To date, my beautiful daughter and her husband Shaun have given me five amazing grandchildren (three granddaughters and two grandsons), all have different characters and are a joy to be around. If you need a pick-me-up, they are the people to be in a room with.

When I think of times in my life when my brain was in turbulence, and that has been quite a few times, I remember how, when I took time to think, write things down and reassess the whole situation again on my own, I'd come to realize that it's okay to say that everything is not okay, and to open up and speak to the right people. You see I struggled with pride. I was always a proud person. I would never ask anyone for anything. I spent quite a few years in the company of people who told me that you do not tell anyone about your business, people will talk about us. I realised that it is not just me who has to face day to day situations when you speak to other people. The fog that is clouding your mind lifts, so that you can see a brighter outcome within a network of people willing to help and support you.

I have encountered three types of people in my lifetime. One is toxic people, the second would be family and friends, and the third are people with the same mindset as myself. Now, understandably toxic is a very strong and harsh word, but I think you'll know what I mean when I say, that I've come across people who do not want to see you do well, they don't want to see anyone else do well, and are constantly having something negative to say about other people. Unfortunately for them, they are people who just have not reached or may never reach a place of understanding within their minds and hearts of where we need to be to have inner peace within ourselves. I gracefully choose not to be around people like this. I choose to not let anyone cloud my thoughts like I used to. These days my thoughts and my thinking are less clouded because I have taken ownership of my mind.

The second type of people that you will have in your life are family and friends where I find myself in my comfort zone. When I am around friends and family I relax more and have learned to have fun. Yes, I said, I have learned to have fun. That is something that took me a while to do, as you will see.

199

The third type of person is the person who is of the same mindset as you. These are people who have learned to love themselves, believe in themselves, trust in themselves, believe in others and thrive on helping others. Over the years I have been fortunate to meet people who set goals for themselves. They are passionate and driven in their life's work but always take time for others. I surround myself with people with the same mindset as myself. I now find myself collaborating with people worldwide, moving forward with my career and continuously self-developing. Having a network of likeminded people around will guide you through life in a confident manner and someone will always lift that cloud, even if it is with a kick in the butt that you may need. I have been grateful for that kick many a time.

I have struggled with ill health over the last 20 years of my life. I put a lot of it down to stress. When your marriage comes to an end and you realise your home is in jeopardy, your job has gone and you don't know how to survive, you worry constantly about where the next meal may or may not come from. When you worry and stress about day to day activities in your life, your judgement gets clouded over, your brain function lets you down, you are in turmoil and it is just a vicious circle.

In 2011, I found myself in the Circuit Court listening to a judge telling me that I had nine months to vacate my home. When I arrived home that day, I was in a state of shock and distress, but most of all I felt like a failure. I had tried to wipe my tears away before my children came home from school, but no matter what face I put on, my children saw through me. I had already decided in my mind that my children would go and live with their father. I was just going to disappear, as life held no meaning for me without my children. I had never contemplated suicide before that day. There was an almighty cloud surrounding me and I could not see through it. When I explained to my children the outcome of the courts, they all had suggestions, one being that the eldest son Darren, would leave school and support the family. I will never forget my youngest son's face when he told me that he did not care if he lived in a tent, as long as he got to live with his mammy. My children saved my life that day, and I swore to myself that I would never let my children down again and we as a family, made plans to move. Darren, continued with his education and is now a self-employed Electrician in London, who only this year purchased his first home at the age of 24 with his lovely partner Mickela.

Five years later in 2016, when the *For Sale* signs went up on our home, I found myself in a situation, where I had to face the consequences of my financial failings. I had read different articles about the governments bail out of the banks and this time, I was the one who felt had been failed. I looked into what was happening with in my case with the bank and within a week I had been to the High Court in Dublin and put an injunction on the bank stopping the sale of my home. From then on it was a waiting game. It was up to the bank to make the next move to get the injunction removed. The best thing for me to do at that stage was to move back into my home, but because of the bank's failure to secure the property, it had been broken into, ransacked, and completely destroyed. All that was left was a bare shell.

Christmas of that year, I received a call from my son Darren who asked me to join him in the local plumbing store. When I arrived, he was looking at two stoves and he asked of my opinion of which one I would like. I pointed to the plain one suggesting that it would be easier kept clean. A member of staff approached and put my name on the stove with sold written beside it. I turned to my son for an explanation and he said, 'Merry Christmas Mum.' — another person who believed in me, so I thought it was about time I started to believe in myself.

We moved back into our home on the April 7th, 2017 and I still had not heard anything from the banks. One day I was in Dublin with a friend, and after having lunch I stepped outside for a cigarette. Whilst I was standing in a doorway, I looked down at my feet and I saw three small white feathers. My heart skipped a beat and the first thought that came into my head was *go to central office in the High Court and check my case file.* I did and I found that the bank had been sending letters to the wrong address for me and were on the verge of taking my home again. That led to me showing up to the next court hearing. I associate seeing white feathers with my father being close to me, guiding me and leading me in the right direction. To this day, when I see a white feather, I react to whatever thought comes to me and my gut instinct is to follow it through. It has never let me down.

The barrister was surprised to see me that day. He aggressively tried to proceed with the case, even though it could not be heard because I had not been served. I had to repeat myself a few times until the judge took on board what I was saying. When you have not been served to be in court, but actually show up in court, your case cannot go ahead. Even though the case only took a few minutes, I stood with my head held high, determined not to cry, holding my hands on a table to stop the shakes but from my waist down, my legs were like a kango drilling holes in the floor, but I did it. The case was adjourned.

I spent two years in Dublin fighting my case in the High Court. I met numerous people from all parts of the country. One in particular was the Daly family in Kilcoole, Wicklow. Bill Daly was a kind, caring and funny gentleman who took me under his wing. Bill was like a second father to me. We spoke and bantered at length in the comfort of each other's company. I was given a key to Bill's home to come and go as I pleased. I was able to take extra shifts as a security officer in Dublin, which aided me in covering my expenses of the courts. It was home from home, as I was welcomed into the warmth with my tea, dinners, and my favourite biscuits. It is amazing who comes to you when you need someone and how they build your confidence and keep you motivated in your times of need. Going back to what I said about that third type of person in your life. Bill and his son Mack were in the same mindset as me. Over that period of time, I hid my fears and emotions from my children as I did not want them to worry. Bill and Mack and his partner Labhaoise knew exactly what I was going through, as they had gone through similar themselves. Bill would phone me weekly to check in on me. He would always start with, 'Well Mrs. Mac, how are ye doing?' The last conversation that I had with my dear friend Bill Daly, was him jokingly talking about the two of us going to the festival in his home town of Swinford, Mayo, where I was to save him a dance. Bill had been in ill health for a while and was in a facility for respite care before returning to his own home again. A few days later I got that awful call on the 17th June 2019 that shook me in my standing. There would be no more dancing. The COPD (Chronic obstructive pulmonary disease) had finally taken its toll and Bill was at peace. I have Bill to thank for believing in me, reminding me often of how far I had come and to keep going. 'For a young one you have it in you', he'd say. Bill built my confidence and reminded me of how resilient I am. He also kicked my butt when I was feeling down, knowing I had it in me to make my life better than it was. Thank you for the tears and the laughs. I will be forever grateful. Rest in Peace Bill.

Over the two years, with numerous court cases we finally came to an agreement that a deal would be done with the bank. The bank believed I owed €260,000 in debt. I offered to pay €60,000, which has been accepted. It was tough going over those few years, I mainly always appeared in court by myself. Once I had my youngest son Dean with me, thankfully. The previous weekend had been hectic as I was working double shifts in the Donegal rally as a security officer. That same weekend, my second youngest son Ciaran, had been involved in a hit and run accident and required surgery on his ankle.

I was pushing through that weekend to just get it over and done with. Thankfully, my son's surgery went well, so after finishing my last security shift in the early hours of Monday morning, I headed for the High Court in Dublin to fight my corner again. When I arrived with virtually no sleep from the previous Thursday, exhaustion kicked in and I went downhill. What kept me going you may ask? Any parent will tell you, when your back is against the wall and your children need you, you will push on through, just like I did. I took the courage to speak up that day to the Judge and the banks legal team. I knew my limits and I also knew that I had way surpassed them. I had a chest infection working on me, exhaustion was already there, and the vomiting had started because of the coughing. The banks legal team that day, did everything they could to help me present to the judge a fair reason why I should be given an adjournment. The judge took one look at me and asked me was I the person who had been coughing in the hallway. She made a point of telling others in the court that I had made the journey from Donegal whilst unwell and exhausted from working, but I still showed up. The judge said I was a fine example to others who take the courts so lightly. She commended me, gave me an adjournment for four months and wished me a safe journey home after asking if I required any medical attention as she would be happy to assist. I saw a different side to the courts and the people in it that day. My experience that day changed the way I looked at the courts and the way everything around me changed.

My last court case was in May 2019. I knew from early that morning by the way other cases were going, that the judge was in no way going to award me my case. During the lunchtime I walked up and down the courtyard, my thoughts scrambled in my mind, panic set in, so I made a phone call to someone, who I knew would make some reasoning of what I had to tell them. After that phone call, I walked calmly back into the courtroom, sat down, and watched everything that was going on. I very much had a 'Feck it' attitude. I have always taken pride in being an honest person and I was not going to change that day because of the powers that be in the courtroom. When my case was called, I stood tall, all 5'5" of me and I faced the judge. When the judge asked me if I had done all my own paperwork I said, 'No, of course not, I'm not a solicitor.' The judge was taken aback by my reply, as I guess he expected me to skirt around an appropriate answer, as others had before me, so as not to have to bring anyone else into the equation who had helped with any paperwork. The judge had a lot of questions for me about my case and how I came to be standing in front of him. I answered him honestly and at times I respectfully disagreed with him and gave him my reasoning why. Within 5 minutes the judge told me that by being present in his courtroom and being as upfront, honest and respectful as I had been, he would willingly grant me my home but as the law in front of him suggested different, he told me that the court order would have to go back into place at this time. The bank's legal team informed the Judge that the possession order was over six years old and had to go back to the original court for permission to execute

206

the order. I stood smiling. The judge asked me if I knew something that he did not, and I replied, 'Yes!' As I was obviously standing very confident about going back to the Circuit Court in Letterkenny, Co. Donegal, the judge suggested to the banks legal team that maybe it was their time to bring down their barriers and speak to me and do a deal. We do not want to see any more people on the street he said. To this day there has not been any further correspondence with the banks, as I had been put on a list to be dealt with before the Covid-19 pandemic. I am in the process of gathering €60,000 for a one-off payment for my home. I am an entrepreneur and I have business ideas coming to fruition. I have used the time out Covid-19 brought, to study and improve my self-development. I believe wholeheartedly that when the bank gets round to contacting me, that I will have the money waiting, because I will not stop until it is sorted.

After that court case, I learnt to face things head on and found a solution to any issue that arose. I had worked in security for a few years. I loved my job. I dealt with people from all walks of life and I always enjoyed good conversation. The greatest perk of the job was being able to help people, to maybe go that little bit further to help when you did not need to. It did me the world of good to laugh with people. I really enjoyed the craic! But no sooner had life started to level out it came down with a bang!

During the time of the court case I was troubled with another issue. I could be in conversation with a colleague and I would not be able to finish my sentence, no matter how hard I tried to remember what

I was saying or what I was maybe trying to say. It just was not happening for me. I became embarrassed but more so worried, about what was going on within my mind, trying to figure everything out only lead to more fatigue, which then led me to leave my job as a security officer. At the time, I would spend my days wondering why I had come into the kitchen, so I would try to backtrack and go into the room that I had left to go into the kitchen, to see if it would kick start my memory, as and why I left that room to go to the kitchen! I knew I was under stress so could have put it down to that, but there seemed to be something else, something much bigger. I had got to the stage that I could not remember names or something I had spoken about an hour previously. It was so upsetting, and I eventually came to the conclusion that I had dementia. I felt my life had been viciously cut short and I realised that I was not going to be able to hide this condition from my children for much longer. Suicide was very much on my mind. I did not want to put my children in the position of having to put me into a home and that I would not recognise them after that. To me, at that time, would have been devastating for them.

In February 2018, I began to experience severe breast pain. I took all sorts of over the counter pain relief and after a week of unbearable pain, thinking that there was something terribly wrong I approached my GP. He asked me what age I was. At that stage, I was 48. 'Oh, that's menopause Christine.', he said. I looked blankly at him and said, 'Meno what?' I had heard the name menopause, but I had never associated it with myself. I thought that it was something old ladies may experience. The doctor offered me HRT (hormone replacement therapy), At the time, I did not know nor care what kind he gave me as I didn't give him a chance to explain. I just told him that I was not taking those chemicals. I left to return home and see what Doctor Google had to say. There was so much conflicting evidence, but what I did realise was that I did not have dementia and that I could survive this! I just needed to find out how to do this the natural way without taking more chemical prescriptions, which for me would lead to other complications down the line. I already had more than enough going on without those!

The more I researched, the more confused I became. I bought numerous different vitamins, lotions and potions from different network marketing companies and all the while all the symptoms I was experiencing hit me like a steam train. I attended menopause retreats in the UK which were attended by other women, who were very flamboyant in saying that they sailed through their menopause and a few others who said that they would not be without their HRT. On listening to other women's conversations, I learned about specialist menopause doctors who were available in the UK. I started to concentrate on finding a specialist available in Ireland. This led me to more research and I realised that I could look after my menopause, because it was my menopause, it was my responsibility and I could do it the natural way with the help of a specialised menopause doctor.

Now, I live in Donegal, but I travelled to Bray, in County Wicklow to attend a consultation with Doctor Deirdre Lundy. How I was treated, listened to, all my symptoms explained and why I needed to replace my hormones and how it could be done was no less than five-star treatment. Before I attended Doctor Lundy, I had already made up my mind as to what treatment I wished to move forward with, and Doctor Lundy was completely compliant with my wishes. It has taken one full year for my hormones to level out, because my symptoms were so severe and I had so many, but even within the first ten days of having started my treatment, which was a little bit of Oestrogen gel derived from yam plants, rubbed on my inner thigh, my night sweats and my hot flashes started to decrease and within a week after that they disappeared completely! Now my mind took a lot longer to come back to me, but that was where I concentrated on where I wanted to go with my life, visualising, setting goals, pushing myself forward and also helping other women with their menopause. Eventually, I got back on track set up a support group called, *The Irish menopausal Mammy'* on social media. It is a support group where women find out factual information about menopause, the right way to replace their hormones and also how to change their lifestyles to live the best lifestyle that they can going through their transition into menopause. Now, having equipped myself with the knowledge I needed to finally take positive ownership of my life, I have reached a place in my life that I feel I have a way forward. I am no longer controlled by circumstance or hormonal challenges. I am back in the driver's seat!

Earlier this year, whilst the country slowed down due to covid-19, I had started to study different programmes, so that I could have a completely different career change. I realized after years of people telling me how much I had helped them, that I could actually make a living and do it full time. So, I have trained as a Life Coach. I am also qualified in CBT (cognitive behaviour therapy) and I am a menopause mentor. My intention is to educate and support other women to transition into menopause and not have to go through what I went through. I have designed online mentorship programmes for menopause ladies for the workplace.

During covid-19, I took the opportunity to really sit down and study without distraction. When the restrictions lifted for the first time, I went to the beach for a walk. I came back with a broken ankle, but I did not let that stop me either, I just put a stool under the desk and elevated my leg. I finished my courses with great delight, and I am thriving on helping other women as I see their stress dissolve and their health improve and protected for the future. I am passionate about menopause, so much so, that I am working on bringing a menopause specialist doctor to Donegal and any other county that may need it as well.

While I am passionate about menopause, I am still a single mother who needs to provide for her household, and I have found myself building on business ideas constantly. Like with the menopause, I do my due diligence and do not jump into anything at first glance. Now I find myself in a position where life is good, I am good. I can see where I am going. I visualise constantly every day, when driving in the car, should it be about my financial progress, my good health, my nutrition, the car I am driving, places in the world I am going to visit etc. And I will! I sometimes even shocked myself at how determined I am. When this does happen, I just smile knowingly to myself. I smile a lot these days. I understand how and know where I am going to take myself at the end of the day. I am my own creator. It is up to me to take myself where I need to go. I create my life, my mind, my body and my circumstances. The baseline for where I am today, is my own self-belief. I do not listen to other people's opinion of me if it is negative. Their opinions are none of my business.

I have a five-year plan. I look back on my life and I have learned by the mistakes that I have made in the past. I now move forward with confidence with my own self-belief. Taking care of my mental health and my thoughts every day, has got me to where I am. One of the things that I have learned, which is very important, is to gracefully say no. I don't have to do anything that anybody thinks that I should do. I give it some thought, then I make up my own mind. I've realised especially through covid-19, that I can have very profitable businesses from home working online. I have put business ideas on paper, worked it out, thought about it and I have taken the jump to progress with it. My goal this year is that by January 2021 I will be a six-figure income earner. I believe in myself. I have taken action and I never give up! Doing this takes a lot of hard work but that is something I have never been afraid of and I never will be. I have reached a stage in my life where I know that it is okay for me to come first. I know and I believe that I am a valuable asset and that I'm worth it, all just because I believe in myself and I surround myself with likeminded people. I am worth it and so are you. Just believe! I do! Me and the little white feather.

Take notice and believe.

My father, Edmund McGonagle, was and always will be my biggest inspiration in my life; he has given me a strength to get me to where I am today. My father was a trained mechanic, a driver and a machine operator. Basically, there was nothing that I remember, that my father could not do. He was a pleasant, calm, sincere, honest individual and nothing mattered more to him than his family. I was only child, so I was daddy's girl. If there was a car bonnet to be under or a truck to drive, I was there. Not surprisingly, I was in the driver's seat from an early age.

On the 4th of June 1991, when I was 19, my father went to work in Letterkenny and did not return. At the time I was in London, working in an Irish bar and my uncle Patsy and his family came to visit me. Unknowingly I got excited when they walked in the door, but my excitement turned to anguish and despair when the news broke that my father had an accident back home. I rang the hospital that my father had being taken to and I was told by an ICU nurse that, if I wished to see my father alive, I was to return home immediately.

After a night of Inconsolable tears, my uncle Patsy and I returned to Ireland. At that stage, my father had been flown by helicopter from Letterkenny to Dublin's Beaumont hospital to a specialised ICU. The following day we all travelled as a family to visit my father, not knowing what to expect. I spent nine days by my father's side willing him to open his eyes. But on the 15th of June, after numerous tests, we gave permission to switch off his life support.

This was the time in my life where I had reached complete devastation. My only go to person was gone. There was a funeral to arrange, family arriving from the UK, but the worst part was when my father arrived home with the undertaker. I vaguely remember two of my uncles holding me up outside the house. It took maybe one to two hours after that, for me to realise what was going on around me, but I found the strength inside me to get up, keep going, and do my father proud. There were times that were very difficult over those next few days. One especially, was when my father needed to be attended to. Because of the circumstances in which my father had died, he had to have a post-mortem. Some of his scars had started to leak fluid so he needed to be made presentable again. So instead of calling for the undertaker, myself on my father's youngest brother Owen, decided to do what was needed for my father. Owen briefly closed the wake, while I prepared to clean my father. My uncle Owen and I spent some quality time with my father, cleaning and making sure my father was presentable as we knew he would have liked to have been. With the support of my uncle Owen, I carried out a last act of love and kindness for my father. For some reason, that I did not know then, I felt emotionally stronger, than I had been in a very long time.

People in general, may think that they would not be missed at a funeral, but from my personal experience, when the family are leaving their home with their loved one to take them to their final

214

resting place, to see massive crowds is humbling but also powerful. To see the respect from other people, for your family and your loved one. That people take time from their busy lives to spend that very personal time with you, is something that you cannot thank people enough for.

From leaving our home and walking through town, on the mile-long road from Buncrana to Cockhill chapel, I walked behind my father's hearse. I read one of the readings at my father's funeral and I stood strong that day, even though inside my heart was broken. Looking back now I realise that my father was there with me, reminding me of the strong person that I was, and that strength has stayed with me 'til this day.

For years I have grieved for my father. Asking why him? I made bad decisions in my life that I feel I would not have made if my father had been with me, guiding and supporting me. I had no emotional support from anyone. I had plenty of family on my mother and father's side. But as I had previously said, I was proud and I didn't let anyone see how much I was emotionally hurting. My mother at the time of my father's death was an alcoholic, which was another cause of worry for me. Thankfully now she has stopped drinking and she is leading a good life, but we were never close like I was with my father.

Over the years there has been signs that my father has been around me, but I never really took them seriously until the time I was at rock bottom. On my father's 20th anniversary, my first grandson, Noah, was born. That day there were tears of joy and gratitude. From that day on, I have not looked back. Now when I see a white feather, I instinctively act on the first thought that comes to my mind. I know that it is my father guiding and support me in everything I do. It was those three little white feathers that got me to where I am today, to be in my home, secure and happy. I know my father is proud of me. In my thoughts, I regularly speak to my father. Should it be in a way of just wondering what would he think of this, what would he think of that, what would he say? It is also from this time that I learned from my little white feather, that with the first thought that comes to my mind, I act on it and it becomes reality. So now I am very careful about the thoughts that I let go through my mind. A lot of the time I have to keep myself in check of how I think and say. With my experience, what I think becomes my reality! So be careful about what you let your mind think and what you tell yourself. Always be your best friend, support yourself, be kind to yourself, push yourself to do the best you can, positively visualize what you would like to see happen today, tomorrow, or next year. Listen to what other people say when they are giving you encouragement and support, because they believe in you. Let those people's words into your mind and believe them for yourself. The power of belief changes everything. So, if you ever see a little white feather on the ground, just take a moment and give a thought of who may be watching over you. Take comfort and strength moving forward with your life, as I certainly have.

CHAPTER 13
You are Worthy

by Anne Canavan

In the immortal words of Amy Winehouse, 'I cried for you on the kitchen floor.' I couldn't have been more broken and emotionally beaten in those moments; my self-esteem chipped away with one derogatory comment after another; laughed at; made to feel I wasn't enough; not attractive enough; not a good enough cook; you name it I can guarantee I felt that I had been labelled as not good enough over the last 10 years.

I was always a confident person; game for any new activities, try everything life has to offer at least twice; see as many wonders of the world as possible. The insidious nature of Gaslighting is so slow and stealthy that you don't realize that your confidence is being stolen, one little piece of you at a time, and it's only in the last ten years that I have experienced this. I'm going to take you on my journey of from Broken, to Better, to Brilliant. But first let me tell you a little about myself.

My name is Anne Canavan and as a story writer I'm going to invite you all to sit back and relax while I tell you a story ... and hopefully make you smile a little.

I'm a left-handed right brainer, imagineer and creator. I like to build castles in the sky with my imagination.

I was born on the London/Surrey border to fabulous Irish parents. I had a great childhood. An early memory of mine is saying to my dad that I was going to collect one million items and hold a jumble sale in the garden and if I sold all these items, I'd be a millionaire, Rodney. I left my all-girls convent with one GCSE in English, a B+ the only subject that I was good at and captured my interest and imagination. I spent most days playing truant.

Somewhat surprisingly, I had the choice of two jobs; one in the BBC and one in the Civil Service. I listened to Dad's advice and took the job for life in the Civil Service. I still wonder what my journey would have been had I taken the job I really wanted in the BBC.

Perhaps in hindsight the lesson is "Listen to your heart. Your heart knows where it's going" Your Dad doesn't necessarily! (smiley face emoji)

I was always fascinated with inventions, products and innovation. I remember very well sitting at my work desk and desperately trying to invent something. As I'm no rocket scientist it was going to have to be something simple like the paper clip.

In 1987 I travelled to New York and stayed with my aunt who was a private nurse for the widowed Mrs. Belle Linsky. Belle and her late husband, Jack, were Russian immigrants in the early 1900's. As a young man Jack worked in a stationery warehouse and came across the stapler. He thought it rather bulky so he set about innovating it and making it more user friendly.

As a result of their amassed fortune over the years they donated $60 million to the New York Metropolitan Museum of Art at which there

218

is a whole Linsky Wing which houses much beautiful art and sculptures. I decided that this was DEFINITELY the lifestyle for me and tried even harder to *'invent'* something.

Over the years I did various jobs. Front of house at the Old Vic Theatre which I ADORED. This gave me a real passion for theatre. I sat in on every performance six days per week and, matinee included, twice on a Saturday. Each show ran for six weeks and I never tired watching the live performance.

My favourite play was *After Aida*, an operatic play about Giuseppe Verdi and the pressure put upon him after his attempt to retire from composing. Continued insistent prodding from his friends eventually resulted in one of his greatest masterpieces, the opera Otello. All good things come to those who don't retire! The Welsh National Opera provided the operatic voices. This gave to me a love of Opera which I carry with me to this day.

Richard Griffiths (the foul tempered uncle of Harry Potter) played Verdi, along with Ian Charleson (Chariots of Fire) and Zoe Wanamaker.

I then worked for Browns of South Molton Street, high end fashion, as HR Assistant and Reception. I worked for Sidney and Joan Burstein. He was a self-made multi-millionaire.

Joan was revered in fashion. In fact, when I first watched 'The Devil Wears Prada' I thought it was about Joan and realized later that it is about Anna Wintour. Indeed, my job wasn't entirely unlike the role played by Anne Hathaway. I kid you not!

I learned so much from Mr. Sidney. Every day was an assault course for survival. It was a cutthroat environment. He had lost all his money and had come back bigger and better. I really admired him even though he was a tough task master. He WAS NOT going under again! He is still my most revered boss and it was a privilege to work for him. Unbeknownst to him he was my first mentor.

On the next step of my journey, I moved to Moville, Co. Donegal, a second home as I had always spent the summer holidays here and have extended family close by. This is where I learned to 'colour outside the lines' which makes me very happy. I love living in Ireland. There is a freedom here which I have never been able to find anywhere else. An ease of being; with not so many grids and straight lines to adhere to.

Together with my now ex-husband we started a chartered town planning business. He was the planner. I was secretary, admin and anything else I was needed to be.

In 1993, together, we built a holiday hostel from the ruins of an old outbuilding which opened late and missed the summer season. Three weeks later our second daughter, Grace was born. Suddenly we had two electricity bills …. two of everything bills!

Being self-employed we often fluctuated between feast and famine whilst holding our breath for outstanding invoices to be paid. I remember standing in front of the unlit fire, holding my new-born baby and contemplating which items around me I could burn for fuel. However, we opened an account with a local shop and got two bags of coal that day on one month's credit by which time we were back out of the Red. For a while. Huge sigh of relief.

It was at this time that I suffered a very mild bout of post-natal depression. "No wonder", my doctor told me. I was often up until 3am on my hands and knees perhaps staining a wooden floor in anticipation of the dreaded arrival of the Fáilte Ireland Inspector to approve our hostel opening.

This reminds me of the morning of Cressida's due date. Our B&B guest politely enquired as to when my baby was due. "TODAY" was my answer. She almost choked on her Donegal sausage. I survived. We did what needed to be done.

Fast forward to the year 2000 we happily opened the Hostel doors to 20 male asylum seekers. This is the best job I have ever had the privilege to do. It was both rewarding and humbling and I learned so much with cherished memories to look back on. We became a blended family and I'm still friends with some of them 20 years later. I learned gratitude on a whole new level. What we had and they did not … but together we had fun, adventures and laughter.

We have 3 beautiful daughters and the youngest, Lauren had her own Nigerian nickname of Ajanacooo (phonetic spelling) which she has tattooed on her arm as a fond memory of this very special time. This means little warrior. I could talk for hours about this period in my life and how much I learned from different cultures even though I had grown up in a multi-cultural city.

Sadly, the marriage dissolved a year later, in 2001.

I then met the father of my son. Another journey. Let me just say that it's my opinion that SOMETIMES alcohol can do bad things to good people.

We lived in Russia for three months in 2013 before moving back to Ireland after a four-year stint in England. Almost immediately after moving back here he just upped and left, possibly because of logistics but nonetheless, I felt cast aside; it seemed that I no longer served a purpose in his life.

I was now a single mum and had to provide for us. So, I took a job in a local hotel as a housekeeper, cleaning bedrooms, as the hours suited. I got eight-year-old Dmitry to school and then started work at 10am. This was a new experience for me. I rolled up my sleeves and happily got on with what I had to do to feed my family. I found great joy in this job as the ladies were an absolute hoot. Every day it was like being part of a sitcom. Dinner Ladies, Julie Walters and Victoria Wood, spring to mind.

Each day on my eight-minute drive to work in my battered and rusted old grey Seat I practiced gratitude. I was grateful for my children and the health of my children. Grateful for my car. Grateful for Granny's house in which we lived and still do. Grateful for my job. Grateful to be able to walk and work.

The reason I was so excited at the prospect of going to work each day was because exactly one year prior to this I had been knocked down by a car and suffered a broken bone in my back, a broken knee, nerve damage and a severe concussion. I was pretty much a prisoner at home in England from December 2012 through to April 2013.

My house in England was rented out at this time and I saved as much as I could to get my second idea, the Snotblots™ made in China via a UK company.

Then! Disaster struck. My tenants decided to wreak havoc on my beautiful home in England and not pay the rent. A battle ensued. Now I only had my income from the hotel which was minimum wage and casual labour. Sometimes only two or three days per week or worse, one. Again, feast or famine. I'm seeing a bit of a recurring theme here.

I tackled this as I do most of my battles, like a game of tennis. They would bat the ball to me via their hostile emails. I would respond, batting the ball back to their side of the court and wait for the ball to return. They could afford a solicitor. I could not.

In the meantime, I would throw myself into painting walls with great gusto as I was renovating the house at the time on a shoestring budget. My two tools were a hammer and a big old knife. I cut up an old carpet with this knife in order to remove it in pieces. I hammered out anything else that got in my way! Great memories. Great tools.

I didn't spend all day worrying about the problem. I took action each morning and then got on with my life until that dreaded proverbial ball bounced back to my side of the court. After much perseverance it was Game, Set, Match to me.

During a week's annual leave from work in the hotel I informed my ten-year old son, Dmitry, that we were going on 'The Best One Day

Holiday Anyone Has Ever Had in Their Life'. We were going to the Ulster Folk Park outside Omagh. We couldn't afford to stay even one night in a hotel. This was just one more famine episode of my life. And it definitely was *'The Best One Day Holiday Anyone Has Ever Had!'*

Upon our return from our miniature vacation I excitedly called work re my rota for the next week. I learned that I was scheduled for one day only. Out of sight, out of mind. Gulp! I decided I'd worry about that next week. But all this time I was progressing with my Snotblots™

Now back to the inventions:

After my first daughter Cressida was born the floodgates opened and I had so many ideas. I found needs that were just waiting to be filled. "See a need, fill a need" – I can do that!

My first idea was a clip to assist in breast feeding. Fueled with my newfound enthusiasm I made a phone call to the National Breastfeeding Association or some such body. When I informed the rather starchy lady on the other end of the phone about my fantastic idea, she shot me down with, and I quote *"breastfeeding is the most natural thing in the world and it certainly does not require the assistance of any device. Goodbye."*

In my infancy of this phase of my life I retreated, completely crushed, and put it to rest. I still have it on my list of 26 items currently swirling around in my head and on my paper list; some of which have manifested into real tangible objects, some of which are 3D images and some prototypes.

Next came the Snotblot™ These were born out of necessity and fun; to eliminate the snail trails on kids sleeves and to promote good hygiene. I have also written 15 short stories about the Snotblot™ characters. I see them as akin to the 21st Century Mr. Men, each with an underlying moral to the tale. These are aimed at young children.

I was one of twelve people picked from thousands to meet Anita Roddick, founder of The Body Shop and my hero, with whom I had a one-hour mentoring session at the British Library in London. She loved the stories.

I did approach three publishers who politely declined my works of art and I promptly retreated from the literary world to lick my wounds before I learned that JK Rowling was accepted on her thirteenth submission. Perhaps the time is now to blow the proverbial dust off and try again. Could this be the right time, taking into account our current climate, to promote and assist good nose hygiene with a bit of good old fun?

I was the only female member of the Wessex Round Table of Inventors. The other members were all exceedingly academic gentlemen generally hovering around the age of 70. There was a lot of talk of patents owned. They tolerated me; this female disruption to their inventors' club, very well indeed and made me most welcome.

I tried very hard to make Derry the Snotblot™ Capital of the World by trying to get them manufactured locally but it just didn't work out – yet.

Chester Greenwood Day, the first Saturday in December each year is celebrated in Farmington, Maine where the young 15-year-old invented the earmuffs out of cold necessity. Necessity being the mother of invention as I know only so well!! Today they have cop cars with giant earmuffs and general celebrations. What an opportunity to create a festival to bring fun and revenue if there were a similar Snotblot™ Festival here. Not to blow my own trumpet, or nose, just a bit of fun.

I am also currently writing a fantasy story which I would love to be televised. Writers block is a revolving bedfellow of mine. But I persevere. I have always been a storyteller. When the girls were young, I made up stories for their eager little ears. Usually about witches and scary castles and thunderstorms as we were a little like the Adams family living in a real haunted house, whether you believe in ghosts or not. Seeing is believing!

Gratitude has always been a part of my life and I truly believe that when I was still grateful for having very little and sometimes almost nothing, something amazing happened.

I WON £1 MILLION POUNDS and a fantastic holiday to Song Saa Private Island in the EuroMillions Raffle on Friday the 28th of August 2015 a date indelibly etched on my mind!

Earlier that evening I was washing my car in front of the house and chatting to Tony, my neighbour, about the EuroMillions and past winners. I jokingly declared that I thought it was about time we brought the EuroMillions to Moville. Little did I know it would arrive a couple of hours later.

It was 1am and I decided to check my ticket on my laptop which I never did. Tickets usually languished in my handbag for a few weeks before I would eventually check them. At first, I didn't believe my eyes. I checked and re-checked and then checked again and maybe one more time; just to be sure to be sure. When it did finally register that indeed I was not hallucinating, my first emotion was extraordinary jubilant shock. I ran upstairs and woke my daughter Lauren to share the fantastic news. It took me 15 minutes to convince Lauren that I wasn't lying. As this was one of the previously mentioned 'famine' periods in my life I couldn't unplug my ancient laptop from the wall and take it to show Lauren as the battery had long since given up the ghost and would turn off as soon as it was disconnected from the wall socket. So, I had to convince her that this was not indeed a practical joke and to come downstairs and see for herself.

We both fluctuated between belief and disbelief and back again several times. We sat up drinking tea and making lists of the people we were going to help and share our good luck with. It was an incredible night. I was truly blessed. "Feast" was back in my life. Goodbye "Famine."

Despite sitting up until 5am with my daughter, Lauren, unable to comprehend this incredible stroke of luck and unable to sleep, I nonetheless went to work the next day in the Redcastle hotel and continued to clean rooms, bathrooms, toilets and make beds for guests. It was a bank holiday weekend and incredibly busy and I didn't want to let my work colleagues down. I worked my weeks' notice and some extra as they were short staffed. And didn't tell a soul.

Initially we couldn't tell anyone about our win because we had to wait until the following Friday for the Camelot representative to arrive from mainland UK. We had a lot of fun "babysitting that little pink slip of million-pound paper." I bought my ticket in Sainsburys in Derry; with my last two pounds for that particular shopping trip. Money may not buy happiness but it's certainly true it does provide amazing freedom for which I am eternally grateful.

Returning to my inventions, I have a list of 26, as I said, ranging from the quirky *'everyone needs one of these'* objects like a spider catcher, a hoover attachment, an app, a chair for the elderly, a unique buggy for a child, some fashion items and festival accessories to name but a few.

This is my passion. My fire in the belly. But I get in the way of myself because my passion is creating and not so much the practical side of business. What I hope to achieve is to license my products and to be the Joy Mangano of Ireland. My favourite film, *Joy*.

Please don't think that my life has been a bed of roses. It hasn't but I have had so many truly remarkable moments in my life for which I am so thankful and as time is a constraint here, I can only convey a part of my story. I am a survivor. I am an inventor.

But I hear you ask, 'How were you broken?' As I referenced in my opening statement, I was hurt and broken. As with us all we have our outer persona and our inner journeys of struggle and angst. That was my outer and this is perhaps my inner.

228

BROKEN

Feeling Vulnerable and Afraid

The feelings of vulnerability and fear are normal. Everyone at some time or another feels these emotions. I definitely have. I still do. I feel vulnerable every time I show my products. How will they be perceived? My stories, will they be ridiculed? This is the work of my soul and it pierces when I feel rejection.

One of my favourite TedX talks found on YouTube is Brene Brown and her 20-minute presentation called The Power of Vulnerability. Vulnerability and fear are part of our life, they are normal feelings. To quote Brene Brown:

'Connection is why we're here. It's what gives us purpose and meaning to our lives. This is what it's all about. Connection, the ability to feel connected is neurobiologically how we're wired. It's why we're here". Shame is the fear of Disconnection. Is there something about me that if other people know it or see it that I won't be worthy of Connection? Shame is universal. We all have it, the only people who don't experience Shame have no capacity for human empathy or connection. No-one wants to talk about it and the less you talk about it the more you have it. What underpins Shame is excruciating Vulnerability. In order for us to have connection we have to allow ourselves to be seen. Really seen.'

We persevere as best we can. I have always worn my heart on my sleeve and shown my inner self. It's what makes us wholehearted.

We All Need Love

But the love needs to be healthy, balanced and reciprocated. Two people traveling in the same direction but not necessarily intertwined every step of the way. I love with my heart on my sleeve, open and wholeheartedly. Why play games with such a sacred emotion?

When I was in the failing relationship I mentioned at the beginning of this chapter and "cried for him on the kitchen floor" I was at my lowest ebb. I loved a man who did not reciprocate my feelings. It seemed to me that everything I did wasn't good enough. I felt that I was ridiculed every step of the way. Even my breathing seemed to annoy him. After years of this I was broken and the constant rejection I felt took its toll. I felt unworthy, unloved and unlovable. I was told I was ugly.

The lowest point of this time is when I actually purchased Scent of Eros, a pheromone which claims to boost our 'likeability' an indication of how invisible and very unloved I felt.

The Power of Hope

Hope is a powerful emotion. Without hope love dies and parts of us wither. H.O.P.E. Hold On, Pain Ends.

> *"If you lose hope, somehow you lose the vitality that keeps*
> *, you lose that courage to be, that quality that helps you*
> *go on in spite of it all. And so today I still have a dream."*
> *– Martin Luther King Jr.*

230

"Hope is medicine for a soul that's sick and tired"

– Eric Swensson

BETTER

Value Yourself

I have learned to value myself. This has been an inward journey in which I have found peace and tranquility. I have learned that I must love myself first. If I cannot love myself how can I expect someone else to?

I might add that I used to love myself, but this was taken, and I felt my trust was destroyed and shattered into a million little pieces. No sacred love should be dashed in such a cavalier fashion.

I am now like a piece of beautiful Japanese Wabi Sabi pottery, I have glued myself back together and I love the joined-together pieces, the cracks which are the veins that have been glued with care are beautiful reminders of how strong I am and how far I have come. I am grateful to have had the opportunity to rebuild myself, just the way I want to be. The cracks of my life are now filled with love.

Indeed, my house is named Wabi Sabi House; Japanese wisdom for a perfectly imperfect life.

See the following short 48 second YouTube video if you are interested in this ancient and wise philosophy:

What is the Japanese philosophy of Wabi-Sabi?

Claim Back Your Power

I claimed back my power when I decided that I'd had enough. Enough of people using me, gaslighting me, discarding me, lying about me, physically and mentally abusing me. Enough!

The first book on my journey was *You Can Heal Your Life,* by Louise Hay. This was a powerful moment for me. The first step into a whole new realization. Another book which really resonated with me was *Co-Dependent No More.* I got to Page 8 and thought, 'That's me.' I changed my thinking and changed my co-dependent behaviour. Knowledge is power. Knowledge can lead to freedom.

As a result of reading that book, I have always ensured that my children are not co-dependent as I believe that we learn this at a young age. "Is Mummy/Daddy in a bad mood?" and our day typically revolves around the mood of significant others. It did for me; perhaps because I'm an empath by nature.

Question What People Think, Say and Do:

Because Honesty, Integrity and Truth are fundamentally three crucial factors in my life, I tend(ed) to believe what people tell me is the truth. Sadly, this is not the case and I have been burned multiple times.

Accept Yourself – You Are Worthy!

This was a hard one for me. I had to deconstruct all the negative messages which I had been fed and which in turn had formed a foundation of my core beliefs. However, with a little help from my books and the teachers whom I sought out I downloaded a whole new set of beliefs. It's daily work. It's a journey of discovery. Some days I'm back at square one.

BRILLIANT

Turn Experiences into Opportunities.

My new-found single life prompted me to utilize my time in a more constructive manner. I was gifted with so much more "me time"

I took this as a golden opportunity to delve into my inner self and do all the things I had previously put on hold whilst administering the greater part of my energy and lavishing my precious emotions on a one-way relationship.

Turning lemons into lemonade.

In November 2019, broken but also Wabi-Sabi'd up and not knowing which direction I wanted to go I decided to attend a seminar one evening at the invitation of Hugh Hegarty.

I was totally captivated by an amazing individual who so eloquently gave me a road map with all the signposts pointing to success. All I had to do was make a choice. The choice I made was to sign up and to a Mastermind Course and I am so glad that I did make that choice. Who is this amazing person? Pat Slattery, also an author in this book.

As a result of my decision on that November night I am now sitting here writing my chapter, having met Pat's amazing wife, Donna Kennedy, who is the facilitator of this, our collection of life journeys.

Become Creative

I love to create. I love innovation, inventions, writing and dreaming. This is my passion. I have been blessed to have been given the time and opportunity to explore and delve into my innermost creativity.

I am currently writing a fantasy story. It's like meditation to me. I can enter my magical kingdom and paint whatever I like. Pure magic. Pure transcendence. A short holiday for the mind.

I have resurrected my 26 ideas, my Snotblot™ stories; my imagination is free to roam wherever it pleases; creating previously unheard-of lands and beings.

Imagine the Possibilities

George Bernard Shaw sums up Possibilities for me in his quote:

'Some men see things as they are and ask Why?
I dream things that never were and ask, Why not?'

Possibilities abound us. What possibilities are you not seeking out by not taking a chance? Sometimes we have to jump and grow our wings on the way down.

'You have to take risks. We will only understand the miracle
of life fully when we allow the unexpected to happen.'
– Paulo Coelho.

If I imagine what my Possibilities could be it is to have my products selling and my stories published. To quote George Bernard Shaw, "Why not?" Overcoming adversity, finding success and being recognized for your achievements. There are people around, cheering your victory. You can succeed in your goals. You can receive the accolade due to you. You can show others what you're made of and can gain their respect. Stay humble.

Trust Your Gut

I always trust my gut. Unfortunately, each time I have given in to people who approach life more logically than I do and I have taken a detour from my gut feeling I have 100% of the time been burned! Ouch!

Shine!

One of my Snotblot™ stories is about Solar Snotblot. He loses his smile. It's about shining. It sums up the shine in life for me and is available on my Facebook page, *Snotblot - Say Bye Bye to Runny Noses.*

I will finish with a fitting quote about story writing from an amazing lady, Lisa Nichols:

'Sometimes you can't fit in your future because you're too full of your past. A new story can't be born because you're holding onto the old story. The moment you put some "extra" on your "ordinary" now you've got "extraordinary." And when you can see that little version of you,

that little girl (or boy) who's looking for validation; "Am I beautiful in my uniqueness?" "Can I change the world?" And when you look eye to eye with an example of who you're becoming, all of a sudden you stop asking the world for permission. You stop wondering, do I fit in this story? And you realize that you're the author of the story; who you are, your "extraordinary", is waiting to be born through you."

CHAPTER 14
How to turn a Can't into an I Can – with no plan!

by Nadia Buju

I left my country, Romania, for the first time in my life at 24-years-old. I had attempted to go to Germany with a visa to one of my mom's friends, but I couldn't receive the visa from the embassy because my country wasn't in the EU on that time, but after a few years my country didn't require visas to travel to Europe anymore, so a group of friends and I promised each other, that we would go to where the first of us went "outside". We never thought about what we were going to do in a strange country, we had no plan of action, but we knew that we wanted to be "outside."

One of my friends and two of her brothers went to Spain and in a few days all three had found jobs in a wood factory. A couple of weeks later she rang me and said that there was another job available in the factory and I could get it. I didn't even think about what I might do there, because I had never worked in a wood factory before. I didn't know how to speak Spanish and I hadn't even a place to live. Nevertheless, I just booked a bus ticket. I thought the bus would be the easiest way to travel as I had never been on a plane before. Before I knew it, I was in a minibus with seven strangers traveling over 3000 km to Spain, which took us about 35 hours. I was about to start my new life.

I arrived in a small village in the south of Spain, Villa del Rio, Cordoba. It was the prettiest and most beautiful village you could ever imagine! After nearly two days and two nights sitting on a minibus, I was sweaty, bloated, tired and cold, but when the driver opened the door to for us to get out that didn't matter. I remember the huge wave of heat and the smell of olives in the air, there were so many lovely colourful flowers and I couldn't believe my eyes when I saw real oranges trees. I asked the driver if I could eat one. He said I could but that it was not very nice to pick them from the trees. I picked one anyway; I just wanted to make sure that I wasn't dreaming. And it was the sweetest and tastiest orange I had ever eaten in my life!

My friend was waiting for me at the bus stop with her Spanish boyfriend. He greeted me with an 'Hola'. I was very surprised, and I asked her what "pot" this guy wanted because I didn't bring any with me. She started to laugh, explaining that 'Hola' means 'Hello' in Spanish. In my language it means pot! I thought it best that if I was to be in an unknown country, I better at least know how to say hello in their language! I was that kind of girl.

We went to the house where I supposed to stay with my friend and his two brothers, but to my huge surprise it wasn't a house, it was a barn, where years ago the owner of that property kept food for her animals. So, there was my new home, just one main door and no doors to our "bedrooms". We had curtains instead of doors. We slept on some old mattresses and I used some of my clothes and a towel to cover myself instead of a blanket or a duvet. Nights were really hot in Spain, so it wasn't that bad.

I was just so excited about starting the job I was promised. But of course, not all arrangements made over the phone from a 3.000km distance happen as they are promised. I was soon told that the owner of the wood factory didn't accept strangers to work in his factory anymore.

So, there I was – no job, no Spanish, no job experience, and no plan. My mom asked me daily to go back home, but I didn't want to give up on my adventure. At 24, I wanted to see what I could get out of what could be my only adventure trip.

I decided to stay and help my friends with their housework. I cooked, hand-washed the clothes and cleaned. I wondered what life in Spain might bring me. I also began to look after the owner of that property, an old lady who lived in a small cottage on the same property, cleaning her house and our garden, picking fresh strawberries, watering the wild flowers and bushes around. And to my surprise, and my friends' too, in less than three months I was able to speak Spanish!

Within a short time, we made some new friends in the village and one day a guy came to ask my friend's brothers if they wanted a job in the north side of Spain in construction. He suggested that we, the girls, could work there as cleaners, and in less than a week we moved to Pamplona. It is such a lovely city with many festivals, including an

239

event involving running of bulls. Basically, you run in front of a small group of cattle that have been let loose on a course of a sectioned-off subset of a town's streets!

I was so happy that we moved there because at last I could sleep in a normal bed, take a normal shower, earn my first wage and start to have a normal life.

I stayed in beautiful Spain for four years and had lots of adventures. I learned many things there about the importance of being honest, ethical and trustworthy, about working hard and being ambitious, about being grateful daily and loving yourself, lessons that have meant so much to me.

Then in 2004 my boyfriend travelled to Ireland and he asked me if I would like to go there too. Honestly, 16 years ago I didn't know much about Ireland, just that there were lots of sheep in Ireland and that Dublin City had 10 bridges in the middle of city. But my boyfriend told me that I could potentially earn a lot of money in Ireland, more in a week than the monthly income I was earning in Spain at the time. I didn't hesitate to accept his invitation. I just made the decision, without asking myself what I was going to do in Ireland and what job I might have, not forgetting that I had no English! It was like when I first went to Spain – impulsive.

So, I left my lovely "amigos", the sunny weather, the great tapas and the lovely Latino music. I left everything behind and on a rainy autumn day in November 2004 I arrived in Dublin. For the first few days, I was speaking Spanish with bus drivers, hoping that they might know some Spanish, trying to settle in. All the streets and the houses looked the same to me. The rain never stopped, and a few umbrellas went upside down because of the wind. My shoes were soaking wet nearly every day, but I didn't complain and didn't feel sorry for what I had left behind, because my mind was now on how I could make the monthly income in a week.

My only job experience I had was that I loved to clean. So, before thinking about learning English, I asked the tenants who shared the house with us to help me write some notes so I could offer my cleaning services. I went door-to-door and put my information in the letter box, which included my phone number. I knew if someone was to call me and speak with me in English, they were enquiring about cleaning. I learned how to ask, 'How many hours?' and 'How much do I charge per hour?' I learned to say, 'Text the address please.' Ha ha ha!

And so, I started my lovely career in cleaning, and when I say lovely that it the truth. I really do love cleaning. I worked so hard, and I was so committed and dedicated, that in less than six months I surpassed the monthly income which I earned in Spain. I did a full week of cleaning here in Ireland from 8.30am 'til 9pm sometimes, six days a week.

In my first few months I had a funny incident happen with a very beautiful and posh client that I have. When I spoke something in English she always asked me to repeat it, as my English was learned by reading newspapers and books, listening to radio and TV shows. I didn't go for any English classes as normal people do, so if I said something wrong (and I did a lot), she was there to correct me, not in the friendly way other clients did. I always felt very nervous when I had to talk with her. One day I went with her to do a deep clean in one of her rented houses. She said that we are going to take a break and that she was going to buy a coffee and a sandwich. She asked me what kind of sandwich I wanted and I told her that I preferred a kitchen salad one. I focused on not saying something wrong so she wouldn't have to ask me again, in her usual 'Excuse me!' or 'Please repeat!' voice, with a condescending look on her face and laughter when I couldn't get the sentence right. I often wondered *'Did I say wrong? Why was she laughing? Why did she ask me again?'* She turned to me and said, 'Are you sure you want a kitchen salad sandwich or a chicken salad one?'

I felt such a huge dis-connection in me. But after a few days when I spoke with some of my friends, they told me a very similar story. One of my friends went for a kitchen-porter job interview. She spoke with the manager and tried her best to make a good impression, to explain that she was really good at cleaning and that she knew how to "degrees the chicken", how to use hot water on "chicken", and so on, until her manager made signs with his hand to stop talking about the chicken. He couldn't laugh and told her that she didn't have to wash any chicken because the chicken would be cooked in the restaurant and that her job was to clean the KITCHEN!!!

When I realised that it was not only me making these funny mistakes, I wasn't so hard on myself. When I got mixed up, I'd pause and say to myself 'Relax, Nadia, everyone is learning and learning from our own mistakes could be funny sometimes, with nice memories to tell to your kids or nieces.' Maybe, if I knew months in advance that I was going to Ireland I would have had a bit of time to learn some English, but my decision was so quick that I didn't even have time to tell my mother that I was going so far away, in a plane this time.

In less than a year after starting my lovely cleaning job, I had so many clients that I couldn't take them all on. One day as I was drinking a cup of coffee with one of my dearest clients, I told her that I couldn't take on any new clients, because I was fully booked 10-11 hours almost daily. She asked me a very short but powerful question, 'Why don't you open your own Cleaning Company?'

'OMG...Who. me?' All my paradigms started to shoot in my mind like an automatic gun... 'Who do you think you are to even think that you can dream to have your own company? You have no experience in making any kind of business, your English is not good enough to do this, you have no car, you never drove on the left side of the road, sitting on the right side of the car...What do you know about running a business in a strange country? Where are you going to find clients? How are you going to choose good employees? Who is going to do your accounts for you? Where are you going to buy materials and supplies? What do you know about all of that?' And so on, the voices in my head never stopped, until a few days later when I decided that I was going to do it. I didn't know how, but I decided that I would do it!

I think the most important part, the part that gave me the most determination, was my vision of when I would get married and have my own kids. I wanted to have the freedom to stay at home with them, I wanted to have the freedom to travel wherever I wanted, without asking permission. for a few weeks holiday break, I wanted to not worry about my income, to be independent, to have the freedom to decide if I wanted to go work or not. I have to say that I love cleaning as it recharges me with satisfaction for the great job I do with my team. I visualised myself doing the work and now I have all I visualised after 14 years in my cleaning business.

I continue with my visualisation routine as I know how powerful it is. It is so easy and relaxing to dream. Just before falling asleep, after my gratitude ritual (I say what I am grateful for every single night as a prayer, but some people prefer writing) I close my eyes and imagine what I want my life to look like. As Bob Proctor said, '*If you can see it with your mind, you CAN touch it with your hand.*' You don't have to be in a lotus position or meditating on a mountain's peak, and you don't have to spend hours in an extremely relaxing atmosphere, to visually keep it simple and align the vision with your inner self, with your deepest wish and with your purpose in life.

What is amazing is that I still have some clients that I had even before I started my business. It can be hard nowadays to be in a marriage for 14 years, or to keep a relationship for so many years, but can you imagine how great it is to know you have loyal clients over so many years? I asked myself many times how I made it, how I was able to do it, how I could build something without a plan (even a small one), without any resources and with all my old paradigms in my head. How was it possible? One of my clients told me that she had asked herself and her family how a girl arrived in Ireland with just a small suitcase, no references at all (which even 15 years ago were really important), no English, no nothing... and she still succeeded?

And I will tell you HOW all of this was possible, and I will tell you that even you can do anything you want in your life, you can have the freedom to get what you want, you can start your own business, you can achieve any type of independence you want, you can break any addictions you have, you can regain your own health (mental or physical), you can be who you want to be, not someone your mother might want you to be, not the one your partner might want you to be, not the one your children might want you to be. You can be the one you want yourself to be. The most important question to ask yourself (and answer) is WHY? Why do you want to have all that you do, why do you really want to do this thing, how are you going to feel if you have all of those things that you wish for? You have to decide first what you want, see if it is aligned with all your core values and that you don't interrupt anyone's life, trust it that it is going to happen and leave the Universe to work for you and help you; you don't need to know the exact step by step how-to, just have an approximate date in your head to get there, but trust that the Universe is going to bring it to you and the exact people and resources will help you get there. You have to connect with your creative ability. In my case, this was simple because I enjoyed cleaning since I was a teenager. My mom (God rest her in peace) asked me and my only sister, 'Who's cooking and who's cleaning today?' I always jumped up with a loud voice, 'Me, me...for cleaning!!!' And I was really relaxed cleaning the house, I always felt great satisfaction after each job was done.

I do have to say, that things aren't always as simple and easy as they look, because sometimes you have people around you who might judge you or criticise you, people who don't empower you at all, who don't trust you, who ask you why you don't do the things how they think you should and why you have to do things your way, for example. Or perhaps people who make you feel that you are not worthy or you are not smart enough to do the thing you want, who make you feel that you are too ugly or too fat to do x,y or z, who make you feel that there is no point to learn any other new skill because you are not young enough anymore, who make you feel that you neglect your family on behalf of doing business, who ask you why you have to participate in so many meetings and trust new and strange people and the list can be endless. I know all of the above because I have met people in my life who I felt tried to drag me down when I went a step up, or two steps, and maybe there I found the power in myself to always prove and show myself that I CAN do anything I want in life. I never gave up, even if it was difficult.

Living your best life is a matter of becoming open, becoming like a sponge for new knowledge. I did many courses over the years and, after I learned some English, I learned many more new things. I have had a life with so many great and powerful experiences, and cannot wait to share them with more and more people, because I think they might help so many other individuals to empower them to dare to live their dreams. I am positive that you have your own life story, and that you have something special to share with others. Believe and know that you are worthy, you can do whatever you want, just dare to dream! You have to let go of any negative belief about yourself or how others see you with their critical eyes. Don't accept anyone's limitations or conditions, you are unique, and no one can compare to you.

You can do anything you want in this beautiful life. Be authentic, ethical, trustworthy, perseverant, committed, grateful, kind and loving toward yourself and others every day.

LOVE YOU ALL!

CHAPTER 15
If Only

by Chris Wojnar

It was 2012 and I was 58 years old. Sitting in a psychiatric unit, surrounded by people suffering with one mental health issue or another, I wondered how I, once an astute businessman, got here.

The nurses in the hospital had listened, in a very caring way, to all my troubles of how I felt I had let everyone down. I had a troubled mind and suicidal ideation seemed to be a very real solution. The message the nurses gave me was always the same, *'Stop being so hard on yourself, it will take time and baby steps forward, but possibly years before you will recover.'*

I felt lifeless, I just couldn't see past my problems. Then one Sunday evening after dinner my phone binged. It was a message from my eldest son, Adam, and it included what looked like an x-ray photo. At first, I didn't know what I was looking at, but I soon realized that it was a scan of my first grandchild! I felt very emotional, in an elated kind of way, now I had a reason to hold on. I immediately shared the photo with those around me and received congratulations from all. That scan was the first baby step back to my family.

I started out in a family business, third generation at 13-years-old, and then full time at 17. This was, on reflection, good timing as the company was going through a rebuilding phase and we started with the first shop in Capel Street, Dublin 1. My journey through school was not at all inspiring. I was not of an academic mind or chose not to be at least. I got through the education system playing rugby. This was when my first leadership genes came to the fore, being selected as captain for the under 13s and I retained the role to the end, winning the first trophy St Andrews had won for a very long time, and beaten in the final of the final of weaker schools senior cup .

My brother and three sisters all worked in the business at various times. My brother and I had been joint MD of the company and took over full control of the business when Dad passed away, in 1993 at 63. We had not just lost a father; he was our mentor and chairman and the void he left took many years to fill. The full control and responsibility were now in our hands. My brother and I worked closely together and for the next ten years grew the business past the ten million sales mark and to trading out of thirty outlets.

Wigoders was the first specialist wallpaper shop in Ireland, established in 1783. We as a family have been very fortunate to inherit the brand and the business has been very kind to us. There were long hours and a lot of heavy lifting, both mentally and physically on the journey, and we had a lot to learn fast. One of the first skills our father taught us was delegation – Give your team the ownership and responsibility, trust and work with them. If you make mistakes learn from them and move on, and let your team know they are working with you, not for you. Some of the best advice we received came from within the business, practical and simple advice. We always had an open door to listen to every member of the team. Having worked from the ground floor up from 1972, the first task I was given when I arrived in the shop full-time was from the manager, Mrs. Kennedy, a lady whom I grew to respect and who shared so much of her sales knowledge with me, and the history of Wigoders. She'd say things like, 'You may be the boss's son, but you'll start the same as everyone else. You'll clean the toilets, tidy up the yard and get the bins out.'

We had great fun working with a team of girls from very different backgrounds, they never let us get too big for our boots and it was great fun. As a naïve and gullible 17-year-old lacking street smarts, the learning curve was a steep one. I was sent into the dry cleaners for a bucket of steam, and on another occasion for the long stand. Having stood waiting for 30 minutes, the girls in Marlowe cleaners laughed and said I'd been standing for long enough! And then on another occasion I was sent to McQuillan tools for a glass hammer. The Christmas parties were legendry and I have the photos to prove it. I enjoyed the team spirit and the way everybody pulled together to achieve the sales target for the day.

Then one day, out of the blue life's first challenge arrived; my parents separated. The importance of the family staying together vanished in a flash. But the message was clear, as cruel as life can be, *"The show must go on"*. I chose to bury myself in the business and followed my mentor, my Dad. I wanted to learn as much about retailing as I could, from those with wisdom in the wallpaper industry. I was shown the negotiating skills of buying and sourcing wallpaper in the UK and we found a network in Manchester and Leeds, mainly Jewish families that were very open to doing business. From the experience I had on the shop floor selling, I developed an

250

eye for good sellers. So, the question I asked my Dad was, 'How *do I know if I am paying the best price?*' I received a very simple answer, which was, '*What can you sell it for? Then divide that number by 5 and negotiate, always leaving something on the table for the seller.*' I was also told about the importance of building relationships and trust with your suppliers and customers.

As our sales increased, we were able to buy directly from the manufacturers and bypass the wholesalers. Margins increased and we expanded the warehouse and distribution base. The retail world was evolving and shopping centers started opening. Our balance sheet was strong, and we were approached by the agents and developers as potential tenants. We were considered to be a strong covenant. They played the supply and demand game and we signed contracts that, with the benefit of hindsight, were very much to the advantage of the landlord. There were 5-year-upward-only rent reviews, which were subject to market rents and there were loading and disregard clauses. We learnt our lessons the hard way and in later years we were able to have break clauses included in the contracts. The lesson is to pay for good professional advice! And so, we changed our legal office and property agents to specialists in the commercial property field.

The buying trips with my farther to the UK were short and fast, often driving long distances between factories and clearing houses to source good product. He taught me how to know when it was time to start the negotiating and we learnt how to look for the stock that you want to buy, rather than the stock the seller want to sell, which

251

takes time and instinct. The goal was to buy at the lowest price, while understanding that the seller was trying to get the highest price. It was a matter of waiting until the timing was right before showing your hand. We had to understand in simple terms what we had purchased and what the potential return was going to be, what the difference between gross profit and net profit was, how to know what to buy and what you should pay, and how to control costs. I didn't understand what the solicitors, accountants, insurance and bankers were saying, and that was a challenge, so I asked how I could understand it, and the advice was basic, *'Buy low and sell at a multiple of no less than five and you will be able to afford all the professional advice you will need.'*

The supply chain was from different sources, some factories, and some brokers. The brokers would buy and sell by the container load, anything up to twenty thousand rolls of wallpaper. They were the outlets for the factories who either had to clear slow moving stock or raise cash, due to a cash flow issue. The trick was to get to the source and have enough selling power to buy directly from the factories. Many doors opened and prices dropped when we asked for the best price for cash up front.

Brand leaders were the easy way to sell, however the margins were too tight, and you could end up working for the supplier. The brands brainwash the consumer and through market-share are able to dictate your margin. As we grew, we were the manufacturer's best route to market and we built strong relationships with our suppliers; many were owned by UK corporate companies, with a local sales director. We built relationships with people, which has been important all through our business life. Always remember to be kind to those you meet on the way up because you'll surely meet them again on the way down!

As the business grew, we installed new systems and became even more professional. We expanded the management team, in-house accountants, HR, marketing managers and buyers. We agreed to negotiate with the sales team through an in-house works committee as an alternative to negotiating with a trade union. We were determined that we were not going to lose our close connection with the people on the front line. This stood to us well as we could communicate the plans for the business to the team and communicate the progress. We held monthly managers' meetings, works committee meetings and Monday morning operations meetings. The importance of open lines of communication and information in your business are often underestimated. Information is key and we required as near to real time sales figures as possible. We introduced a live-stock system barcoding on the back of a database, which was ahead of its time. This gave us the ability to respond quickly to changing market conditions, which in retail can change very fast.

When our financial controller made the proposal to introduce the system, our question was for them to justify the cost and explain the benefits. Sales were at approximately €10 million. One percent of sales equals €100,000, the system increased gross margin by 3%, which equaled €300,000. The cost of introducing the system was

€250,000 with a 1-year payback. Cost and benefit analysis are crucial to every decision of expenditure in your business.

The nearly five decades that we have been fortunate enough to work with Wigoders has brought many benefits to us as a family, but it has also brought challenges. From the early noughties we were faced with new challenges; the business of wallpaper, our main income generator, was going out of fashion. The DIY stores were using white paint as a lost leader to entice customers, and with the property market boom in the mid-nineties the upward only rent reviews were crippling us. We had a good portfolio of leased and freehold premises, but we were fighting an uphill battle. The difficult decision had to be made, to downsize the company and dispose of the properties while the market was strong. It was our view the property boom could not last. Our goal was to do the best we could for all the loyal employees and pay all our creditors. There were other options, however this was our preferred choice. We had worked together from one to thirty outlets, and then back to one outlet on the Long Mile Road. We negotiated loans of approximately €3 million with the banks. We had a property valuation of €9 million, rental income of €400,000, and negotiations with perspective buyers all looked good for our exit in 2007...what could possibly go wrong?

The crash of 2008 brought with it a downturn that reduced spending and the economy went into free fall. We had made a poor choice with a licensee for Wigoders, which ended up being a very torturous legal battle. In 2012 my brother and I were back on the shop floor and reopened the shop on the Long Mile Road and my son Eric joined us. The value of the property had fallen to €900,000, ten per cent of the 2006 valuation. We were now in negative equity. The bank was loading on the pressure and my private life was under pressure, with financial commitments that I could no longer fulfill. This, alongside my partner being diagnosed with stage four breast cancer was the straw that broke the camel's back.

I was diagnosed with anxiety and depression with suicidal ideation and signed into Saint John of God's hospital in October 2012. The perfect storm had arrived. It was a feeling of hero to zero, complete helplessness, worrying where the next few Euros were going to come from to pay the bills. Letter after letter from the bank forcing me into a corner, I was overwhelmed with fear. I had never known what it was like not to be able to support my family, I felt like a complete failure. I had not had a good night's sleep for three years and the anxiety had taken control of my mind and body. I lost over two stone and every morning was as if I had just had a sauna with the night sweats. All I could do was plan my suicide. I didn't want to die; I wanted the pain to stop.

What had led me there were my choices, good and bad. Not only had I made poor choices in business, in my private life I had an affair that led to a very acrimonious divorce. I was married to an amazing person whose love for me was unconditional and I let her down. I deserted 18 years and 5 wonderful sons for someone I fell in love with. I invested my whole self into my new relationship to the detriment of my sons. In my eyes I could see no wrong. I met my financial commitments after the separation and failed as a father, not giving enough quantity time to the boys. The guilt will be with me for the rest of my life. Immersed in my new relationship and running the company with my brother, life was moving very fast. I was blessed with 2 beautiful daughters and burning the candle at both ends long hours in the business and a good social life. Looking back, I maintained a good relationship with all my children and our love for each other came to the fore during my challenging years. It was a difficult road, but with the help of my family, close friends and the hospital, the light eventually went back on.

The routine in the hospital was that you queued for your medication every morning after breakfast. One morning, I was approached by a man offering communion, my response was 'Thank you, however I am a lapsed Presbyterian and not of your faith.' He laughed and asked if we could have a chat later. We met a couple of times a week and he listened to my story in a very caring and nonjudgmental way and built up my trust. One day he invited me to a healing mass in the hospital church and assured me he was not trying to convert me to Catholicism and I agreed to attend. Early in my first confinement in the hospital I had been diagnosed with floppy foot syndrome, which was very upsetting, and the prognosis was that as it was a brain issue and it may be with me forever. I attended the mass and at one point the priest laid his hands on my head and whispered in my ear, 'What are you looking to be healed from?' I said I wanted to be healed from my anxiety and depression. My right foot was getting worse, I had to drag it to the extent that when my sister, Emma, came to visit and as I walked toward her, she broke down in tears. After a couple of visits to A & E they fitted me with a lag caliper, which helped, so I had a limp rather than dragging my foot. Some weeks later when I was walking to breakfast, and had not put the leg support on, I realized my walking was back to normal. I believe that this was a message to me from the healing mass, and my faith had been restored.

After two three-month stays, and the maximum amount of ECT treatment, I left Saint John of God and attended as an outpatient from 2013. My relationship with my then partner was over, and I was homeless. My brother and sisters helped me out until I moved into one of the rental properties that the bank was forcing me to sell, and then to another rental property that my partner was kind enough to help me with, until the bank forced her to sell. My son then found a house and we rented it together.

I was working back in the shop, although more there in body than mind. The battle went on with the bank and slowly but surely we started to rebuild the sales and income from letting out units. The issue was cashflow, for without it there is no financial security. I don't blame anyone for the financial crash I faced. I signed the loan documents and I take full responsibility for being seduced by a financial system that is satanic to its core. The system wants you to get educated, get employment, get married, get a mortgage, a car loan, credit card debt and trap you for 40 years working 40 hours a week and end up in your sixties with 40% of what you need to live on. I call it the 40 40 40 trap, which today looks more like a 50 50 20 trap.

Every month I would collect my medication. It was four different drugs, the strongest being lithium, which had a side effect of shaking hands. Physically I felt my body was falling apart, my memory was impaired, and I was addicted to the medication. My main concern every day was fear that if I didn't take them the anxiety would return. In May of 2017 I was at my regular month's meeting with my psychiatrist and he asked how I was feeling. He said he had noticed a change in me, that my body language and appearance was more confident, and he asked what I had changed. He was somewhat taken aback when I informed him that I had stopped taking the medication. The reason I had stopped taking the drugs was that in March I didn't have the money to get them. He did not understand why I didn't have any withdrawal symptoms and had gone cold turkey without any issues. I had started taking a supplement in February that a friend gave me. I did not relate it to my recovery until months later. (I should make it clear that I do not recommend that anyone reading my story goes against their medical advice). My mind became clearer, the shakes had stopped, and I was determined to take back control of my life. I asked my brother to give me a year to sort out the banks and just let me at it and trust me. I set about building the cash flow and put together a team of professionals who backed my plan. Slowly but surely, the ball bounced in our favor.

We had always has had a non-exec director that we met on a monthly basis, who was our "wood from the trees man", and when

Pat Slattery turned up in 2017 things changed even more for the better. I signed up for his personal development program. When asked by friends why I signed up, and why I was going to the mastermind meeting with all my experience, my reply was that the world was moving ten times faster than in any decade I had experienced, and I felt I had to continue investing in myself, if I was going to keep up. Pat is my coach to this day and will be for as long as he will put up with me! It is my view that whatever your business is, involve a professional who understands your passion and is not emotionally connected to your business. It will give you that clear perspective on how your business is progressing and keeps you on track.

Once I was on track, people started showing up to help us achieve our goals. Patrick Barry, who took over the Wigoders brand under license gave us the freedom to work on adding value to the property and continue our plan. We built a team of professionals to negotiate with the banks. Slowly but surely, with patient persistence we made progress. We set aside the people that were not aligned to our goals and worked with our team. The pandemic has brought a whole new set of challenges and has also been a time to reflect. It has given us time to hit the reset button.

During the period from 2010 to 2017 I had given up my passion for golf. My mind just wasn't in the right state to be able to be able to work on my game. But again, something happened that was another part of my awakening. My daughter joined the junior coaching at our club, aged 11, and because of her interest I started playing a few holes with her. One day on the practice ground Ella was hitting a few shots when a friend came by. He was impressed with her swing and asked if she a junior member. In seeing my difficulty in responding, and knowing my financial struggles, he offered to pay her membership and did so for the next four years. Thank you, Noel Griffin.

Another issue that was resting heavily on my mind was how I was going to continue to pay for my daughter Ella and Lauren's school fees. Once again, my renewed connection with my faith was rewarded with help from my church. Thank you, Reverend John Tanner.

I rediscovered my confidence and went head on into rebuilding myself. My motivation was that I owed a lot of pay-back to all that were nearest and dearest to me. There was no silver bullet; I changed my lifestyle, got up in the morning and had my tasks reviewed for the day, and carried forward. Adding to the list. I took my supplements Vitamin E, stem cell replacement, Noni juice and pro biotic, and I set a goal to sell the remaining property and move to Portugal for the winter months and continue my new interest's in Blockchain technology and in the multi-level marketing industry and as an independent business consultant. I reengaged with my passion for golf and the exercise and being out in the fresh air for 4 hours at least twice a week helped me greatly. I reconnected spiritually with my chosen brand of religious faith and I joined a mastermind group. The challenge was financial pressures and to overcome them I believed that firstly I had to look after myself physically with more exercise, technically building a team of professional advisors, and mentally working with a psychologist and joining a mastermind program. I found new income streams and now I get great satisfaction helping people scale, grow and sell their business or products. I believe in networking and attended as many events as possible. I enjoy everything business and have worked with SME businesses and startups and recently sold a business for a sole trader who wanted to retire. The funds arrived in his bank one week before the Covid-19 shutdown and he has had a smile on his face every time I have met him since. I am currently working with clients in the sustainable renewable energy and tokenization of same, a company recycling clothes to reduce the amount of clothes going to land fill, an artisan producer of health and wellness products, a new brand of clothes with a young man who has the passion to succeed, and negotiating an exit sale for a retail business. I work with three companies in the network marketing industry that have a proven track record and stand up to scrutiny from doing my due diligence. Experience has taught me how to identify the red flags. As in any industry there are good and bad companies and people. The get-rich-quick approach is too good to be true and opportunities usually only reward the early movers. I continue to work with Wigoders and with managing close to 50 units in the Long Mile Road premises, life is full on and great fun, "most of the time."

I was recently described by a client as Altruistic, which does not translate to kindness is weakness.

I have found great strength in my experiences. I am wiser, I am happier, and I have empathy for anyone fighting a battle. I'd like to share my greatest lessons with you here because I know that if you really think about them and live by them, life can take on a whole new positive meaning.

- Advice and opinion.

  In my experience, advice and opinion come from those who are qualified to give it, have professional indemnity insurance and have followed it up with a fee note, all the rest is a point of view and at best bar talk.

- Goals have to be SMART - **S**pecific, **M**easurable, **A**chievable, **R**ealistic, **T**ime boxed.

- Don't take your dreams to the grave, "Die Empty."

- If you've nothing nice to say, say nothing.

- The more I practice the luckier I get.

- A bird in the hand is worth two in the bush.

- Make a gesture of goodwill every day and lodge as many smiles in your heart as possible, you will reap what you sow.

My goal in contributing this chapter is to help you the reader to achieve your dreams, and if one of you found my words helpful and inspiring, I have achieved another baby step forward.

"IF ONLY I KNEW THEN WHAT I KNOW NOW."

CHAPTER 16
Victim to Victor

by Tanya Cannon

Walking down the street in Athlone, I felt a foot taller. I had an extra few bob and I decided to treat myself to a bottle of perfume. I walked with my head held high. I felt important for the first time ever in my life. I was wearing my fabulous new grey suit had my hair washed and straightened, I felt a million dollars.

That weekend, I attended the Women's Empowerment Summit. I felt so comfortable, normal, and connected with everyone there. I was where I was meant to be that day. I was myself in that room, I was right at home there.

A woman called Breeda Hurley spoke on the stage that day, and inspired me by her tenacious resolve, drive, determination, kindness and compassion to help others. It was my third empowerment summit I was finally ready to take the next step, to put my story into words on paper.

Life wasn't always like the picture above, let me bring you back to when I was 4 years of age. I am the eldest of three siblings in our family unit. My parents were married in the 70s, my dad was in the army and my mam was a housewife. My dad had served overseas three times before I was 6 years of age so he was away a lot from home from what I can remember. At the time Dad was violent at home and when he returned home from overseas, he was more violent in his manner and generally not particularly good to anyone of us. Mammy got beatings and as time went on, they got more serious. Abuse became a heavy issue in our home but eventually the marriage ended.

It was difficult for my mother, she tried to manage but got very little support from my father. My mother is an amazing woman but trying to manage three children on your own is not an easy thing to do. Social services stepped in and told her that they would give her six weeks to make everything work and if she couldn't they would take us from her and put us into care. Thankfully, Mam is a strong-willed person and she fought for us. She never turned her back on us, and to this day she lives for us.

At the age of 8 my Dad was kicked out of the army. I was told this was due to his violent behaviour towards his family, and of course his drinking issues. My poor mam got the blame for him being made to leave the army, but we could all see that it was the drink that was the issue and not turning up for work. Even as a child that was obvious. Mam suffered a lot from depression at that time and she was convinced that everything that happened was her fault. Although it wasn't, her spirit was broken from the whole thing. And so was mine but not just because of family reasons.

At 7 years of age I was playing outside my home. There were young lads playing around too. Although I knew some of them to see, we weren't all friends. It was a case of play with whoever was out on the green. We all went up to the train tracks that were not too far away from my home. Seven of the lads pulled me under the train tracks, lured me into a shed and abused me. I have a scar on my arm to this day from where they the burned me with coal from under the tracks. I remember screaming from the top of my lungs, so loud that I could be heard over the trains passing. An elderly man that was working further up on the train line heard me and followed the sounds. I'll never forget the big, tall grey-haired man standing in the doorway, shouting at my abusers. He got rid of them and saved me. He rang the guards and then brought me to the hospital for treatment where I spent several days. The guards called to my house to get my mammy. They knew where she was as they were regular callers to the house.

Those lads struck a second time and raped another girl, not long after me. The emotional and physical effects of this has stayed with me all my life.

But out of the ugly time in my life something beautiful happened. Mam met a man called Hughie. He had long red hair and a beard and when he saw my mother on the street, he did his best to find a way to get her attention so he could speak with her.

After about 2 years he eventually got a date with her and became a solid member of our family for 23 years. I was a little rebellious at that time as I was probably jealous of his and my mother's relationship. Mam and Hughie had a fantastic relationship. He treated her like a lady, he treated her with respect. Of course, it was a rocky start in the relationship due to my mother's years of mistrust and abuse, but through thick and thin, Hughie stood by Mam and they were very happy. He was a very patient sort, generous and kind to me. I could tell him my secrets before anyone else, he had my trust. He bought me to my first disco, he taught me how to drive, and he opened my first Credit Union account to help me save my money. He acted like a biological father.

Hughie was self-employed. He had his own cleaning company. Mam took the calls and he did the jobs. He cleaned everything from chimneys to windows and gutters. He was a good businessman and he showed us what it was to work hard. He showed us what good work could do for you and if you worked at anything you could have anything in life. His work ethic was phenomenal, and this brushed off on all of us in our later lives.

At the age of 14, I went down a rebellious road. I started mitching from school, looking for constant attention, some attention in the wrong places, attention from Mam and Dad, when he was around, and attention from Hughie. I looked for attention from everyone. I was on a slippery slope. At the age of 17, I decided to drink a bottle of Vodka straight. I drank the whole bottle and went to bed. In the middle of the night I started to vomit in my sleep. Hughie was the only one who heard me and saved me from myself that night. At that time, I also took an overdose and again Hughie was there.

Somewhere along that time, I decided to leave home and head to England to live with my dad. He moved to London when I was 12 and stopped drinking a couple of years after. He had set up a successful cable business with 150 staff under him. He was always asking me to come over so this last time I did.

At first everything was normal; he wasn't drinking, things were good, and everything was very polite. But even though he wasn't drinking,

267

as time when on his behaviour became more aggressive and his language more colourful towards me. On the other hand, on good days, he would bring me to Westend shows and out for meals but only he felt like it. This was the father I remembered and at times, I was embarrassed by him. It was tough.

I thought by going to London that all my problems would be solved. Dad constantly spurred me on to join Al Anon, a support group for families of alcoholics. I was not into this. I listen to his account of what our life was like, which didn't sound like a life I knew! He always said that the family breakdown was not his fault, that he sent money home from the Lebanon and he wondered what happened to it. He constantly asked questions like 'Why did Mammy do this, and all of my money gone?' and 'Your mother took everything that belongs to me.'. He convinced me of it, and then I thought it was all mammy's fault. I was really brainwashed. What I do know now is that my mother would go without rather than asking for anything from anyone. I only came to learn this later in life.

I had spent 2 years in London with my father and at this time he was quite the businessman. Joe, one of his staff, walked into my father's home office one evening and that's where my next chapter starts.

Joe and I fancied each other from the first time we saw each other. This was my first real relationship and from the outset my father had warned him to stay away from me. Joe and myself had a great relationship and we still do to this day.

Early in our relationship I fell pregnant but at that point our relationship was still a secret from my father. When he did find out about us, he hit the roof!! When he threatened to hurt Joe we decided to move out and move in with each other for safety. Two weeks after I moved to a new place I didn't feel very well. Joe was concerned so he brought me to the nearest hospital. My dad was called as he was my next of kin. When he came to see me, he brought all the colourful and insulting language he could muster to the hospital with him. The doctor told him that I was pregnant, which only made the situation worse. He called me all the whores' names under the sun, and he didn't know how to stop. Joe decided that we couldn't stay there in London as the tension was too much, and he certainly was not going to leave me with my dad. I was never as lonely in the world as I was then. We decided to move back home to Ireland. It was during this time that I had lost our baby. I named her Mary and even though I never held her in my arms she will always be my little angel in heaven.

One day I was on the way to Mullingar with Joe at the age of 21. We were involved in a serious car accident. Joe had pulled me from the car, even though he was injured himself. By this time, Dad had returned home for a short time. Someone had called him about the accident, and he happened to be closer to the scene than my mother. My father entered my life again.

Joe and I were engaged at this point and were living life like any normal couple. Like everything I had done in my life, my dad had an issue with me marrying Joe. Joe and I began to argue over the fact that my father was back in my life. Joe was terrified of him as he threatened him more often than not. After a 4-year relationship, we split up and went our separate ways.

My father seemed to have this effect on all men in my life; he had a knack of destroying any chance of happiness that I could ever hope for. My father was the jealous type and I felt he had destroyed chances of relationships that I had. As much as he didn't want to be in my life, he didn't want anyone else to be there either!

At the age of 24, a particular house on my street went up for sale. When I was younger, I was often in the house and often remark that someday it would be mine. My boyfriend at the time and I decided to buy that house in a whirlwind romance. All was going very well until he had an affair with a girl at work. That finished the relationship, but we still had the house together. I fought a three-year battle and I won back my house. My friends at that time thought I was crazy buying house; I was too young for this after all. On 31st of August 2020, I'll be in my home 23 years and by Christmas of 2020 I'll be mortgage free — I'm only 46 years of age!

Around the time of my accident I was working for a cleaning company. I did this for 15 years. I had a lot of responsibilities at the time in the company as the contracts were high-end factories. A promotion came up in the company and I applied for it. In the interview the director asked me, 'Where do you see yourself in 5 years' time, Tanya?' I jokingly remarked, 'In your chair' and quickly clarified that it was a dream of mine to be the director of a company in few years' time. I didn't think at that time that I would be in my own director's seat in A1 Cleaning and Maintenance Services.

I made myself a director of my own business at 32 years of age. I gave it to myself as a birthday present — my birthday present to me! I didn't get any outside help to do this, I had my own way of making it work. I remortgaged my home for €50,000 and I bought stock from a friend who owned a cleaning products company, to the value of €30,000, to get the business set up. He told me to pay him back whenever I was ready, but I had him paid back in 7 months. Business with A1 Cleaning was good. I was lucky I got to build my business before the crash in 2008 and even though the recession hit, my priorities were always my business. I would rather pay an electricity bill than go out on the lash in town; my business was my baby. I was single for 5 years until 2012 when I met a man. We stayed together 7 years but there was never a full commitment, so it inevitably ended.

I choose to attend events like the Women's Empowerment Summit or motivational speaker events etc. These events were my support network. The summit helped me focus and I loved it.

Now, in 2020, I have my goals set in place and I am working to be debt free by Christmas. I will also have a new Jeep and a new fireplace in my home. These are some of my personal goals. Hard work is paying off for me, I control what I have, and I control what I do. It has been said that I have a real "fire in my belly attitude" towards my business and its future. I want to be able to help people have the right products for the right jobs. I want to help people. I want to help people with A1 Cleaning recommendations because I do the job right. Not only that, I want to help people through speaking my story. I want to be able to uplift people, people who are like me, who were once in my boat, to help them be the best they can be. Never be afraid to live your dream, stick to it and it will come! My last business dream is to add another revenue stream to A1 Cleaning and Maintenance Services. I have plans to step into a different side of A1 Cleaning and build on the foundations for this part of the business and bring it to great heights. This is my pension pot plan.

I love what I do but all my life I have been a caretaker for everyone else in different ways. The only time I was my own caretaker was when I went to look for counselling to help me deal with the many different traumas that were in my life. My priority now is for my future is me. I now realise I am beautiful and worthy of everything great!

There is one secret that I have covered up for most of my life and it has thrown up many challenges throughout my business. It has stopped me putting myself forward for a lot of experiences. I am dyslexic. As a businesswoman, I have found it very difficult to put a sentence together that is grammatically correct. Spelling could be very erratic. When writing, I could see a full sentence of words, but a lot might be missing in reality. The last 3 or 4 years I have surrounded myself with people who are patient, helpful, caring and kind. They would go out their way to help me with words, and how to spell etc. I found ways around hiding my dyslexia (Google is great!) and I got people to read important pieces to me to allow me to listen and take it all in properly.

Writing this chapter has been the most daunting experiences for many reasons but the biggest challenge has to be my dyslexia. There is a lesson in this for all of us – there is a way around everything. If you have a big enough reason to find your solution, your goals will always be met!

My burning ambition in life is twofold, one is to be a Secret Millionaire and the second is to have the courage to empower people to be the greatest version of themselves. I am very proud of myself. I am in a very good place in life and business is good. I am very grateful for what I have, where I work and where I have come from. I am so thankful for my family and with every learning moment that I have had.

In the future I would like to see myself in a steady relationship and to be happy and content in myself. I see the new leg of my business taking off financially and I would like to sell it to another cleaning company so they could grow it further. I don't want to be up a ladder at 50 years of age!

All my life I have had the ability to turn a negative into a positive, I chose to be the **victor** of my life, not the victim. I am happy in my life today. I have planned for a great future. I have a couple of things to iron out, but that's no problem. I'll meet them head on too!

In memory of Hughie Martin

27th April 1998, age 42.

RIP

CHAPTER 17
Declutter Your Mind

by Sharon McNulty

As a Professional Organizer and a Gold Certified KonMari™ Consultant, I help clients declutter and organize their homes and businesses using the KonMari Method™. This is a relatively new way of tidying and its creator, Marie Kondo, explains that when we tidy using the KonMari Method™, we will never need to tidy again. That's right, we will never have to tidy again! She believes tidying should only happen once in our lifetime.

KonMari™ is a structured method and there are certain rules we follow: We tidy by category and not location, we chose only those items we love or those we need and, we let the rest go with gratitude. We declutter in a particular order —clothes, books, papers, miscellaneous and finally sentimental. KonMari™ is at the heart of empowerment, clients learn how to surround themselves with items they love. In the process of achieving a tidy home, they achieve a shift in mindset and, as they declutter their homes, they also declutter their minds.

'Your home should be the antidote to stress, not the cause of it.'
– Peter Walsh

When we find ourselves in a mess, it can feel overwhelming. Physical clutter leads to emotional clutter and when supporting clients through their tidying journey, I hear many of the same emotions come up time and time again.

The word most commonly used by clients to describe their feelings amidst clutter is 'stress'. This is understandable as research shows being surrounded by clutter increases the stress hormone, cortisol, often referred to as the 'fight, flight or freeze' response. Cortisol has kept us alive since the beginning of time. Thousands of years ago cortisol gave the caveman that surge of energy to escape the sabre toothed tiger.

While it's healthy to have a small amount of cortisol, being stressed on a daily basis can be harmful to our health. Chronic high stress leads to a poor attention span, lack of focus or clarity. Our brains are distracted and try to multi-task; we take longer to perform tasks which ultimately lowers productivity. Incidentally, the neuropsychologist Dr Rick Hanson, found that chronic stress can change the structure of our brain, making us hyper-sensitive to stress and so the cycle continues. Stress turns into dis-ease in our bodies, which in turn creates disease. Research shows that stress causes weight gain, anxiety, depression, cancers, diabetes; the list is endless.

It is harder to focus on emotional conversations amidst clutter, and this can lead to negative behavioral effects for ourselves and our children. We are easily irritated and often reactive. This is evident when we observe children in a messy environment. They are chaotic in their play, have reduced concentration and difficulty regulating their emotions. Clients often talk about feeling fatigued, yet they have difficulty falling asleep at night. This is no surprise as they tell me their bedroom is far from relaxing. Cluttered bedrooms and insomnia are bedfellows (pardon the pun) and it is difficult to have a productive day while feeling exhausted and overwhelmed.

Clients often speak of having neither energy nor motivation to tackle their homes. They feel dissatisfied with it but can't move forward. This is the "freeze" response to cortisol. So, if you are feeling overwhelmed, be aware that this feeling is perfectly normal and felt by the majority of people at one time or another. Take a moment to have a look around you today and consider how you feel when looking at your surroundings. Now you know there is a reason for you feeling this way, it's time to tackle it and make some changes.

Our physical mountain (the clutter) represents our mental clutter, and when we superficially tidy we are simply moving items from one place to another and not addressing the problem. Likewise, when we don't want to address something emotionally, we 'sweep it under the rug' and profess we will deal with it some time. That time rarely comes and, as time goes on, this rug becomes a mountain of things not dealt with. The thought of dealing with what lurks under the rug is scary and therefore we keep putting it off. The KonMari process helps us go through what we have been avoiding and helps us face things head on.

Today's consumerism encourages us to buy more than we need, and the 'Buy two get one free' strategy leads us to stockpile. We feel we are saving money, yet it has the opposite effect. We never get around to using them and we buy what we already have, either because we can't find it, or we have forgotten we have it. Disorganized paperwork and mislaid bills cause us to accrue late fees for missing payments. Many times, when tidying their homes, my clients have found out-of-date cheques and vouchers tucked between the pages of a book or nestled in a pile of paperwork. They continue to receive items that they signed up for months ago and they haven't the time or energy to cancel them (or may not be aware that they are still being charged for these).

Buying things makes us happy momentarily but we don't appreciate what we have when there is too much, in fact it often evokes feelings of shame. In today's "perfect"–social media world, we catch a snapshot of everyone's tidy, organized and uncluttered homes. This is often in stark contrast to what lies behind the camera lens but, it's enough to create feelings of inadequacy and low self-worth — 'Others can manage to keep their homes tidy why can't I?' When clients get overwhelmed and give up, this reinforces those feelings, thereby creating a self-fulfilling loop.

Now I am not talking about hoarding here, I am exploring how everyday mess can affect our daily lives. This relates to the home that is surface tidy with bulging cupboards. Even though others can't see inside, *we* know it's disorganized. This is the home with unopened boxes in the attic from the last three house moves and, the home with paperwork spilling out onto the kitchen worktop.

277

We spend precious time searching for items and most of us can identify with the feeling of frustration at not being able to find what we are looking for.

It is hard to find joy and serenity amidst clutter and, embarrassment at having visitors over often leads to isolation and loneliness. These feelings of shame can lead to anxiety, which is further exacerbated by isolation. Clients know that it will take time and energy to manage the clutter but don't have either as they are already frantically spinning plates. Avoiding it makes it bigger both emotionally and physically.

In today's society we are also conditioned to want instant gratification, we want results straight away and when it doesn't happen, we feel irritated and frustrated. When we press a button on our computer, we expect that page to appear in front of us instantly and we keep pressing the button (with fervor) until it does. We need to learn the skills of consistency, persistence and faith. Tidying your home is the first part and will give you these valuable skills which are transferrable to other areas of your life. Turn up and tidy a little every day (consistency). You must do this even if you don't feel like doing it (persistence) and know that this will come together (faith).

Do it right!

You can superficially tidy in a short time, yet it will return to its previous state very quickly, if you declutter half-heartedly. A half-hearted effort will get half-hearted results, and this increases the possibility of rebound. If you have been tidying this way for years, your results will show how effective it is. How about trying something that will help you fall in love with your home (and life) again?

For me, the completion of the KonMari Method™ has resulted in so many positives. I completed my KonMari™ journey several years ago and I now live in my serene home with items and belongings that I love. My home is so incredibly easy to keep tidy! Everything I own has a place and this serenity sparks immense joy for me on a daily basis.

Did you know that on average we spend 40 minutes each day searching for items in our homes? Imagine how you can spend those 40 minutes once you finish tidying your home! What would you love to do with this extra time each day? Take a moment and write it down...

_____

_____

_____

_____

_____

_____

_____

Where to Start

From experience, most people don't know where to start, they just tidy room by room or cupboard by cupboard, but what they're actually doing is moving their stuff from one place to another and this is ineffective. It will never stay tidy and before long it is as bad as ever. They resent putting energy into keeping it tidy because the results are so short lived, and they often feel frustrated with family members who are blissfully unaware of it or indeed, in their eyes, the cause of the mess.

We accumulate our belongings over time and therefore to properly declutter your home, to go through every item you own will also take time. We need to do it in its entirety, so it doesn't rebound. The timeframe for tidying depends on the amount of possessions you own and the time you can allocate to tidying. It takes weeks to declutter and organize an average sized family home, if they work full time however, it took me around 5 months to complete my own home, as I could only devote the weekends to tidying.

To be effective, Marie Kondo recommends that this should be done quickly and efficiently and so I provide daily intensive decluttering support to clients in order to complete it in one week. Alternatively, by engaging in my 6-week-course or with my online planner, other clients can complete this journey at a gentler, but steady pace. Regardless of the time taken, the critical and most important element is to keep working at it.

Tackling the mess can be overwhelming physically and mentally and there are items in our homes that we do not love but feel obliged to keep. 'We might need it someday' is the most common fear but, that day never comes and, if it did, chances are we have forgotten we had it so would have to buy it again. When we tidy similar items together it allows us to see how much of each item we really have, and we ultimately realize that we will have enough and will not go without.

Another reason we hold onto these items is because we have 'spent our hard-earned money to buy them' and feel it would be wasteful to let these items go. We decide we could sell them and recoup some of the cost but of course this doesn't happen as we don't have the time.

Think of those items that were given to us by loved ones, those expensive items we never use or the pre-loved items from a supportive friend. Items that have an emotional connection may be difficult to let go of. Each item evokes either positive or negative memories and often it seems easier to hold onto the item than deal with the emotions attached to it.

All of these feelings are understandable however, if guilt, fear and "what if" are your reasons for keeping items think again. Be grateful for what they did for you in the past. They got you to where you are now, but do you need them for your future higher self? Letting go of what doesn't serve you, (physical clutter, toxic relationships or our thoughts), leaves room for items you love. When you surround yourself with items you love and with supportive people, you are raising your vibrations and attracting more fabulous things into your life.

The more often you practice letting go the easier it will be and when you know you can do this in one area of life, you realize you can do this in every area of your life. Change your self-talk, refuse to be judgmental or self-critical as you go through this journey. Negative thoughts don't serve you so let them go.

Your Why

Most of us have too much stuff and we just don't even know where to start. Our overwhelm leads to paralysis and inertia and, if we stay in this state, we make it into something bigger than it is, both physically and emotionally. Yes, your home may be messy, but be mindful that the messiest things lead to the best results because you can see great improvement. Don't waste energy feeling guilty or embarrassed. Be kind to yourself and focus instead on getting started.

A great exercise to help you do this is to sit in your favorite part of your home and close your eyes for a few moments. Take a slow deep breath and relax. Think about your ideal day from the moment you waken in the morning, consider how you feel as you experience a calm and serene room with everything in its place. As you reach into your wardrobe to choose your outfit, feel your joy when you see your beautiful clothes. Go through every moment of your ideal day in detail right through to your night-time routine —how your bedroom looks and feels as you drift off to sleep.

Then open your eyes and write down your ideal lifestyle and how your home will support your ideal day. This is so powerful and, in my opinion, the most important part of tidying. Having a clear image will help keep you motivated, and this *"why"* will keep momentum going and be the driving factor pushing you towards your finish line. On those days you don't want to tidy, revisit your ideal lifestyle and remember your *why*.

What is your why?

_____

_____

_____

_____

_____

_____

Now you know your Why, where do you go from here? Well, remember the saying 'The only way to eat an elephant is one bite at a time.' The same goes for tidying, break your tidying into manageable chunks. Set aside time each day to work on it, draw up a plan of action and stick to it. If you want this strongly enough you will do it. Once you know what you want, and have your ideal vision, get started and keep moving towards it.

I motivate and encourage my clients each step of the way. It may be worth considering getting an accountability partner, someone who is nonjudgmental, who you respect and who will keep you moving towards your end goal. Send them photos of your daily achievements and they will cheer you on. Remain consistent and these small steps will get you towards the end goal of completion and satisfaction.

Choose a treat for when you finish (and no you don't need to buy anything). When completing the book category, one client decided to keep many of her cookery books even though she never cooked (she never had the time). However, on seeing these books proudly displayed in her bookcase ignited her love for cooking. Then and there she set a date for a dinner party with friends. This was her treat and kept her moving towards the finish line.

A home is a reflection of the mind, with everything on the inside reflected outwards. When we have serenity and calm in our surroundings, we create an environment that soothes and quiets the mind. The act of decluttering our home is cathartic, it allows us to become introspective and helps build our mental strength. As we become more tranquil, we gain deep inner peace.

Letting Go

For many, the thought of "letting go" of our belongings is scary. Some items hold an emotional attachment for us; they are special because they hold memories, both positive and negative. They reflect who we are, our journey travelled and, represent a piece of ourselves. So, when letting go of an item, we worry we may lose our identity.

Many clients doubt their ability to declutter and are nervous of how they will make decisions. I explain that, yes, you need courage each time you take a step towards something new but suggest they see it as a challenge- accept it and get to work. Challenging their self-doubt will change the loop playing in their mind and, over time they realize they can do it. Our innate instincts then kick in, they are always there but, often we have difficulty tapping into them and listening.

Fear of failure is another stumbling block for clients. I often hear them say they have decluttered many times before, but their house has never stayed tidy. This reinforces their story and they procrastinate. This is a self-fulfilling prophecy and in their minds they have already failed before they have begun. This is the same for every area in our life, if we do what we've always done, we'll get the same results. It's time now to change it up somewhat and try a new approach.

I appreciate that whenever we tackle something new, we overestimate the time, energy and courage needed. But if we have step by step plan to follow, it makes it so much easier. This tidying method provides just that and, as long as we follow the steps, we won't go far wrong. The only thing we need is a desire to make a change and persistence and everything else will fall into place.

Tidying is not about having a home that looks like a show-house, it's certainly not about perfection, it's about achieving a home that you love and that brings joy into your life. I believe we should embrace imperfection, use our intuition to decide what we love and grow confident in our decision-making abilities.

The tidying method I use encourages clients to concentrate on keeping only those items they love or those that they need and, they let go of the rest with gratitude. But how do we find out what we love or what sparks joy for us?

Marie Kondo suggests we hold each item in our hands, pay close attention to how we feel and focus on the response that item elicits inside us. When something sparks joy, we experience a thrill through our body. It may prompt a special memory or make you happy when you see it or touch it. If you're not sure what this feels like, consider if you would buy it again or spend time and money getting it repaired. Ask yourself if this item will bring you closer to your ideal lifestyle.

Patterns

Clients are amazed by how much personal growth they have during the tidying process, and they start to see themselves from a different perspective. As they go through their tidying, patterns emerge. Quite early on they gain an understanding of their previous shopping habits. There is always a lightbulb moment, where they realize why those clothes are hanging in their wardrobe and generally their thoughts, fears and unresolved issues go hand in hand with them.

As they hang the clothes, they love in the wardrobe they gain confidence in the colors, shapes and style that suits them, and they end up with a curated collection of items they love. These patterns are often the catalyst for change. Their mindset changes from one of lack to one of abundance and they make a definite decision to shop mindfully in the future.

I am reminded of a lovely client who had a wardrobe full of clothes she didn't particularly like. She explained that most of them were bought on a whim when shopping with her best friend. She realized all too often she let people talk her into doing things she didn't want to do or buying items she didn't like. Many of the items in her home were not her style and "inherited" from other members of the family. These were all well intentioned of course, however, she kept them out of a sense of duty and lacked the courage to say "no". She realized she was a people pleaser and made a conscious decision to have her voice heard in the future.

Our hopes, dreams and aspirations for the future lie amongst those clothes you're expecting to get into or in the case of another client, her reading material. She kept every edition of a slimming club magazine for past few years, yet she remained the same weight now as then. She also came across 23 starting packs for the same slimming club group. This was her lightbulb moment. She realized the desire was there for change but, it wasn't strong enough to follow through. She would start in a flurry of anticipation and excitement but couldn't sustain it. On reflection she realized this was the same for every aspect of her life. This was a powerful self-reflection; she discarded the magazines along with her guilt and is now on her way to a fabulous body regardless of what the scales say.

Clients have clarity because the mental clutter has somewhat diminished and they trust in their decisions. They keep items that resonate with their passions and, Marie Kondo explains, that often when tidying books clients see patterns emerge and consider a new hobby or change career. Now just because clients are aware of a pattern, they may not be ready to act on it just yet and that is okay. We all do things at our own rate. The process allows for self-reflection and empowers us to make informed choices when we are ready to do so.

It can be quite difficult to visualize the impact that tidying can have but be aware that tidying your home can change your life in more ways than you would ever imagine. The change in both your home and lifestyle encourage you to make good choices about future purchases and you start to shop mindfully, only letting those items that you love into your home.

Once you question your belongings and have surrounded yourself with items you love, you realize how amazing you feel. You want that feeling to last and therefore hold everything else in your life to these same principles. This happens organically and before long you question your beliefs, lifestyle and set new exciting goals in your life.

This is so powerful and in my opinion is why this method is truly life changing. After tidying our homes, we reflect on what else in our lives doesn't bring us joy. We reassess relationships and friendships and consider how each person affects us; are they supportive and understanding, do they inspire us to be the best version of ourselves?

This can be challenging because we invest so much time and effort building these relationships, however as we let go of toxic and negative friendships, it's like a cleansing of our mind. We remember to thank them in our heart for the past friendship and wish them well for their future. By doing so we are open to meeting people with similar interests and values as ourselves.

Making Decisions

If you're unsure how to make decisions, rest assured this is the easy part as you chose only those items you love or need. You take each item in your hand, one at a time, hold it close to your heart and decide if you love it (if it sparks joy). You only need to decide for one item at a time, so this takes the overwhelm out of it. If you love it (or need it) then you keep it with confidence and if it doesn't meet the mark you thank it and let it go.

I have often been asked why we thank each item, after all they are inanimate objects and not aware we are thanking them. Each item has been in your life for a reason, we needed it at a time but don't need it now. We thank them for bringing you to where you are now both physically and emotionally. While you are dealing with your physical belongings, you are also mirroring this with your emotions and you are letting go of those things that aren't serving you now, i.e., the person you used to be and negative memories attached to your belongings.

One of my clients who had difficulty with the spark joy concept chose to make her decisions based on the person in her ideal vision, the person she wanted to become. She asked herself would this person wear, use, and love each item. This worked well for her as she was making decisions that would lead her to her ideal lifestyle.

Regardless of how you choose what to keep, you learn what is important to you and have a greater appreciation of those items you are keeping. As you tidy your home, you will experience a shift in mindset, and you will hone your decision-making skills. Trust in the process and this will be evident as you go along.

When we declutter our home, we hold each item and decide whether we love it or need it. If you consider how many items we own, thousands of decisions are made by the end of our tidying journey. Most of the time it won't matter if we get it wrong, after all we can buy another roll of sellotape if we discard ours in error. But what about those decisions that we're just not sure about?

As we tidy, we come across sentimental items that can stop us in our tracks, those items that have a special meaning behind them. It is tempting to sit and reminisce there and then, however it will derail our tidying, so we place them in a separate pile and go through these at the end. If you try to make decisions about sentimental items at the start, you will keep every single item, worried that when discarding the items, we will lose precious memories that can't be replaced.

By making the small decisions when they don't really matter, you will be more confident about those difficult decisions. You begin to trust your intuition and learn what to place value on. It's a cathartic experience because things that may have been holding you back, things that you have been holding onto in the past both physically and emotionally, you're now letting go of and you are saying that you don't want to bring that into the future.

When you're not frantically rushing about you are more relaxed and more likely to notice and appreciate all the beautiful items you own. I love seeing the transformation in my clients as a result of the transformation in their homes. Recently I worked with a client whose opening remark was that she had no clothes in her size that she liked. Within the first session, she turned to me and exclaimed how looking into her wardrobe was like shopping in a boutique where she loves every item. What happened in those 4 hours to create such a dramatic difference? She fell in love with her clothes again.

Another client started our session not liking any of her clothes and she stored her good clothes in a spare room (that she never entered). As we completed her tidying, there was a shift in the way she held herself, she grew confident in her decision-making and, I noticed that as she placed items in her wardrobe, her hand would linger on each item affectionately. Again, this transformation was evident within a few hours of starting her tidying.

When we choose what we let into our homes, we are careful what we let into our body and mind, which in turn will lead to self-care. Completing your tidying will certainly free up precious time and you can use this time as you wish. You can take time for personal development, spend time with loved ones or enjoy a new hobby. This further raises your vibrations and allows space for creativity to flow.

When we enter a cluttered room there's a shift in our body both physically and emotionally; it makes us feel sluggish with little motivation and we adopt a pessimistic mindset. The energy in that room is stagnant and our vibrations and energies are low. This energy is disempowering, it holds us back and prevents us from living our lives to the fullest.

When we avoid dealing with physical clutter, we avoid dealing with it emotionally and this energy becomes stuck. Whenever there is discord or when we hold onto items to please others it impacts our energy and lowers our vibrations. This also relates to those unopened boxes in the attic, even though they're out of sight, we hold them in our minds constantly and this lowers our vibrations.

One of my clients is a prestigious seamstress and her reputation meant people travelled long distances for her services. Several years ago, she had to take time off work due to an injury and therefore her craft room wasn't used. During her recovery time a close family member died, and she inherited most of their belongings. Unsure how to deal with them, she placed them temporarily in her craft room and there they stayed unopened until our tidying session. This room held negative connotations, it lowered her vibrations and she never entered it as she felt a sense of dread when she was there. She had no inclination to sew and therefore had not worked since the accident.

The process of decluttering helped her separate emotions from their physical items.

Her focus was on keeping those items she loved and being respectful when letting go of those she didn't love. This gratitude completely changed the energy surrounding these items to a positive and healing energy which in turn raised her vibrations. With higher vibrations, she could experience greater joy and excitement and by the end of our tidying she had created a calm, serene craft room that she was excited to enter. She displayed her beloved items where she could see and appreciate them knowing that when we are grateful for what we have, it attracts more of the same into our life.

Create a Space of Value

When I completed my own tidying years ago, letting go of such vast quantity of items (and the emotions attached to them) was a turning point for me. I made a promise to myself that moving forward I would only bring an item into my home if I absolutely love it. I don't feel the need to keep up with all the trends, I see the value in those beautiful items I surround myself with and have saved a fortune doing so.

In today's consumer society it is all too easy to keep buying. When we see that 'shiny new must-have' item in the shop window we get a rush of Dopamine and Serotonin, the happy chemicals. Buying that item momentarily satisfies an emotional need and we leave the shop delighted with our purchase. However by the time we get home, that feeling of anticipation and elation has passed and the item is set into the back of the wardrobe with a vow we will wear it someday, knowing in our hearts that the tag may never be taken off.

However, whenever we surround ourselves with items we love, we realize we don't need to buy something to make us feel fulfilled, we know that *we* are enough. When we learn what we love and what we want to have in the future, we know nothing outside of us will ever equate to our worth inside. This is empowering!

As we surround ourselves with our treasured items, it can be an emotional and spiritual journey. We restore harmony to our homes, which can be a freeing and exhilarating experience. This shift in perspective fosters a new relationship with what we accumulate. We appreciate.

CHAPTER 18
The Busy-mess Mind-set

by Therese O'Connor

Once upon a time there was a girl who came from a good country family, brought up on the values of respect, integrity, hard work and honesty. Her Father was a farmer and her Mother worked all through her childhood. She wanted for nothing; she had food, security, love and all the materials things that she could ask for. Being a part of the community was important in her family. As a teenager, she used to read at weekly mass, she was a member of the local Irish dancing club and like her other family members got involved as much as she could in other local clubs and events. To everybody she was confident, bubbly and outgoing, but inside she felt insecure and that she didn't belong. She lacked self-belief. She had what a lot of people longed for but there was something bigger that she couldn't figure out – She needed to find out what that sense of belonging meant! That girl was me.

Masking the insecurities of my busy mind

From an early age, I had what I now call the busy-mess mind-set syndrome – always a series of questions, stories and comparisons racing through my mind. Why couldn't I be popular like the other girls? Why do I feel stupid every time I contribute to a conversation? What if I wasn't here, would anyone care? Why can't things come naturally to me, like they do to others? What if I lost weight, would that make me pretty? Why couldn't I find a handsome boyfriend or in fact any boyfriend? Why wasn't I intelligent like the other girls? Why is my hair so frizzy? And the questions of self-doubt kept creeping up on me throughout my teenage years. I'm sure these feelings resonate with many others, but goddamnit I found it hard. In my eyes I had no sense of identity and I loved comparing myself to others, which didn't help. The self-talk in my mind wasn't a pretty sight.

In school, I wasn't one of the popular girls; I really had to work hard to fit in, which resulted in me always feeling like an imposter and not being my authentic self. Where things came easily to most people around me, I felt awkward and out of place. It took me 5 series of swimming lessons before I could take off the arm bands without sinking! It only took my two brothers one class to learn! I was 27 before I had the confidence to drive; they were about 17 when they drove. Get the drift? Sometimes phrases like 'stupid' and 'Can you not just do that?' were said, mostly as flyaway comments, but to me, at the time, it added to my lack of self-belief and my self-worth. My mind became busy with negativity. And the only way to escape it was daydreaming.

I imagined that I lived on a tropical island, with the man of my dreams (Brad Pitt made a regular appearance!), that everybody knew and loved me (I was popular!), and life was like paradise. I would fall asleep at night to that dream. It was my bubble of belonging and happiness! As I really didn't have anyone to share my thoughts and feelings with, my mind became my best friend, and the dreams gave me a sense of release.

It is healthy to have positive dreams

They also gave me a space to prove people wrong. I remember, when I was about 13, a comment was made to me – *'Therese, you will not amount to anything, as you don't play sport, sport makes the person'*. To put that into context, I really did try to play sport; Camogie, Rounders, Athletics and Tennis. I was reluctantly a member of the local Tennis club growing up, and I was an average player, but from others' perspectives I was awkward, clumsy and very much out of my comfort zone. However, following that comment, I was determined for that person to be proved wrong. I was going to find my sport! And I did, through the medium of stage. From the age of 13, I regularly performed in talent shows and competitions. In fact, I represented my Parish, County and Province on several occasions in competitions such as Scór na nÓg and Readoiri for reciting poems written by well-known Poets.

*'If I were a lady, I'd wear a hat that all the street would be lookin' at.
I'd have a lady's maid, do ye mind, who'd button an' fasten me dress
behind.'* - If I were a lady, Percy French.

I finally found my belonging, my moment when I felt I was me (being on stage), even though I was always playing the part of someone else. The more competitions, I entered, the more I won and the more my sense of belonging I felt. The library in my mind started to

297

fill with pages of positivity, confidence and developing belief. I found my sport and it made me the person I am today! The 'can't', was replaced with an 'I can, I will, and I did!'

Determination helps push past the busy mind

At 17 I left the small village to move to the big city for college. It was a new adventure, and little did I know it would be the beginning of me finding myself. My mind was opened to new experiences, new learning's and new people. New and exciting questions were replacing the negative ones I had held in my mind. There was a sense of curiosity and exploration. Suddenly, the girl from the country with poor self-confidence was popular, and I felt like I belonged in a group with like-minded people. I was being invited to people's homes, going to concerts, parties and weekends away. I developed close friendships at last and finally found trusted confidants that understood me and allowed me to get the thoughts out of my busy mind without judgement. I remember a friend saying to me once you are the friend that I link to going shopping. I asked her what she meant and she quickly said, I have a friend for every area of my life and if I want to go clothes shopping, I ring you. While I do love shopping and keeping up with fashion trends is one of my favourite hobbies, I was still insulted. She only saw shopping as my value to our friendship. However, it got me thinking, and I realized that your friends have their individual strengths, find that strength and there is the hidden gold for your friendships. Find your inner circle, the friends you can confide in and you know that you are being listened to and heard without being judged. Yes, it is also important to find the friend that you can go shopping with too!!

The Importance of an Inner Circle

I studied Hotel Management in college and like my earlier years a lot of things didn't come naturally to me. I remember accidentally nearly stabbing the Chef during kitchen service one day and for 4 years she did not forget it! I was awkward in the bar classes and could never get the pints just right —the same with opening the Champagne bottles. Not only that, I nearly took someone's eyes out one night in restaurant service. While that all seems funny, it wasn't to me, the questions of self-doubt started to creep back in. I questioned whether I had made a mistake in choosing hotel management as a career. I really hoped I hadn't. In my mother's eyes, I should have a pensionable job in the Civil Service, where I would be there for at least 25 years and probably still living in the village. While that all sounds great and would definitely give me the security I longed for, I knew it wasn't for me. I remember it being said to me one day *'Therese a job is a job, you are not meant to like your job, as it is just a way to make a living.'* Of course, I disagreed. But now I was starting to think I had made a mistake – What if my mother was right? Should I just get a pensionable job and stay in it? Have I selected the wrong course? What happens if I drop out? Again, the seeds of self-doubt churned in my mind. However, the drive and determination to prove everyone wrong took over and I began to look at it differently. Hotel Management is not just about food and beverage, there is accommodation, reception, sales and marketing and the list goes on. All I needed to do is find my niche. Before too long following work placements, I realised my strengths were in dealing with people, analysing figures and developing plans and strategies. Therefore, roles in reception, conference, events and sales and marketing suited my personality and skill set. At last, I had a direction and the mental noise started to have more clarity. I had found my niche.

Over the years, each event became like a chapter of a story in my mind. Whenever another situation triggered negativity, it would remind me of my previous failures and mistakes. When I do well at something and I am about 70% there, the file opens in my head and says '*Ha, Ha, Ha, you are not going to finish this?*' and brings me back about 10 steps. And I never get there. Like a chimp in my brain the nonsense talk would present itself, '*You never did it right before so why would you do it right now?*' The more the self-talk influenced my thinking and actions, it prevented me from putting myself forward for bigger jobs and projects. Of course, now I know that constantly telling ourselves negative messages, limits our belief in ourselves and our abilities to reach our full potential. Thankfully, and even I might have taken the longer scenic route to get there, my thinking is so much better now and I can live my best life. I now understand that to be our best selves we must step out of busy negativity and change the self-talk script to a positive one. We are all, including you, worthy of living our best lives. Growing up I was a huge Spandu Ballet fan and I constantly had Gold on repeat. In the last 10 years of my life these lyrics have resonated more with me, and now have deep and real meaning to me. The reality is I am Gold and You are Gold!

Always believe in your soul, you've got the power to know you're indestructible. Always believe that you are gold.

There have been times in my life that I didn't like myself very much and this opened up other pages in the library of my busy mind. However, I always had that inner drive to change that. Therefore, my personal development journey pushed me out of my comfort zone on many occasions. Firstly, there was my addiction to online dating in order to find a soul mate that met by values, interests and manage to stop me from getting bored! This was an interesting experience; I met self-obsessed fridge lovers who talked about fridges all night, another whom every time he turned his head his toupee slid to one side, another said 'but' so many times I counted 500 'buts' in 20 minutes, another turned up in a Christmas jumper in the middle of March and spent the night talking about his mother, and the best of it all was the guy who had the checklist of what his mother wanted in his ideal woman. What is it with Irish men and their mothers? I obviously didn't pass as I never heard from him again. Well, isn't that his loss or maybe a great escape for me? There are many ways I could have looked at these experiences, especially in a negative way. However, my synopsis was, I am okay the way I am and if I am single for the rest of life, that is okay too. I'm independent and actually now enjoy spending time with myself. More importantly, what I did learn to do is actually like myself. My journey of self-discovery also led me to join many spiritual and meditation groups. One Saturday afternoon, I ended up on Sandycove Beach with 20 Yogis humming a mantra that I certainly didn't understand, while holding hands and being watched on by the bewildered audience on the beach. They probably thought we were cracked and for many years I thought the same about these groups. In saying that, I didn't return the next Saturday but after years of exploration, I have found the type of meditation and spirituality that helps and gives me clarity daily.

The power of meditation

In the present day, busy mind thinking kicks in occasionally, and if it does, it usually happens on my way to work. I get into my car around 7.45am every morning for my 1-hour commute to work. I listen to PJ and Jim on Classic Hits radio on the way, as I love testing my knowledge or lack of knowledge in the Breakfast Table Quiz. But if my mind goes into busy mode, I don't even hear the questions; the planning, judging, remembering, analysing and yes probably overanalysing, commenting and pre-empting the day ahead make the radio just fuzz in the background.

One question after the next, always with the same theme of trying to understand and solve questions about **ME**.

How do I...

- Stay motivated?
- Become happy?
- Live my best life?
- Find a man and live happy ever after?

Why do I...

- Let others bother me so much?
- Worry about what others think?
- Have such lack of self-belief?
- Let my emotions take over?
- Prevent myself from reaching my potential?
- Feel so worthless in certain situations?
- Feel I need a man, to live my best life?

Why can't I...

- Keep the weight off?
- Stop worrying?
- Get people to see my life from my perspective?
- Deal with difficult people?
- Earn more money?

And the list of questions is endless and goes on and on....

My working day involves a lot of thinking, managing projects and people. That kind of thinking is useful but emotional overthinking is where problems can occur. It increases stress levels, drains energy, and even puts up barriers to achieving potential. I was the Queen of overthinking! However, I have learnt over the years, that when you're preoccupied by thoughts and emotions, you experience life through the filtered (and sometimes blurry) lens of your busy mind. A busy mind can be an overwhelming place to live. A calm mind is achieved when you know how to deal with that overwhelm.

It's important to deal with overwhelm

According to the Oxford Dictionary, overwhelm is defined as having such a strong emotional effect on someone that it is difficult for them to resist or know how to react. In today's society our work lives have become increasingly demanding, presenting us with ever more complex challenges at an uncontrollable fast pace, so it's easy to feel overwhelmed. The important thing is to get to know your mind and understand the triggers that might lead to overwhelm. There are some key factors to consider:

- Slow down

    When the mind is filled with 'what's next' and numerous competing deadlines, it's easy to miss the radiant colour in the changing leaves, or the twinkle of lights in a display window, or the curiosity in the eyes of an innocent child. I have always lived with a sense of un-needed urgency with the concept of wanting everything done or in my life now. However, living by this principle has been one of the many causes of overwhelm in my mind. To overcome this, I have learnt through the many mentors I have in my life, I need to be more conscious of my actions. How often have you used the phrase, 'I am crazy busy' or something equivalent? Are you just going from one task to another, so you can tick off your checklist? You are getting things done but unaware of what is going on around you? No sense of control, no pause, just busyness. The modern-day reality is that everywhere we look; we are exposed to advertisements, news, emails and senseless posts on social media. We are constantly told and persuaded to buy that, go here, stay there, and eat this. It's understandable therefore, that our mental hard drives become overloaded. Every day, a busy mind tries to absorb and remember the onslaught of information coming across your mental screen. In our overstimulated society, living in the busy mind can lead to mental exhaustion and fatigue, chronic stress and even depression, it leads to a weakened state. It speeds through life and doesn't slow down to take even a few seconds to tell you to, mindfully place your phone and keys in the same place, set your coffee cup away from your laptop, or notice the stop sign in front of you. Being busy doesn't necessarily mean that you are being productive. Slowing down, allows you to engage in every moment.

- Move out of Autopilot

Many of your daily activities are repetitive, like brushing your teeth, getting dressed, checking emails, and having a shower. The thoughts streaming through your mind tend to be repetitive as well. Many of today's thoughts were yesterday's thoughts—they keep replaying in your head. For example, you might think, 'I have to pay the phone bill,' over and over for two days straight until you actually go online and do it. The script for autopilot is often a thought loop that keeps running in your head: 'I need to lose weight,' 'I need to earn more money,' 'I need to get fit,' and so on. When you're on autopilot, you think the same thoughts over and over without being aware of it. Living on autopilot is exhausting and will leave you feeling drained at the end of the day. However, it also doesn't mean you action any of it! To empower yourself you must step out of that repetitive autopilot pattern and engage in every activity consciously. As I mentioned above, I have always lived with the sense of busyness and I am never just doing one thing. Even when I am cooking dinner, I am also emptying the dishwasher, probably on a call, analysing the activities of the day and the TV is a noisy blur in the background. Recently, I started to be more present in my activities and now when I am dicing onions, I am consciously dicing onions and experience every tear and every action of the knife on the chopping board.

Believe it or not, dinner is now more enjoyable because I am present and my meals are made with more thought and love. I now take the time to enjoy my meals and allow myself the time to eat, out of autopilot mode.

Being present allows for a more purposeful life

- Get balance in your life

Here is a confession; I have never had a work-life balance. Up until recently, I have been a workaholic! Don't get me wrong, I love all the other areas of my life, but work always seemed to take priority. Why? This is easy to answer; because it is the one area in my life that I know I am good at; it gives me confidence and I am seen as the go-to person. What I have come to learn about myself is that I need recognition and work gives me this. Hence, I throw myself into every project 110% and my personal life takes a back seat. But this isn't healthy as I have also learnt. It leads to unwanted stress and fatigue, which results in missed social occasions, mood swings and extreme burn out. I have now come to realise the importance of self-care and getting balance in my life. In fact, by having regular 'me' time, eating healthy, spending time with friends, ensuring I exercise and meditate often, actually have improved my work performance and have completely eliminated burn out, stress and fatigue. Work-life balance promotes clarity and gives you the confidence and permission to work as hard as you can in whatever area of your life you need to prioritize. It also makes it much easier to make decisions because you will do so based on a clearer perspective.

Be present in every moment. Your problems are not your identity. With some adjustments and a willingness to consciously develop your mind, you can gain the clarity you need to live your best life. Here are some things that may help you do this:

1. Accept the Feeling for what it is

Has fighting your feelings of being overwhelmed ever helped you delete them? Probably not. It is normal to experience some form of anxiety when you are in a situation that is bringing you out of your comfort zone but fighting feelings doesn't help change them. Changing how you represent and deal with what is triggering the feeling is much more impactful.

It is important to learn to be **NEAT** in your life (The Chimp Paradox, Prof Steve Peters). Always remember that it is **Normal** to have emotional outbursts and activities that even though you try you will not always manage well. Therefore, you should always **Expect** this to happen from time to time in your life. **Accept** that you are not perfect and understand the emotional chimp in your mind is very powerful. **Take care of** the outburst appropriately by apologising if you have affected others, or importantly by forgiving yourself if you feel you have let yourself down. If you have negative emotions, by implementing NEAT, it allows you to turn these emotions round and use them to move forward. Start thinking of ways that you can positively deal with negative emotions rather than engaging in them. A common phrase that has become my mantra is Accept, Move on and Deal with it.

2. Develop Empowering Thoughts

Pay attention to what you are telling yourself. When we are in situations where we feel we have no control, we probably have unrealistic thoughts that ignite a stressed-out reaction. When you have what seems to be an endless to do list, is your mental noise saying, *'I will never, get this done, it is impossible?'* According to Psychologist Deibler, that's a damaging thought that can lead to distress and anxiety and it prohibits you from problem-solving and taking action. Therefore, you need to learn to create and develop positive helpful thoughts to counteract the negativity and overwhelm. For example, change your mental noise to *'I may not get it all finished today, but if I make a plan, prioritise, break it down into steps and delegate where I can, I will likely get it done and it is achievable'.*

3. Change your multitasking mind-set

The definition of multitasking is the ability to deal with more than one task at the same time. Why do we have to always be completing many activities simultaneously? Why can't we just focus on one thing at a time and get them done well? Being constantly crazy busy, leads to stress and overwhelm. Therefore, we need to change our expectation that everything has to be completed right now. Delegate, if you can. Why do we always think that we must do everything ourselves? Share the load and minimise the stress and anxiety. It took me years to master this as I always felt I had to do everything and no one else could do what I do – what a load of rubbish!!! Take the load off.

4. Focus on the present

We are all so busy thinking about what may or may not happen in the future, that we do not appreciate what we have in the here and now. Thinking about tomorrow leads to unnecessary worry and more anxiety, as what needs to be done seems unachievable. Be more conscious of your thoughts; catch those negative ones and replace with positive ones immediately. Be aware of your surroundings. Every day, I spend 1 hour each way on the M18 driving to and from work. While I always keep within the speed limits, I usually do drive at the limit and quite frankly don't notice anything around me but just focus on getting to and from work on time (on Autopilot). However, one day for no apparent reason I drove slower and suddenly I started to observe houses, hills, colours in the sky, signposts and even car registration numbers in front of me. Up until then I was floating through my journeys and never took in my surroundings along the way. Now, I pause and take a careful look at what's going on and I absorb the information that comes to me. We live in an interesting and incredible world. Slowing down still gets me to work on time by the way! Slowing down and being conscious of the present, eliminates overwhelm, helps you see facts and brings clarity, which for me also helps develop my creativity. My advice is to live in the present and schedule time to plan, from the results of today's actions and observations.

5. Support system

It is important that you have a network of friends, family, professional colleagues and peers that you can turn to for emotional and practical support. However, remember, those in your support system should help you reduce stress, not increase it. They should support your goals and efforts to achieve them, not belittle or undermine or ignore them. Here are some ideas for building your support system:

- Volunteer - Identify a cause that is important to you and get involved. Volunteering can give you the gratification of taking action to further your values and will bring you into contact with others who share your interests and ideals.

- Take up a sport or join a gym or an activity/hobby you like to do. This is good for your physical and psychological health and it may also provide the opportunity to build new friendships.

- Start a book club or an online group in an area that you have interest in and invite some people to join who you don't already know well. Discussing interesting ideas and sharing thoughts and observations is a wonderful way to make new friends.

- Make an effort to get to know some of the acquaintances you see on a regular basis.

- Say yes to invitations. See each invitation as an opportunity to meet new people and build new relationships to perhaps add to your support system.

- Join professional organizations. Taking this step is good not only for your future career but it will also extend your social network to include others in your field. Sometimes friends in the same profession can understand the stresses you face better than anyone.

- Use online resources. Social networking sites can help you stay connected with friends and family. There are also many sites that can provide specialized support if you are going through stressful times or changing circumstances in both personal and professional situations. However, make sure to stick with reputable sites and use common sense about making arrangements to meet people in person that you have only known online.

6. Breathe

Deep breathing encourages our body's relaxation response. When you are in a state of overwhelm, follow the below steps:

- Take a deep breath in through the nose, filling your diaphragm for 4 counts.
- Hold for 7 counts. The carbon dioxide levels in your blood are starting to increase, slowing your body down.
- Exhale slowly through the mouth for 8 counts. The heart rate and blood pressure decreases, promoting an instant sense of calmness.

Continue this for approximately 5 minutes and you will be ready to deal with the situation at hand. Conscious breathing calms the mind

7. Connect with Nature

Simply, spending a few minutes a day in nature will help you shift beyond your busy mind. You'll start to feel more settled and clear, more open and limitless. Beyond your busy mind, you meet life head-on. Beyond the mental noise of thinking, thinking, and overthinking, there are no masks to hide behind and no filters to alter your perspective. I am very fortunate that there is a nature reserve just across the road from where I live. It is amazing that when I am stressed or anxious, by spending only 20 minutes here helps me clear my mind and get a more focused perspective. My senses are used to their full potential and my experience is different every time. Nature is wonderment and really helps ground me and clear the thoughts that have been circling around my busy mind. My advice to you all is to have a go to place just like me that you allows you to get out of your busy mind even, slows you down for a few minutes and helps you refocus.

8. Get it on paper

Allowing thoughts and to-do lists tumble around in your head is not productive. The reality is, without calmness and clarity, nothing gets done. Get thoughts out of your head and on to paper. Don't worry about the format, just get them written down. Once on paper, it is less overwhelming and increases the chance of the tasks actioned.

Break it Down Step-by-Step

'What we think determines what we believe, what we believe influences what we choose, what we choose defines what we are and what we are attracts what we have. If we are not happy where our past decisions have brought us well then the place to start is our current thinking process. As we add new knowledge, we will continue to define our way of thinking, actions and philosophy. As our beliefs change so too will our choices. From better choices come better results' (The 5 major pieces to the life puzzle, Jim Rohn).

Let's now look at the steps involved to help you achieve better results:

1. To get better results in our lives, you first need to **look at the way you think** and the difference between your thoughts and the actual facts. Let's take an example; you

have been invited to an interview for a fantastic job, what are your initial thoughts? Are they mostly negative or positive? I can tell you that over the years I have gone for many job interviews and mostly the first thought I had was; I am never going to get this, as there will be stronger candidates than me. What this thought immediately did was stress me out and get me worked up and caused me to probably under perform in the interview. In most cases, I didn't get the job I really wanted and then the cycle of other negative thoughts began and I stopped applying for the jobs I really wanted, as I felt I wasn't good enough. To be honest, my thoughts were my worst enemy and I attracted only what my thoughts allowed me worthy to attract. However, this has changed and now I expect positive outcomes in every meeting and encounter. I focus on the facts and not my thoughts and emotions around it. Remember, your thoughts and emotions are not real, the facts are. Be aware of the thoughts you are telling yourself if they are negative look at the positive facts around it and change your way of thinking immediately.

2. The next step is to **set goals**. It can be daily, weekly, monthly, or yearly goals and these should be for all areas of your life. However, it is important that your goals are measurable. A mistake that many people make is to have broad, immeasurable goals. For example, I am going to lose weight, I am going to earn more money, I am going to save

money, I am going to buy a house. Do these sound familiar? If so, did you ever achieve these goals? My guess is that you probably didn't. My advice to you is to set goals that have a quantity and a time frame. Instead of saying I'm going to lose weight change it to, I am going to lose 2 stone within the next 3 months. Immediately you have created mini milestones as now you know that if you lose 2.5lbs every week for the next 12 weeks, you will exceed your goal. Write down your goals and display them where they are clearly visible to you, so as they are constantly your focus. I have my goals pinned on a noticeboard in my bedroom and they are the first and last things I see every day.

3. To achieve these goals, you now need to **create an action plan**. What steps are you going to make every day to help you get to where you want to be and on schedule? Again, make them measurable and write them down. As you tick off completed tasks, celebrate each milestone. These are mini wins. Enjoy the journey to completing your goals.

4. **Identify what you do have control over in your life** and focus on that, to help you achieve your goals. What you don't have control of is out of your hands, so deal with it and act on the other.

TOTAL CONTROL	Your attitude
	Your effort
	Your mind-set
	Your knowledge
	Your determination
	Your work ethic
	The way you treat others
	Your wellness
	Your language – verbal, and body language
	Your decisions
	Your beliefs
	Your behaviour
SOME CONTROL	Your schedule
	Anticipating daily challenges
	Your home environment.
	Your work environment.
	Your support team.
	The result
NO CONTROL	The weather
	Thoughts, actions and opinions of others
	Your body shape
	The past
	The future
	Other people's happiness
	The traffic
	The news

Why worry about things you can't control when you can keep yourself busy controlling things that depend on you? Appreciate the adventure of not knowing what might happen next and have the strength to know that what you do have control of will help you through it no matter what twist is presented to you. Every experience is a life lesson and helps you grow.

5. To move forward it is necessary to **break the habits** that may have been holding you back until now. Admit you have bad habits, identify them and write them down. Be specific. How much do you indulge in this habit and how does it affect your life? The longer you've been addicted to the bad habit the more difficult it will be to give it up. However, the bad habit may hit your physical and emotional health. It could be preventing you from achieving your goals and dreams for a better life. Tiny changes can have remarkable results and help you move close to achieving your goals. Remember earlier in the chapter I said I used to be a workaholic? This also led me to have a few bad habits such as eating unhealthy food while working and avoiding exercise. This meant, I slowly piled on the weight and then the rollercoaster of emotions and negative thoughts started swimming around in my busy mind. I wouldn't go out because I didn't like the way I looked. Ignoring your bad habits might seem like the way to avoid them but

eventually, these habits catch up to you. My bad habits held me back from moving forward until I started making small changes such as walking to work instead of getting the bus, always bringing my lunch with me instead of buying the usual chicken fillet roll in the local Deli and most importantly being aware of my self-talk. These small changes completed consistently, allowed me to get to my ideal weight within the timeline I set in my action plan. The physical changes impacted my mental thoughts positively.

6. Determine the **benefits versus the costs** of doing or not doing something. Confronted with options, most people make the decision based on affordability (money or time) and then perhaps continue the decision-making process by looking for other opportunities that may be cheaper and more affordable. However, most people don't look at the cost of not doing the first option. The cost of not doing it could far outweigh the cost of doing it in the long term. For many years, I always looked at the immediate cost of doing something and always went for the cheaper option. However, what I have learnt is that investing in something that has a higher monetary cost makes me value it more and empowers me to succeed to achieve my related goal versus spending low but frequently. Guess what? You spend more long term on the cheaper option, with little results. Therefore, when you have options don't always look at the

cost instead look at what desired results that option can bring to your life.

7. Every day and every action should be an opportunity for **learning**. If you don't succeed on the path you set out on, remember that there are learning's to be had from failure. I am a big believer that on your life journey, you need to make mistakes and have certain failings. If you don't make mistakes you don't learn. However, it is important that you learn from your mistakes. Learning can come from many sources such as experience, attending courses, from others' mistakes, from coaches and mentors and online sources. Take all opportunities to learn new skills and knowledge to move you further towards your goals.

8. One thing I have discovered in my life, is that life should not be an on off switch. If you go off path, use the **dimmer switch** and start back fresh immediately. Have you ever started a diet on a Monday and by Thursday you have scoffed 2 bars of chocolate and had a takeaway? What do you say to yourself? Ah sure that's this week gone, I will start back again next Monday. Does this sound familiar? Let me ask you this, why wait until Monday, why not hit the dimmer switch and start again immediately? If you make a mistake, start again straight away. Don't let time keep passing by, as the longer time passes there is a greater chance that you won't get back on track.

9. Constantly *review* your goals and by having measurable actions it is easier to monitor if you are on track or not. However, it is important to have the courage to make changes when you have gone off track. Don't be afraid to go back to the learning and dimmer switch steps, you are on a journey not in a race and sometimes you need to go back a few steps to move forward.

The Importance of Mental Clarity

The next step on the journey of overcoming the busy-mess mind-set is to get the clarity. Imagine a life with less confusion and doubt. You can make better decisions, become more self-aware, trusting and healthier.

Clarity is important in our lives because:

- It minimizes doubt and increases self-confidence and self-awareness.
- It stops you feeling frustrated as you have less confusion going on in your mind.
- It brings you through a process of self-reflection which helps you identify your strengths and work on your weaknesses.
- It helps you move forward in your life and make plans and goals for the future.
- It allows you to make better (and faster) decisions that are aligned with your core values.
- It helps you get out of feelings of being stuck in a rut.
- It gives you a purpose.

- It brings more energy and focus to your day.

You will feel empowered to make decisions you feel good about. I appreciate it can feel tough to get there, with so many distractions and stressors floating around us, but you can get there and it's worth the effort!

To start getting clear about who you are, what you want, why you want it and how you are going to get it, ask yourself these questions and be honest about the answers

- What area of my life needs clarity – health, finances, family, relationships, career, and home?

_____

_____

_____

_____

_____

_____

_____

- What exactly do I feel unclear about in this area?

_____

_____

_____

_____

_____

- Why do I need clarity in this area?

  _____

  _____

  _____

  _____

  _____

  _____

- What information do I need to help me get clear?

  _____

  _____

  _____

  _____

  _____

- Who can help me in gaining clarity?

  _____

  _____

  _____

  _____

  _____

- What is making me anxious?

  _____

  _____

  _____

  _____

  _____

  _____

- How is my physical, mental, and emotional health being affected?

  _____

  _____

  _____

  _____

  _____

  _____

- When am I most happy?

  _____

  _____

  _____

  _____

  _____

- Is anything draining my energy?

_____

_____

_____

_____

_____

_____

- When do I feel most fulfilled?

_____

_____

_____

_____

_____

Get your thoughts on paper through journaling. This clears space to welcome clarity. Journaling helps you to organise your thoughts and ideas in a coherent way. Frequent journaling establishes patterns of thought and behaviour which can be addressed once identified, whether it be to work on or use more of. There is no right or wrong way to journaling, it is personal to you. Some examples of ways to use journaling are:

- Brain dumping – just write down everything that comes into you mind. Give yourself a time limit such as 10 minutes

- Lists – write out a list of 20 things that make you feel anxious, frustrated, confused, happy, fulfilled, mentally drained, grateful, or overwhelmed
- Capturing specific moments in detail regarding what you felt and experienced
- Unsent letters – these are great to help you work through what you are feeling now. Examples of types of letters are of forgiveness to yourself, advice to your younger self or to a person who has either positively or negatively impacted you
- Biographical summaries – written in an objective way without judgement or biases

It is important that you always reflect on what you have written. Note the language you have used. Is there a lot of *I can't* and *I never*? My advice is always challenge your never and can't. What if our nevers and our cants are what we want most, but because we don't want to be hurt or hurt others, or fail or expose ourselves to disappointment, we keep them in the never and can't file? As soon as you think, 'I could never do that' or 'I can't go without this' challenge them. They are usually exactly what you need for absolute clarity.

Look at the Possibilities with Clarity

People with greater levels of clarity are more successful, happier and have better self-esteem. The more clarity you have, the easier it is to know what to give our energy and attention to daily. If you don't focus on getting more clarity, you can find yourself falling behind in what you are trying to accomplish. This means you won't achieve the things you want. If you had clarity, imagine what you could achieve in your life? *'What would you attempt if you knew you could not fail? '*- Robert H. Schuller. Imagine that for a moment if you actually had a guarantee that failure was not an option and you were destined for success. What would you do? The possibilities are endless! Or are they? Did only one or two ideas come into your mind? Most of us have only one or two specific dreams we'd love to pursue, but we usually don't because what if we fail, then what? We don't want to face failure so it's easier to keep our dreams parked and every so often tease yourself with the idea of your dreams. However, note success isn't a sure thing but neither is failure. And how will you ever know what will happen until you try? And with clarity think of all the possibilities available to you.

Over the last 6 months I have really realised how logical, real and practical I am – the fuzz is starting to get clearer. My life purpose is unravelling in front of my eyes. The years of feeling a lack of belonging, a sense of frustration and confusion is finally getting clearer. The questions in my mind while still busy, is a different kind of busy – it's my daily and weekly action plan – the practical steps for what I need to do – not a self-criticism of **ME**. That clarity has come due to my years of working on my personal development. Yes, the crazy meditation groups formed part of that self-realization journey. What this clarity has opened up for me is the self-belief to follow my dreams of having my own business and hence the development of *Blueprint Solutions*. I now help business owners design a plan to get positive results for their business, by using my 25 years plus experience in business management. I help support individuals gain clarity, growth and success in their business, just like I did for my own life, by never giving up and pushing through the negative fuzz in my busy mind. (Want to find out more visit www.blueprintsolutions.org)

My final advice to you is don't be afraid to invest in you, no matter what it takes. Push yourself out of your comfort zone. Trust me the result will be a huge personal gain – it was for me. As my teenage (and yes it continued into my adult years!) celebrity crush Jon Bon Jovi has been singing for the last 15 years...

It's my life

It's now or never

I ain't gonna live forever

I just want to live while I'm alive

My heart is like an open highway

I did it my way

I just want to live while I'm alive

It's my life

It's your life, so live it your way, the best way.

Believe in yourself because you are worth it!

CHAPTER 19
Spin it!

by Veronica Bodano

'Your life is a journey'– it's a phrase we've all heard and, in many cases, including my own, we roll our eyes to it. I did many times, until one day I realized what it really meant!

Let us rewind my journey back to 17 years ago, a Sardinian girl finalising my studies in Milan, Italy. I was on my scooter (a green Aprilia scarabeo) and I had to decide where to start my professional life - in Italy or in Ireland. I was at a crossroads, leaving everything dearest to me like my family, my friends, my culture, my food, and my sunshine for the unknown in Ireland but with a work opportunity.

I was scared and unsure. I was leaving my area of comfort to enter a new learning zone. I stopped and consciously started thinking. I wanted to avoid the overwhelming fear of change. I wanted to positively visualise the opportunity I had, and I wanted to feel that it was my choice. Suddenly that brief take of consciousness and control changed the "lens", I had an opportunity to enrich my life to learn and steer my scooter to Ireland. It all clicked when I stopped listening to the scared voice inside me saying 'You will not make it' and I started asking positive questions to myself 'What are the great things that could come from it?' Then excitement filled me, making me

329

think about the next stage of my life journey. I was ready. I left the most important people in my life in Italy, but after some reflection this change no longer scared me - it excited me! If I could, thanks to the excitement, I wanted to fast forward to watch myself crossing the finish line of this new stage of my life. Now, after 17 years in Ireland, my life has gone through many phases. I have crossed many finish lines. I got a post-graduated master's degree in business, I worked in several companies, I was promoted, I bought my house, I got married to a caring Irish man and have been blessed with my healthy and beautiful son, Leo. Wow! It is way more than I had planned initially. I was only going to Ireland for six months to a year for work experience! My journey has elongated more than I expected and certainly looking back, I crossed finish lines I never thought I would, and all these stages felt like individual trips with their own challenges and gains. Never in a million years did I think I could do all that. Now my life is incredibly enriched. At times I still feel I have more "hats" than I can juggle, but I have grown up. I was the Italian girl looking for an experience in Ireland. I am now a professional, a wife, a mother, a person with life in Ireland and strong family connections to Italy.

That said, I made a fundamental mistake in every stage — I questioned my ability to handle what I was doing. *'How could I balance it all? How do I get it all right? How can I be great at all of it? How can I achieve excellence in each of my roles?'* I felt the pressure to be everything to everyone all the time. For years and at times still now, I suffered from

"Super Woman" syndrome, which truly placed an enormous pressure on me and how I tried to fulfil my different roles in my life. 'I' tried to do it all alone, but the 'I' needed to learn to ask for help. The social pressure, guilt, and mostly the stress I placed on myself to perform, resulted in time being scarce and ultimately not taking care of myself. I have not been carving even a moment to do the most simple acts of selfcare: I did not dedicate time to my passions like painting and dancing, I did not have any headspace or time for relax and unwind after a busy day – like having a bath, going to the hairdresser, watch a series without multi-tasking, and more. When the house was quiet, I would try to complete all the pending choruses for the wellbeing of the overall household, instead of taking some of that time for me.

I had to learn that in order to take care of myself, I needed to start with spending time on me. If I do not show the importance of self-care, what message do I send to others? Is it like stating that there is no need nor importance to prioritise myself, am I the last of the priorities?

To start with I had to remind myself to ask for help and that I am not alone. This was a necessary step to make time available for me. My mindset was changing, it is okay for responsibilities to be shared. I needed to learn how to be self-compassionate, to let go of the guilt and the pressure, to be grateful and proud of everything I do and to check on my daily routine. I had to let go searching for 'that' perfection, which does not actually exist, in my work, in my personal life, in my role as a mother, a sister, a daughter and a friend. Accept that it is okay to be myself as I am, in all my roles. It was like going to the gym, a gym for self-love to gain the realisation that the "imperfection" is okay. The feeling that what I can achieve is enough, and that to seek "perfection" you just need to be you. I had to take the time to stop, evaluate, and instead of believing that my efforts were not enough, start appreciating them.

Imagine being on a spinning bike. You push one leg at a time and slowly the challenge becomes less and less difficult until the force that slows you down dissipates. Then the wheels suddenly spin, your legs are lighter, like a breeze behind you and everything accelerates. You get a feeling of relief, relaxation, and joy that those difficulties disappeared. You have made it! But there are also moments where you feel defeated, tired, and floored but you keep going. In both scenarios there is a very important part – the recovery! When you get off the bike, it is like finishing a moment of your life, you need to give yourself time to recover. It is an act of self-love, and without it you suffer. You can always get back on the bike again, but that resting period is essential to progress. It makes you stronger by having time to ground you experience. Translating that to daily life, I realised that giving myself "recovery" time for self-care was key to a happier more self-accepting life. Sometimes it was not easy to get back on the bike, either I needed more time to recover or I needed a way to get inspired for a new start. I created a 5-step process that inspires me for a new start.

- Step 1. **Visualise my success**

   What will I gain by doing this at the end? How beautiful will it be when that mountain is climbed? How will I feel on the top? By using a few more questions, I help my brain discover it. It is important that I am convinced, I truly see it, I see the colour, I see the shape, I feel the emotion that this achievement will bring me. It is like experiencing it before going for it, this helps me to be sure and to be empowered by the feeling of "wanting it".

- Step 2. **Find my energy, remove energy drainers, and take control**.

   This is an amazing exercise that I learned from Donna Kennedy, I complete the "Wheel of Health" to allow myself to have a peek under the bonnet and see if I am equipped to take this up.

   This exercise scores 14 categories to help assess where I am low in energy. It helps me to focus the attention on the areas that have the lowest score. It allows me to evaluate what is in my power to improve. It helps me to acknowledge which of these areas are out of my control but are still impacting me and I should be more sensible around them. One massive learning has been that if I cannot change the area, I certainly can change the way to look at it.

NEEDS

Taking an example of COVID and the level of *safety and security* I felt since the pandemic started, I rated the area 1 out of 10 and had no possibility to impact any part of it. Instead, I had the possibility to change the way my emotions were around it. For example, I stopped fueling my brain with news that was not trusted. I almost stopped any social media and consciously watched only legitimate news sources. Also, I ensured this activity was clearly a cadence in the day or week, to avoid an emotional build up. I started being grateful for the fact that I was actually safe, and I could continue my life in this global crisis.

NEEDS - *Example*

As a first stage, I focused on lowest areas focusing on ranks of 4 or less, I also would limit my focus to 4 - 5 areas at a time. Then, I would repeat this audit every 2 weeks to a 1 month. Either I would continue my focus to elevate those same areas or if improved enough, I would focus on others. There is always a fluctuation in the rank of needs, but by assessing it you could acknowledge them, and see if a simpler or more structured fix is needed.

- Step3. **Make time**

For many people, this step defines the success or failure of the entire process. Many of us struggle to carve out the necessary time to support our personal needs. When I look back at all the different "hats" in my life, it seems that I never had enough time. The only way to accomplish what I planned meant sleepless nights until sunrise, trying to carve another day out of the night. This has proven unrealistic as we all need sleep to operate better.

At this stage I decided to assess how and where my time is spent, and out of the total time - how much of it I was dedicating to myself. The review was shocking, and it explained why after my Wheel of Health, some areas ranked so low.

At the same time, I was not ready to change all my life around. I had commitments, I was not ready to stop helping people, but then how could I fulfil my own needs? I started reviewing the list of commitments, activities, and projects to see how I can repurpose them to allow for a win-win. I was looking at how my needs and the duties can be completed together.

Initially, I thought it was not possible – in my head if you want to do something you need to give it full focus and you cannot mix – but as I did not have any other alternative and I could not change who I was, I decided to test the low risk areas. For example, when the working day is over, my little 3 ½ year old rightly wants time with my husband and I, no alternative accepted. As long as he wants time with us, I really want to embrace it, as in the future we will not be as interesting to him. The plan normally is to sit for 1-2 hours with him playing cars, horses, and any other game in his playroom. This is a precious moment but after a full day of sedentary working, after work is my only time to do some physical exercise, it's not easy. Here comes the opportunity to combine needs. Spending time with my son is a must, but can this time also become my physical exercise? The answer is yes, I ultimately bought a trampoline. My son loves it and 15 mins jumping on the trampoline is one of the best exercises, it boosts cardiovascular health, improves endurance, relieves stress and tension, giving better balance to both of us, coordination, and motor skills. So, it is an absolute win-win!

I admit it takes conscious effort to make the connection and define how two activities could work together but it is fully worth it. Start with a list of your wish activities and then draft your weekly/monthly routine and some matches will emerge. If you cannot find enough matches to give you the satisfaction that you are dedicating enough time for you and your dear one, then another level of decision might need to be considered.

- What should you reduce or stop? (social media or TV time, procrastination, time to people that drain you or do not leave you with much)

  _____

  _____

  _____

  _____

- What can you delegate or ask help with? (cleaning, tidying, gardening, babysitting, cooking, shopping, planning)

  _____

  _____

  _____

  _____

- Is the family load balanced with your partner and closer family? (share house responsibilities, swap house responsibilities, jointly complete house responsibilities, ask or pay someone to give you time back)

  _____

  _____

  _____

Either by pairing needs or by re-evaluating your time and load, you should be able to start a plan that includes more you in the plan!

- Step 4. **Make it grow as chain mechanism**

  I suddenly realised that as soon as I did something more for myself, an inner energy gets created and it fuels me to do it again and again, to push for this time investment to continue. I feel proud, grateful, and energised. All of this has an explanation since it is proven by scientific research that acts of kindness are good for your health. The warm feeling of wellbeing that sweeps over you when you have done something kind is not just in your head, it is in your brain chemistry. It releases hormones that contribute to your mood and overall wellbeing. It could be *oxytocin*, occasionally referred to as the 'love hormone' which aids in lowering blood pressure, improving our overall heart-health, increasing our self-esteem and optimism, which is extra helpful when we are anxious or shy in a social situation. Also, it could release *endorphins* in the brain, which is a natural painkiller improving mood, depression, and anxiety. Finally, this feeling of kindness would stimulate the production of *serotonin* which helps to heals wounds, calms, and again increases happiness.

  For me it is such an inebriating feeling that the boost of energy keeps me surfing on the top of this wave for hours, bringing me to achieve weeks of neglected actions in just a few hours. This is the proof that you should not underestimate what your inner self could give you back. Ultimately, you need to start it, but your body and system would reaffirm the act by thanking you, rewarding with an inner chemical sponsorship for doing more. I'd like to use a phrase from Sarah Bernhardt as it is very fitting to explain this dynamic, *'Life begets life. Energy creates energy. It is only by spending oneself that one becomes rich.'*

- Step 5. **Commit to it**

Even the sincerest effort could fade away in the space of a few days, simply because older and more established routines take precedence. Our older ways could feel easier for us, we could all just fall into existing habits. Everyone has a way to execute their resolutions which then would solidify as a new life commitment. For me personally, I need to see it, have it visible and use a system of reminders to be able to stick to it. As a first step I normally socialise the new habit with my family and people that need to be involved. I share with the clarity the importance for me, and clear actions for all parties involved. This is for me the most important moment as I am creating a contract of mutually agreed actions and timelines. To bring another example to life, my quality time with my husband has not been the same since we had our beautiful boy. Everyone would agree that these are normal circumstances, but we were not satisfied, we wanted still to have the pleasure of each other's company, having an uninterrupted adults' conversations and relax together. So, twice a week on Tuesday nights and Saturday mornings we have asked for help. One time my husband's family helps us and on the other occasion we pay for someone to help us. This recurrent support gives us space to plan and schedule activities for us. Being a foreigner in Ireland, I know that we do not have the full family circle nearby to help us but for that reason it is important to leverage other circles of friends and colleagues. And sometimes I have realised by offering help once, three times more returns come your way.

Check In!

Throughout my self-care process I also learned the importance of being self-aware and never complacent, especially in times where you can see the goal but it's not happening as quick as you'd like. Having a regular check-in gives clarity and allows you reset and progress.

I found myself in this situation during quarantine; I wanted to achieve so much, to do so many things and I could not make them happen. Even though my brain was focusing and seeing all that I could gain from completing those actions, I did not have the inner power to do it. It was again a moment to assess my level of energy and needs, so I used the "Wheel of Health" to review. I needed to understand which section of my needs required care, was it the Emotional, the Spiritual, the Mental, the Physical, or a bit of all of them? Why could I not progress?

After repeating the ranking of the 14 elements, I realised that my Physical elements were extremely low, I burned the candle at both ends, taking care of many tasks without asking for enough help and forgetting the basics. I was only sleeping 3-4 hours a night, not drinking enough water, not exiting the house so limiting my fresh intake of fresh air and sun, and finally eating many foods that were not energising me with goodness and vitamins.

When I would get the time to do what I liked, the time would fly off my hands, my concentration would be low, my effectiveness poor. Unfortunately, I realised I did not have the physical capability needed to execute. It felt like I got dressed ready to go for an epic cycle and then I slept on the bike, which meant the time was up and I did nothing, I did not move a centimeter forward, I was still in the same place but with a lot of time lost. As U2 would say I was "Running to Stand Still."

This has been a constant in my life, I took my body and brain for granted. I would squeeze them to the extreme. In fact, I have been constantly praised for an incredible work-load capacity. And now I see it, to what cost, to the clear drainage on my inner energy resources which I have forgotten to replenish. I can say I have been playing a dangerous game for many years.

The good news is that simple actions helped me to revitalize my state, by simply reinstating a positive routine of 7-8-hours sleep, forcing my water intake to a minimum of 1.5 litres with whatever tricks to flavour the water, finally watching my diet and adding natural super-foods which helped as strong sources of vitamins, minerals, fibre, and other nutrients to give me a big nutritional punch.

What I learned is that if we do not learn to listen to and act on our needs, no-one is truly able to do it, apart from us. It becomes crucial to master the conscious act of self-awareness and self-care. I was in a negative loop, I was trying harder and harder, but my body was the limitation and I could not believe it or did not want to believe it.

No matter what section you need care in, learning to listen internally or creating a routine of assessment could diagnose punctually where some self-care could bring you back to your optimal or better level. Please remember to check-in with yourself!

Give yourself a Chance

Being Italian, I love the expression "Rome was not built in a day". Even though I really like the saying, it seems I used it as an inverse motto in life; I wanted to push reality and achieve everything as fast as possible and to do it at whatever cost. Well, now the costs are not only mine, I have responsibilities to my family and to my friends. So, after learning about my energy sources and taking care of energy sections, I am focused on not burning my candle both ways again.

However, sometimes life throws you surprises and obviously you cannot do more than deal with them. My most recent surprise, to call it that, was breaking both legs during this quarantine, while leaving the house for first time to bring my son to his first playdate in the park. I will spare the details, but I would only mention that it was as simple as stepping out of the car, stepping down from a high curb and snapping two legs in a drain.

The initial thought, due to the unbearable pain, was "game over." If I had to compare it to the pain threshold of giving birth without epidural, giving birth was a walk in the park. What an ironic metaphor!

During the first 10 days of recovery, I understand that the needs I wanted to focus on were not the right ones. I thought I would focus on rediscovering how to restart exercising or going to the garden to enjoy the good summer. Instead my priority became how to recover my basic needs like minimal mobility to at least going to the bathroom, washing properly, getting dressed. I needed to feel somehow "independent". This was incredibly frustrating as before the accident I could do everything blind folded.

Looking back to the day of accident. I could not lift myself, due to the pain in both legs and due to lack of arm strength. That night when I returned home, I could not find a position to sleep, the amount of pain killers I had to take would have tranquilized a horse, with my level of mobility I could not reach the toilet in time even with help. I believe you can understand that only tears and disbelief were my mindset and feelings.

Then, the realisation that my newly created positive routine, matched activities, new habits were not valid anymore. My life had changed without my consent and I could not do anything that I had planned. All those goals and positive images of what achieving meant for me, started crumbling as they looked out of reach. I went backwards in the space of a second, this was inconceivable for me. For the girl that could not stay still I was now mostly forced to stay in bed.

But three weeks after the accident with a bit of thinking, planning, time to heal and a lot of will, and not having to take the medication, I can go to the toilet as much as I need. I can wash and dress alone and I am lifting myself with my arms. I am starting to put weight on one of the legs and I can balance myself standing. I managed to put my child to bed, I can cook a meal and I can correct some of the tidy up done by my husband. I am now planning what else I will achieve in the next weeks.

What a change from the moment when I truly crumbled. I felt it was so unfair after all I did to get in a better place, but that mindset was only stopping me from trying to think what I can do to get better. I wanted to fall asleep and wake up in 6 weeks, when my legs would be healed or wake in few months when I would be fully recuperated. I was letting myself down, instead of giving myself a chance. But I am now telling myself I can do it. It is not ideal but little by little I am making it, a small push at a time and then I will be better and better. I was being my own worst enemy.

The Power of a Push

At the time of this accident I have to admit I had temporarily lost all my self-belief. It took me a few days to snap out of it and source my energy to face my new challenge. I have to be thankful for another powerful exercise from Donna Kennedy about gratitude. Honestly, I could have been in a much worse situation with a head concussion or a trauma, more injuries that might not be easily healable, or my child could have been injured in the process. Thinking about everything that thankfully did not happen, I suddenly felt happier and I felt a wash of positivity around me, which lifted me and my mood immediately.

Also, I have to immensely thank my family, friends, acquaintances, and strangers. The amount of people that had kind words, words of reassurance, words of courage, anecdotes of how I made it in the past and I will make it again, funny comments of disbelief and numerous offers of help and support. These people have always been there, they did not just appear yesterday. It was me that did not reach to them. This time, possibly out of desperation I shared so clearly my feelings, my situations, my worries, and everyone just wanted to reassure me. I never felt anything so powerful.

As per my situation there are moments in life that you need a push, to start something, to believe it is the right or wrong thing, to simply believe in yourself. This push could come from different angles, from the inner you or from outside. Do not discard one or the other, as in the past my inner support would have made me walk a hundred miles, this time it would not have been enough. So, I thank myself to have had the courage to openly speak to people about my situation and I thank all the people that, with kind words or actions, helped me to slowly propel myself forward.

Many of the new activities I propose to myself are not achievable in one instance, to compel to them I need a plan. Everyone is different and I see mostly two categories of people: the naturally structured and organised and the other that needs a supporting framework. I belong to the second category since I have acquired so many "hats" in my life, I need a framework. Also, because I have proven that I seldom put my needs first, I struggle to ask for help, so it is a must to ensure that I have a structured plan with a positive routine in place.

This is not only a schedule, it is more. It may start as mentioned as a calendar, but it includes responsibilities that need to be shared with the people involved. It is a respect-contract to assure clarity and accountability. Then, it would have checkboxes and checkpoints either weekly or monthly, to see if I am moving towards the objectives and to measure improvements. Also, to keep a journal is a great support for me, as sometimes looking back helps me to quantify and be proud of myself. It helps to celebrate all these achievements, both the small and big wins. Sometimes I celebrate just by thinking of accomplishment. Sometimes I would give myself something like time for a bath, or buy myself something symbolic, like one of my many antiques! It then starts the chain-mechanism of energy that generates energy!

All the above makes me deconstruct my mountain of things in smaller pebbles. With my framework, I am categorising and moving all these pebbles. Then every mountain is not an obstacle anymore.

With my plan I feel again a breeze pushing me and giving me amazing momentum to seal any new phase of my life.

CHAPTER 20
Inspiration to Action

by Pat Slattery

When I look back at some of my earliest memories, I think about what has driven me to overcome any obstacle and where I have found inspiration to keep going despite circumstances. Here I will share some of my story, so you may find inspiration that will also allow you to keep going despite circumstances.

As a young boy, I was not used to having very much in terms of material goods or even at times extra food, I certainly did not have many treats.

I have early memories of going to our local shop to collect empty cardboard boxes, so I could cut the shape of my shoes out on them, so I could put it inside my shoes to stop the water from coming through the holes in the soles of my shoes.

I had an amazing mum and dad whom I truly believe did their best for me and my brothers and sisters, in particular my mum; what an inspiration she was to me, even though at the time I did not realise it. My mum received a payment from my Dad's pension of just £70 per week for which she had to use to feed, clothe a large family and also manage household bills.

As a young woman, my mum married my dad who had previously been married and whose wife passed away, leaving him with 9 children. This did not deter my mum, at 24 years his junior she married my dad and took on the role of supporting him and raising his children. She then went on to give birth to 7 of her own children, extending a family of 11 to 18.

The importance of knowing this is so that it will give you a better understanding of how incredible this woman was then and still is today.

We grew up in a council house with 3 bedrooms and by the time I had come along to join this already large family, money and material goods were few and far between, However, my amazing mum always managed to find a way to make sure that we always had enough.

I have memories of my mum walking 4 miles from our home to the largest supermarket and coming home with up to 8 shopping bags full of groceries. She did this because it meant her money would stretch further and she could make sure that everyone in our home had enough, so we never went hungry. This showed me that once you have a desire to do something and that if the desire is strong enough you will do whatever it takes to make sure it happens. My mum had an extraordinarily strong desire to take care of her family. This is just one of many amazing stories I could share with you about my amazing mum.

Moving forward a few years, at 14-years-old I took a job working in a hotel in the city, first I was hired as a dishwasher and shortly after I was given the job as porter or concierge as it is now better known. This meant the world to me, it meant that I would have some money to buy nice things and it allowed me to bring some money home to help my mum. I kept this job and did not go back to school anymore; I very quickly went from a boy to a man.

A year later I left that job and began working as a doorman in a nightclub at weekends, I took a job delivering newspapers during the afternoons Monday to Friday, in the morning I worked in the printing office of a newspaper company, and on midweek evenings I worked as a doorman in a fast-food restaurant. I took a job as a security officer in a menswear store on Saturdays, I became a work-acholic. I discovered that I had a desire to make money, so I took any job I could fit in to the time I had, so I could make more money.

Eventually, I went from working as a doorman to creating a very large security company that in its lifetime generated over €25,000,000. I have since had multiple companies that have generated millions of Euros for both me and my partners. And I have developed strategies for hundreds of companies and individuals to generate both extra income in their businesses and extra time in their lives.

It took me many years to discover how this happened for me but when I look back on my life I can see where some of this drive and determination came from. I had many inspiring people in my life and sometimes without even knowing it they were guiding me in the right direction, there are way too many stories to go into on this to fit into this short story.

One of my greatest learnings or BFO's (Blinding Flash of The Obvious, or lightbulb moments) was when I was attending an event in Ireland. During the presentation it really hit me: Be prepared to change your beliefs often. I am not even sure which of the guys that were speaking said it or even exactly what words were used but the message was loud and clear. It was at that time that I realised I had limiting beliefs, that some of the strongest beliefs I had – I did not even recognise them as beliefs – were responsible for most of my greatest setbacks in my life.

If you are holding onto a belief that doesn't serve you then ask yourself why, why would you hold onto something that does not serve you? Where did you learn that belief? What if you didn't have that belief, what if it didn't exist?

Ask yourself what is going on in your environment. Is it affecting your beliefs? Sometimes, the people in your environment project destructive beliefs, usually not intentionally, and it's easy to take them on as your own.

Growing up I didn't have very much; I came from a part of town where there were just over 6,000 residents with over 80% unemployment. Obviously, this brought its own problems over time as people become frustrated with having very little in life, whether it is finances, simple comforts, enough food or even respect.

Society would stigmatise people with an address such as mine; with such an address you would not expect to amount to much, according to society. Not everybody in society thought this way but that is not what most people in my environment believed.

Before I continue, I must point out that I was truly blessed with some of the people that influenced me in a positive way in my life that certainly played a part on me making great decisions that shaped who I am today. My story is not a sad story, I was extremely happy as a child and have thousands of great memories.

However for the most part growing up the some of the people in my environment would believe that those outside of our community were against us, they were the enemy, because they had more than we did or they lived in nice areas or were able to dress better or drove nice cars, the belief then was that if they knew where we came from they would look down their nose and judge.

This belief came simply because of how society would treat them, most people from this area when applying for a job would try to find a friend or relation with a different address when filling in the application.

The truth is that most of these people were honest people and were always willing and wanting to work and support their families. But the belief, in my opinion, that most people held onto was that people from my part of town would never amount to much. I believed this for some part and it certainly held me back at times. However, when I realised that I needed to change the way I think, I had to change my environment in some ways.

My family were a great support to me and I am always grateful to both my mum and dad for allowing me the freedom to learn and go out into the world and create the belief that I now have today, which is that I can be, do, and have anything in this world that I desire.

I went about learning new skills and building self-belief that I could do what I desire. Here are some of those skills and I wish for you to use these or something similar in your life. Some I have already shared with you but let me elaborate a little more.

The first thing I had to do was re-train my mind. I had to let go of the beliefs that were holding me back. This meant I had to change how I was thinking and to ensure I was thinking of all possibilities rather than focusing on the things that I didn't have. I chose to become solution focused, I wanted to know more of what I *can do* rather than what I can't do.

One of the limiting beliefs I had was that I had no education, and this is possibly one of the most common limiting beliefs, especially amongst business owners. Having spoken with so many people throughout my life, and coached so many for the last 20 years, I have learned that believing you are uneducated really holds people back, creating a sense of embarrassment when asked about qualifications, for example.

Instead of asking what you can't do, ask, W*hat CAN I do?* When someone tells you that you can't do something (and you will meet many) rather than becoming frustrated with them or yourself, thank them for their advice and then ask what do they think you can do. Keep asking this question until almost all the answers you are getting are telling you what you can do. If you find yourself doubting, remind yourself of this: Your *I Can* is far greater than your IQ.

Your I Can > IQ

Remind yourself of your moments of truth, the times when you stood up in the past, when you did something that really had a positive impact. Ask yourself empowering questions, for example, instead of asking what is going wrong, ask yourself what is great about this situation. What are you learning from it? If something is not going right, then ask yourself what you can do to fix it and have fun doing it.

Start your day reading or listening to positive stories or reading positive stories. Find books where strategies are shared that you can apply to your life. Go to seminars where the speakers have already achieved something similar to what it is you want to achieve. Listen to the tips and stories shared here and ask yourself how you can apply these to your goals. Everyday create an attitude of gratitude, asking, *What am I grateful for right now, what is going on in my life that I am truly grateful for, who are the people in my life that I am grateful for right now, what lessons have I learned that I am grateful for.* Create a list of things that you are truly grateful for. Choose to be grateful for the things you may take for granted. Choose to make a positive contribution everyday through your actions and what you do for a living. All of these will help you train your brain to moving towards the outcomes that you truly desire. What I discovered that I consider was my driving force was a message I came across from the great Jim Rohn many years ago. Here I will share it with you. I discovered what Jim Rohn called the 4 emotions that will turn your life around. I am delighted to share them with you here.

1. What have you had enough of?

Once you have decided you have had enough of something, it will change your life dramatically. When I say had enough, I mean it in a way that you feel it in every cell in your body that you truly believe that you have had enough of something that no longer serves you or may never have served you at any point of your life.

For me I guess I had enough of not having enough, I had enough of watching my mum struggle, I had enough of not having enough week left at the end of my pay check, I had enough of walking around a store checking the price of products, at the same time checking how much money I had in my pocket to make sure I could afford what I wanted. These are just some of the things that I had enough of. Ask yourself this, what do you have enough of, what is it that you no longer want in your life?

When I decided that I was going to own business I shared this goal with some people who thought it was a silly idea, people like me don't own businesses, they thought it was funny, the idea that someone of my background would consider owning a business, and for a while I believed them too. Until one day I decided I had enough of playing small, I had enough of people telling me where I belonged and that I could not achieve whatever I put my mind to achieving. I decided I had enough and then I committed to an act that said, "I have had enough".

Once you have truly decided that you have enough then you must commit to an act that says, "I have had enough ". What have you had enough of? Write it out right now! It may be more than one thing.

I have had enough of

_____

_____

_____

_____

_____

_____

Commit an act that says I have had enough.

I commit to

_____

_____

_____

_____

_____

_____

2.Decision

_____

_____

_____

_____

_____

_____

Decisions can be really emotional, this is what gives you the knot in your stomach, knowing that you want to decide to do the action that you need to do in order to get you closer to your desired result.

In order to make progress you must decide. Commit to the decision to take the action that will bring you to wherever it is you desire to be. Sometimes you may discover that you are getting lots of advice, some may be conflicting and this can create confusion thus leaving you in a situation where you are unsure of which decision is best for you.

Here is a simple way that I make decisions.

Imagine for a moment that we are going to enter a 100-mile boat race, and this is the boat that we must use.

We are entering this race to win, so for us to win we must find ways that will make this boat go faster. We will come up with some ideas and maybe even get suggestions from other people.

Some suggestions might be:

- Paint the boat
- Put a sail on the boat
- Put an engine on the boat
- Put more seats so more people can row the boat
- Remove seats to make the boat lighter

You can create an endless list and for sure if you ask for suggestions you will get many. So, how do you decide which options are the best?

Sometimes you can have too many choices and it becomes more difficult to decide.

I always ask myself: Will this make the boat go faster, yes or no?

When I look at any task that may have to be completed I liken it to the boat, I ask myself when it comes to my goals, are the decisions I am making likely to make the boat go faster? If the answer is no, then I remove that option from the list of actions. Sometimes I ask if an action may make the boat go faster is it worth the effort for the result it can produce? if the answer is no, then I remove this action from my list. Once I identify the actions that will make the boat go faster, then this is what I get to work on completing. These are the actions I decide that need my priority.

Once you complete your list of actions that will make your boat go faster, commit to the top four activities that you have chosen, once completed then commit to four more. If you take on too many at once you may find yourself being in overwhelm again, so break it down to four steps at a time.

I have decided to commit to.

1. _____
   _____
   _____
   _____

2. _____
   _____
   _____
   _____

3. _____
   _____
   _____
   _____

4. _____
   _____
   _____
   _____
   _____

'If it is easy to do, Do it easy.

If it is hard to do, do it hard.

Just get it done.'

3. Desire

When you discover what you have had enough of and you create the desire to change and you really feel this desire then you start the journey of achieving all that you want in life and business.

Desire is that feeling you get in your gut that tells you whatever you are thinking of doing is truly possible, it is the feeling of *knowing* that you will do whatever it takes to make it happen, that you will commit to this desire and believe in yourself that you can be, do, and have anything in life that you want to have. It tells you that even though you may not know the way right now, you will find the way, you will do whatever it takes to learn the skills, put in the work, do whatever is required of you to achieve whatever it is you truly desire. I discovered a real desire to grow.

Desire can be triggered by many different things, it may be something you read in this book, it may be something someone says to you or something you have seen, desire comes from inside and cannot be got from an outside source. You must feel it within you. You must want it bad enough. You must want it more than you don't. What do you have a desire for in your life? What change do you really want to have in your life right now? Write it out right now.

I have a real desire to be, do, have

_____

_____

_____

_____

_____

_____

_____

_____

_____

_____

_____

4. Resolve

The Definition of resolve: Promising yourself that you will never give up! Two of the most powerful words you can tell yourself are, I WILL. What are your "I Will" statements? You must tell yourself what you *will* have, not what you hope to have. Be truly clear on what you will have!

When you create your "I Will" statement you are now making a statement of intent. This, I discovered, was a tremendous tool in helping me focus on my goals. When you create your "I Will" statement you are setting your intention, and once you set your intention pay ATTENTION to your INTENTION!

This means that you find out what you have had enough of, decide to commit to an action that says "I have had enough", find the desire inside you to go after whatever it is that you desire in life then set your intention and DO whatever it takes to get there. Grab a pen and complete the following exercise!

I will Be-Do-Have.

What?

_____

_____

_____

_____

_____

_____

_____

Action steps for change.

I am going to do. What?

_____

_____

_____

_____

_____

_____

... in order to get what?

_____

_____

_____

_____

_____

_____

_____

Discover resourcefulness and resources

What action needs to happen for you to get your desired outcome?

_____

_____

_____

_____

_____

What resources do you have or need?

_____

_____

_____

_____

By when, will it be done? Pick a date.

_____

_____

_____

_____

Remember "If it is easy, do it easy, if it is hard do it hard, just get it done."

These tools are what have served me so well in life, these tools have helped me overcome many challenges in both my life and business and I am sure they will help you too.

Play to your strengths

Let me assure you of this. Whatever has got in your way up to now, whatever doubts you have had or challenges you have had to deal with, YOU ARE BIGGER THAN THEM! In order to take control and become a victor you must remind yourself everyday what you stand for.

First thing every morning and last thing at night, before you go into any important meeting, before you meet with friends, colleagues, turn up for work, or meet and greet strangers, remind yourself what you stand for.

365

Create your culture.

Take time to list out your points of culture, think about what you stand for and write them out. Post them where they will be visible. Don't just write them and close the book and walk away and forget them, read them out loud often, read them with pride and feel every word you speak when you tell the truth about who you are and what you stand for.

Share your points of culture with anyone that you want on your team (people who support and influence you in a positive way), let them know what you stand for so when they speak of you this is what they will say about you. This way everyone knows what you stand for and as your team grows they will all understand your culture and you will find that you attract the right people to your team always when you are true and think and behave like a victor. Creating my points of culture has been monumental in the direction of my life. I truly believe in them and committed to living my life by them. Most people I have met struggle to create points of culture so I would like to share mine with you simply for the purpose that you may find inspiration for yours.

1. Commitment ...

I give myself and everything I commit to 100% until I succeed. I am committed to the Vision, Mission, Culture and success of *Pat Slattery International*, Its current and future team, and its clients at all times.

I always recommend products and services of *Pat Slattery International* prior to going outside the company.

2. Ownership ...

I am truly responsible for my actions and outcomes and own everything that takes place in my work and my life. I am accountable for my results and I know that for things to change, first I must change.

3. Integrity ...

I always speak the truth. What I promise is what I deliver. I only ever make agreements with myself and others that I am willing and intend to keep. I communicate potential broken agreements at the first opportunity and I clear up all broken agreements immediately.

4. Excellence ...

Good enough isn't. I always deliver products and services of exceptional quality that add value to all involved for the long term. I look for ways to do more with less and stay on a path of constant and never-ending improvement and innovation.

5. Communication ...

I speak positively of my fellow team members, my clients and *Pat Slattery International* in both public and private. I speak with good purpose using empowering and positive conversation. I never use or listen to sarcasm or gossip. I acknowledge what is being said as true for the speaker at that moment and I take responsibility for responses to my communication. I greet and farewell people using their name. I always apologize for any upsets first and then look for a solution. I only ever discuss concerns in private with the person involved.

6. Success ...

I totally focus my thoughts, energy, and attention on the successful outcome of whatever I am doing. I am willing to win and allow others to win: Win/Win. At all times, I display my inner pride, prosperity, competence, and personal confidence. I am a successful person.

7. Education ...

I learn from my mistakes. I consistently learn, grow and master so that I can help my fellow team members and clients learn, grow and master too. I am an educator and allow my clients to make their own intelligent decisions about their future remembering that it is their future. I impart practical and useable knowledge rather than just theory.

8. Team Work ...

I am a team player and team leader. I do whatever it takes to stay together and achieve team goals. I focus on co-operation and always come to a resolution, not a compromise. I am flexible in my work and able to change if what I'm doing is not working. I ask for help when I need it and I am compassionate to others who ask me.

9. Balance ...

I have a balanced approach to life, remembering that my spiritual, social, physical and family aspects are just as important as my financial and intellectual. I complete my work and my most important tasks first, so I can have quality time to myself, with my family and to renew.

10. Fun ...

I view my life as a journey to be enjoyed and appreciated and I create an atmosphere of fun and happiness so all around me enjoy it as well.

11. Systems ...

I always look to the system for a solution. If a challenge arises, I use a system correction before I look for a people correction. I use a system solution in my innovation rather than a people solution. I follow the system exactly until a new system is introduced. I suggest system improvements at my first opportunity.

12. Consistency ...

I am consistent in my actions, so my clients and teammates can always feel comfortable in dealing with me. I am disciplined in my work, so my results, growth and success are consistent.

13. Gratitude ...

I am a truly grateful person. I say thank-you and show appreciation often and in many ways, so that all around me know how much I appreciate everything and everyone I have in my life. I celebrate my wins and the wins of my clients, and team. I consistently catch myself and other people doing things right.

14. Abundance ...

I am an abundant person, I deserve my abundance and I am easily able to both give and receive it. I allow abundance in all areas of my life by respecting my own self-worth and that of all others. I am rewarded to the level that I create abundance for others and I accept that abundance only shows up in my life to the level at which I show up.

Who are you and what do you stand for?

Write out your points of culture. You may have 8 points 10 points or even 20 points, write them out read them often and feel every emotion you need to feel so you believe. Be proud of who you are and what you stand for. Practice this often and it becomes easier to believe, if you are a confident person and maybe even run a successful business this is so important for all your team to know.

Imagine if all the important people in your life or the best customers understood this about you, imagine the impact it would have when these people speak about you in this way that they tell people what you stand for. Once you embrace this you are creating a value on who you are as a human being.

Once you increase your value as a human being then opportunities will open to you many times, you will get to experience all the things that you desire in life and or business.

You will discover that you are attracting the right people into your life, you will discover that you are achieving outcomes much easier, the outcomes that you desire. This is inevitable once you understand your value.

Take Action

Take immediate action on any positive thought that comes to mind when you want to achieve a goal, don't hesitate; once you have an idea do something immediately that commits you to the goal, it will create momentum and will keep you moving in the direction of the goal. It will also keep your brain focused on moving toward the goal. Most people try to plan all of their actions at once and then become overwhelmed because it is difficult to see the end result. Sometimes you may just need to take the first step.

Imagine this, or maybe you have already experienced this. You have been after a very long day and you are making your way home, you are tired and its very late into the night, you are imagining what it's going to feel like when you get home and get into bed, you can feel the soft pillow under your head as you lay down, you are thinking of this as you get closer to home. You arrive home and all the lights are off. You look up from the bottom of the stairs. What do you see at the top of the stairs? Darkness.

It's like looking up into a dark hole and you can see nothing, however you know that up there is that pillow you have been thinking about on the long journey home, the soft bed that you imagined your body laying down on.

You look down and what do you see? The first step, correct?

You take the first step up the stairs and when you do what do you see? The next step. Then when you take that step, the next step becomes clearer and so on.

Following your goals and desired outcomes are more or less the same, sometimes the path is clear and obvious and sometimes you just have to take it a step at a time, and as you take these steps and move forward the next step becomes clearer and clearer.

Eventually, you reach the top and achieve your goal of that soft pillow.

Remember this when you are getting frustrated if you don't have all the plan figured out. Just taking the first step is sometimes all it needs for momentum to build, and once that happens you will find more *Inspiration to Action* and you will achieve your desired outcome. There is a great satisfaction in realising you are moving toward your goals. And one of the important parts of moving forward toward your goal is to recognise when you have taken some of these steps rewarding yourself. Remind yourself why it is so important to you, do this often. Take this information and apply it! It will change your life!

FINAL NOTE
TRUST IT

by Donna Kennedy

We appreciate that taking steps toward getting the life you want can be a daunting experience; we've all been there. We have all been in that place of standing in the dark, wondering and wanting, but too afraid or too tired to move towards what we wanted. However, and this is where I'm going to give it to you really straight, it's not okay anymore! It's NOT okay to stay in the dark wondering and wanting, it's NOT okay to play small or live in a shadow, it's NOT okay to turn your back on yourself. Sure, you can do it (that's YOUR choice) but it's NOT okay.

All those years ago when I was hiding out in my safe space, I used every reason I could find to keep myself there, and you might be playing some excuses in your mind too. Does this sound familiar? *'I'm not able to do this because..., I can't be because..., I don't deserve...,* yeah but..., it's because they..., I wouldn't be this way if..., blah blah blah.' That conversation is NOT okay anymore. Truth be told, and taking all the fluff out of it, there was only one person keeping me where I was and that was me. I was keeping myself there, nobody else. I could understandably blame the world for not being nice to me, I could get angry at experience and circumstance, but ultimately and honestly, I chose to stay in my safe space because it was easier to beLIEve my excuses than it was to be better and allow myself to BE-LIFE. It was only when I stopped to think that I woke up to life – literally.

It took a new conversation, a shift in consciousness and ego, a trusting of something bigger than myself and a letting go of excuses and fear. If you want to create changes, you will need to have an honest conversation and a different conversation with yourself.

Now, I'm not saying this to ruffle your feathers. I am saying it from pure kindness and love for you. Honesty is part of love. We did not write this book to entertain you, we wrote this book because we care, and we want to inspire you to BE the best version of yourself. You will have noticed common strategies among us all, I'm sure. Why? Because they work! IF you do. You were born to rise and BE-LIFE, not crawl in Be-LIE-fs that don't serve you.

Let me ask you, why did you pick up this book? Why did you open it? Why did you continue to read it? Is it because you know deep down that you are more than you have been settling for? You were never born to settle.

Remember the seed-to-plant we spoke about in this book; when a seed is planted the natural process of LIFE is for it to move out of darkness, grow into the light and bloom. You have that same LIFE force inside you. And just like a flower swaying beautifully in the breeze, you don't have to see the breeze to know that it's there. Just allow it to BE and connect with it. Sometimes all it takes is to be still and listen:

You are here for a reason, BE YOU, BE-LIFE!

AUTHORS

JOHN BOYLE

John Boyle is the owner and founder of *BoyleSports*, Ireland's largest retail bookmaker.

John was the driving force in transforming the betting industry into a more customer-friendly business.

Beginning with one small

shop in Markethill, Co. Armagh, *BoyleSports* is now a multi-billion-euro betting company, with 347 retail outlets in Ireland and the U.K., as well as online and mobile betting services.

Having recently retired from his position as CEO, John still serves *BoyleSports* as Executive Chairman of the Board.

DONNA KENNEDY

Donna Kennedy is a 6 times bestselling author, highly sought-after professional speaker, psychologist, and mentor. She regularly features in media as a personal development expert and her work has been endorsed by many well-known leaders and multi-nationals. Her work has been used by several leading organisations to train staff, and her academic work has been recognised and published internationally by various faculties, including *The American Journal of Psychology* and *The Irish Psychological Record*. She had several difficult challenges to overcome in the first half of her life but she has proven that no matter what your circumstance, with the right approach anything is possible! She has taught her strategies to thousands of people worldwide and continues to positively impact people with her no-nonsense authentic caring approach.

"Listen to this girl, she knows what she is talking about!" - Bob Proctor *(teacher in the book/movie, The Secret)*

"You are going to thank me in your prayers for recommending her to you." -Mark Victor Hansen *(Chicken Soup for The Soul book series)*

"I have been privileged to speak with Donna Kennedy. - Brian Tracy (Eat That Frog)

"Donna's talk in Google was extremely well received. We found her content to be very strong!" - Google, European Head office

Contact Donna: www.donnakennedy.com

PETE LONTON

Mighty Pete Lonton from the 'Mighty 247 'company, is a mentor, entrepreneur, podcaster, coach, property Investor, husband, and father of 3 beautiful girls. Pete's background is in Project Management and Property, but his true passion is the 'Fire in The Belly show and 'project. His mission is to help others find their potential and become the mightiest version of themselves. Pete openly talks about losing both of his parents, suffering periods of depression, business downturn and burn-out, and ultimately his years spent not stoking 'Fire in the Belly'. In 2017, at 37.5 years of age that changed, and he is now on a journey of learning, growing, accepting, and inspiring others.

Pete has the ability to connect with people and intuitively asks questions to reveal a person's passion and discover how to live their mightiest life. The true power of 'Fire in the Belly 'is the Q&As - Questions and Actions!

The 'Fire in The Belly 'brand and show is rapidly expanding into podcasts, seminars, talks, business workshops, development course and rapid results mentoring.

Contact Pete:

www.mightypete.com

www.fireinthebelly.net

www.fireinthebelly.net/podcast

KEN FALCONER

Ken is an Emotional Intelligence Coach, Therapist and Mentor who works with clients from all around the world. He has renowned for his simplistic yet effective approach to emotional wellbeing, attitude, behaviour and mind-set. Whether you are a business owner or someone ready to start your personal journey Ken will coach, mentor, offer advice and encourage you on your personal journey to fulfilment.

Ken has an impressive background in the construction industry but after experiencing his own problems with low mental health, he became interested in personal development. As a result, he not only found personal healing, he found his true passion is helping people get measurable, visible, tangible results in their lives.

His personal change initiated a career as an Emotional Wellbeing Coach and Mental Health Specialist. He is also a Clinical Hypnotherapist and a Trainer of Hypnosis, an NLP Coach & Practitioner and a Time Line Therapy Practitioner. He runs self-awareness workshops, speaks at various events and is well respected for the work he does. One of his rules is keep things simple. Ken is result oriented and many of his techniques are unique and he have helped hundreds; possibly thousands of people make changes in their lives, significant changes, lifesaving changes.

Contact Ken: info@kenfalconer.com
www.kenfalconer.com

KAREN FLEMING

Karen is a Mother, Entrepreneur, Creative writer, and Author. She was born and raised in Dublin, the eldest of 3 girls. She became a mother at 17 and shortly after returned to education to study business and language. For 6 years Karen has been in business in both the Vape and hemp Industry. In earlier years she developed an interest in wellbeing and trained as a holistic massage therapist. Later an experience in her own mental health caused her to embrace transformation, finding inner strength, courage, and authentic self-love. She continues to further her training in the area of mind, body, health and wellbeing. Since writing her first poem as a teenager, Karen has enjoyed writing both fiction and non-fiction. Her vision is to inspire and make a positive difference through her writing, business, and wellbeing programs.

Contact Karen: flemingkaren11gmail.com

HUGH HEGARTY

Hugh Hegarty has gone from the brink of suicide to becoming a much sought-after Business Coach, Wealth Coach and Empowerment Coach.

In his journey Hugh has educated himself in Psychology, NLP, Hypnosis, Wealth Coaching and Empowerment techniques which he has used to help many clients overcome varying issues and limiting beliefs and move forwards into a more successful and enriching life. He accredits his success in his mentorship and coaching programs to the outstanding coaches he has had in the past and currently has, and his desire and passion to continuously learn about the mind and its limitless powers.

Hugh is an expert in his field so whether it be anxieties or phobias or removing limiting beliefs from your life so as you can improve your earning potential Hugh has the solution for you. Check out his private group on Facebook, *Live the Life you Want*, for regular free tips and advice on how to begin your journey to a better life.

Contact Hugh: www.facebook.com/hugh.hegarty1

ED MARTIN

Ed Martin is over 40 years in the property sector and is the third generation of Martin involved in property. He is a popular public speaker and is fanatical about rugby and golf. In 2009 he was made the first and remains the only Irish Captain of the Old Head Golf Links. Ed lives between Dublin, Kinsale and South Africa with his wife Lou. They have two wonderful children.

Contact Ed: ed@edmartinproperty.com

JACKIE MALLON

Jackie is from Co. Armagh in Northern Ireland and is mother to her gorgeous son.

Her passion is to inspire and motivate others to be the best versions of themselves. She is absolutely delighted to be part of this book, with such amazing and empowering co-authors and 6 times bestselling author, Donna Kennedy, to bring that message to many, whilst achieving one of her dream goals.

Jackie's career has allowed her to work with and for some major brands and top prestigious companies in their industry, specialising in Sales and Customer Services at different levels. She is a high-performance employee, exceling in problem solving, focus based solutions, achieving high results, smashing targets and training. She is a people's person, thriving in building great relationships with everyone she meets and works closely in partnership with customers to bring the best value and service to their businesses.

Her favourite hobby is to bake, whether it be scrumptious cakes, cupcakes or desserts. She will always turn out some amazing treats which are enjoyed by many, and which can be viewed through social media sites as Luvva Lil' Cupcake xx.

She loves and thrives on personal development, helping her grow in all areas of her life, whether it be with her mentors, programs, reading, mastermind groups, meditation etc, it all benefits in her continual growth and be the better version of herself.

Contact Jackie: missym@live.co.uk

VIVIAN MCKINNON

Vivian McKinnon's proudest achievement is her 3 children, Garry, Hayley and Sonny. She is dedicating her chapter in this book to them, and her husband, Tommy, for their unwavering love and connection which she feels keeps her grounded and full of gratitude every day. Vivian is a Trauma and Floatation expert, founder of the RAFT programme and an award winning international Public Speaker and Author. In September 2015 she established Northern Ireland's first dedicated floatation centre, Hydro-ease. The idea to open a floatation centre came about during her first float in Edinburgh in 2004 where she instantly knew this 'strange and a bit different therapy' could help other people; especially those living with addictions, physical and mental pain. Since then she has become qualified and experienced in The Havening techniques, Cognitive Behavioural Therapy, a Master Practitioner in Neuro Linguistic Programming, TimeLine therapy, and Clinical Hypnosis, a practitioner of SPECTRUM Coaching, a Laughter Yoga instructor and auricular acupuncturist. She is involved with the Health Care Trust, SMART Recovery UK, PIPS Ireland, and the UK/ROI Float Tank Association. Her experience as a grounded yet dynamic change-work specialist spans over almost 3 decades and it is her belief 'The magic is within you". She acts on this belief by empowering people to use the skills and tools within the life they have, to create the life they desire. Her work is especially beneficial to adult children of substance misuse parents.

Contact Vivian:

vivian@hydro-ease.co.uk

www.hydro-ease.co.uk

PATRICK DILLON

Patrick Dillon is a qualified electrician from Dublin, owner
and self-employed businessman and entrepreneur. He is also a
proud single father to a young handsome boy. His devotion is to his
son and his company. He is admired and looked up to within his
community. His value, respect and trustworthiness is recognised
and commended in his professional and his personal life. His main
interest is self-development and been a better version of himself
every day.

In his life there was a point that Patrick hit rock bottom and there
was only one way out. He had many complex's issues to have to face
in his life, with great persistence and encouragement he has stood
tall and face these blocks in his life.

With support, efficient communication and having taken
responsibility, he has succeeded in overcoming these challenges in
life and been a positive more confident person. Patrick would like to
share his learning and positively encourage each person to not be
scared and have some self-care.

Contact Patrick: patrickdillon@live.ie

CHRISTINE MCGONAGLE

Christine is an author and specializes in educating Menopausal ladies with her Mentoring, Coaching and Cognitive Behavioural skills. Christine is ten years into her own Menopause and has realized the need for more education for women and the GP services surrounding Menopause and the lack of specialized care available. Christine is passionate about bringing change to services to Donegal and surrounding counties. That is why she set up the company, The Menopause Executive.

Christine has a Facebook page called 'The Menopausal Mammy' where support is given in the form of factual information for Menopausal ladies and they can talk freely to each other and privately

Christine is an Entrepreneur who is involved with numerous companies which help people have a more fulfilling life. She is also the founder of 'Wild Atlantic Way Competitions', on social media. Christine has just begun her entrepreneur lifestyle and has many more plans ahead!

Contact Christine:
irishmenopausalmammy@gmail.com
wildatlanticwaycompetitions@gmail.com
Facebook;
Irish Menopausal Mammy
Wild Atlantic Way Competitions

HEATHER LUNDY

Heather Lundy has over 20 years' experience starting as a cub reporter on the local newspaper and has published research, short stories and she is a published author. Following her Granny's diagnosis with dementia in October 2010 Heather was determined to increase awareness of dementia joining Alzheimer's Society in March 2011 where she has worked across Operations, Research, Fundraising, Policy and Campaigns across a number of roles working with people affected by dementia to increase awareness and change society's view of dementia.

Heather is also a Ghost-writer and Editor with a keen interest in helping people write and publish books.

And as a mother of three Heather enjoys hiking, watersports and movie marathons with her family who also provide lots of inspiration for her writing.

Contact Heather: heatherclundy@gmail.com

NADIA BUJU

Nadia is from Romania and moved to Ireland 15 years ago. She set up a cleaning company and it has been going from strength to strength for the last 14 years. She is very ambitious, driven and organized and she likes to keep a positive attitude in all things. In addition to her cleaning company, she has an interest in health, wellbeing and universal laws. As such she has completed several courses in these areas. She received a diploma accredited by the EMCC and ICF of Life and Executive Coaching in Ireland and is a certified essential oil specialist. She is keen to help people who are looking for an alternative solution to their family's challenges and, with a willingness to give people support, she set up a Facebook group called *Holistic Empowerment* to empower others to lives their best lives. Nadia is a kind, strong and enthusiastic lady who believes EVERYTHING IS POSSIBLE and hopes that by reading her chapter you will be inspired to be, do and have more in your life.

Contact Nadia at: nadiabuju@gmail.com

ANNE CANAVAN

Anne Canavan is a writer of fiction and author of the new fantasy story, *In Finity*.

She has also written fifteen short stories for children about the Snotblot characters whom she has created to accompany one of her products, the Snotblot. These stories are akin to the Mr Men stories which she would consider the 21st century version.

A product developer and inventor, Anne has spent the last several years writing stories in her free time, bringing her numerous characters to life.

Anne lives and works out of her home in the picturesque sea-side town of Moville in County Donegal where she lives with her family and three dogs.

Contact Anne: snotblot@gmail.com
Facebook: Snotblot - Say Bye Bye To Runny Noses
Instagram: Snotblot

CHRIS WOJNAR

Chris' background is in a family retail business in the home decor industry specialising in wallpapers with a brand Wigoders, that was first established in 1783 and the first wallpaper shop in Dublin. He and his family built the business from one shop to thirty and back to one. On that journey Chris developed many skills and experience, which he now shares as an independent business consultant to help people develop, scale, and sell their businesses or products.

Contact Chris: chriswojnar@wigoders.ie

TANYA CANNON

Tanya Cannon is director of A1 Cleaning services and supplies. She is also a victor in life. Tanya's story tells of how she has navigated through the turbulence of her younger years, having experienced domestic and sexual abuse, to resolute determination to live her best life. She was born and raised in Athlone, is the eldest of 3, Aunty to 7 children, Godmother to 2 children and supporter of them all.

Tanya's fire in her belly was stoked by her traumatic childhood experiences but rather than loosing herself in the negatives, she embraced the lessons and the positives. Her mind-set for her business is a reflection of her life, packed with persistence, resilience and energy. She employs on average over 70 people from her hometown and has a prestigious client base across the midlands.

Tanya continues to show and share her determination, and her attitude and sassy personality makes the world a better place!

Contact Tanya: a1cleaningltd@gmaill.com

JOAN MC DAID

Joan was born and raised in Co Fermanagh, Northern Ireland, before moving to Co. Donegal where she now lives with her husband and two children. Joan is a Social Worker, Life Mentor, and has more recently trained in alternative therapies. Joan is passionate about enabling others to find emotional and energy healing from within. She believes that everyone has the inner power to change their lives.

Contact Joan: www.connectedprosperity.com

Instagram @connectedprosperity

SHARON MCNULTY

Sharon Mc Nulty is the founder of *Serenity Sparks Joy*. She has three children and works full time so she knows how busy life can get. When her children were young she would spend her weekends tidying but, by midweek, her home would start to get cluttered again and so the cycle continued. For Sharon, a cluttered home was a cluttered mind.

Many years ago, Sharon tidied her home using the KonMari Method™. Now her home is filled only with items she loves, everything has a place and it is easy to keep tidy. She trained as a KonMari™ Consultant with Marie Kondo and now works as a Professional Home and Business Organiser.

Her experience has given her great insight into how clutter affects our minds and, she witnesses the physical and emotional transformation of her clients as she supports them to declutter and organise their spaces.

For clients who feel overwhelmed and just not sure where to start, Sharon is available for in-person and virtual tidying sessions. She has created online courses to help those DIYers who are willing to roll up their sleeves but just need a bit of guidance. She hosts workshops, seminars and employee wellbeing days for groups and businesses.

Contact Sharon: www.educationbysharonmcnulty.com

THERESE O'CONNOR

Therese started her career in the hotel and catering industry back in the 1990s, following the completion of the HDip in hotel and catering management and a BSC in business management. However, over the last 25 years Therese's career has spanned many sectors and different management roles within the fast-paced service sector. Therese has been frequently described as the 'great multi-tasker', the 'glue that brings everything together' and the person that gets things done. Therese excels when given a challenge and has the passion and drive for success and delivering results. In 2020, Therese took the leap in developing Blueprint Solutions with the purpose of giving business owners back their time.

In her free time, Therese has a passion for musical theatre and drama and in the past could be found performing in dramas, musicals and pantomime's with local amateur societies. However, Therese's main passion is for travel and exploring different cultures and how we all interact together. Therese has developed her travelling bucket list with dancing a tango in Argentina, volunteering in an elephant sanctuary in Sri Lanka and finding her spirituality in an immersive meditation retreat in India being the top 3 on her list. All of which play an important part of Therese's 5 year living her best life plan.

Contact Therese: therese@blueprintsolutions.org
www.blueprintsolutions.org

VERONICA BODANO

Veronica Bodano is a passionate professional and entrepreneur with decades of experience in leadership, strategy, business development, business and life coaching. She has wide experience working with any size of local and international businesses either with Profit and Non-Profit focus.

Her academic background is economics and business, but her focus and passion has been in organisational development, people and businesses empowerment.

Italian by birth Veronica has relocated and established in Ireland for nearly 20 years. Curiosity and learning have been two of her guiding principles allowing her to adapt and move across businesses and departments. She has a long-lasting devotion for creating and supporting corporate social responsibility projects in Ireland and globally, many award-winning initiatives. She is radiant and positive by nature, and she learned how to turn challenges into opportunities. While living a new chapter as a mother, Veronica keeps avidly interested to be enriched by meeting new people and new learnings.

Contact Veronica: Veronicabodano@yahoo.it

www.linkedin.com/in/veronica-bodano

PAT SLATTERY

Pat Slattery is no ordinary speaker or coach, leaving school at 14yrs old he began working in the hotel industry, at 15 years old Pat began working in the security industry and built a company that generated over 25million Euro. He has an incredibly positive attitude and outstanding work ethic along with a determination to give 100% to everything he does.

Pat has delivered over 2500 keynote speeches during his 20+ years in the personal and professional development industry.

He has facilitated thousands of mastermind mentoring masterclasses that have helped thousands of individuals achieve their lifetime goals.

Pats talks come straight from the heart, the ups and downs of business and life experiences, he gives practical information that he has applied himself that has driven him to the successes he has achieved in his life and business.

Brian Tracy Author of 86 World Best sellers says "Pat has one of the greatest minds in the world when it comes to personal and professional development"

Contact Pat: www.patslattery.com

FOR MORE INFORMATION, BOOKS AND EVENTS GO

TO

DONNAKENNEDY.COM

Printed in Great Britain
by Amazon